Jo Ann R. Coe
Goutham M. Menon
Editors

Computers and Information Technology in Social Work: Education, Training, and Practice

Computers and Information Technology in Social Work: Education, Training, and Practice has been co-published simultaneously as *Journal of Technology in Human Services*, Volume 16, Numbers 2/3 1999.

Pre-publication REVIEWS, COMMENTARIES, EVALUATIONS . . .

"**A**s social work professionals begin to explore the interface between, and integration of social work practice and technology, they will find an invaluable resource in Computers and Information Technology in Social Work. This compilation of 'cutting edge' research and application of technology in social work practice, presented by the leaders in the field, will be indispensable to practitioners, educators, agency administrators and students of social work. We see between these pages a vision of where the social work profession will be in the new millennium."

Edward Geraty, LCSW-C, LPC
CEO, Behavioral Science Consultants, LLC
Director of Professional Development
Maryland Chapter
National Association of Social Workers
Executive Vice-President
Maryland Society for Clinical Social Work

T0186855

More pre-publication
REVIEWS, COMMENTARIES, EVALUATIONS . . .

"**I**t is vitally important that social workers understand how to utilize information technology in the best interest of clients *and* students. This book provides relevant information that informs both practitioners and educators in social work. Such a book has an important place as social workers and social worker agencies increasingly take advantage of it in practice."

Julie Miller-Cribbs, PhD
Assistant Professor
University of South Carolina

"**C***omputers and Information Technology in Social Work* represents a compilation of some of the most interesting papers presented at the 1998 Technology Conference for Social Work Education and Practice sponsored by the University of South Carolina. The first half of the volume consists of ideas and projects representing innovative applications of computers and information technology for social work practice, and the second half represents similarly innovative technologies applied to social work education. Technologies applied to assist professional helpers in their practices range from the develop-

ment of case-based reasoning for child protective cases to the use of information technologies to transform organizations. Educational applications include Web-based instruction, Internet applications for social work education, and other distance-education considerations.

For anyone who missed the 1998 South Carolina conference, this volume represents an invaluable resource of concepts, applications, and evaluation methodologies concerning the application of information technologies in social work practice and education. I found the selections informative and exciting, and predict that I will return to reread several of the papers, particularly those related to the development of expert systems and to distance education strategies. I am grateful to Drs. Coe and Menon for compiling these important conference presentations!"

Joanne Yaffe, PhD, ACSW
Associate Professor
University of Utah
Graduate School of Social Work

Computers
and Information Technology
in Social Work:
Education, Training,
and Practice

Computers and Information Technology in Social Work: Education, Training, and Practice has been co-published simultaneously as *Journal of Technology in Human Services*, Volume 16, Numbers 2/3 1999.

The *Journal of Technology in Human Services* Monographic "Separates" (formerly the *Computers in Human Services* series)*

Below is a list of "separates," which in serials librarianship means a special issue simultaneously published as a special journal issue or double-issue *and* as a "separate" hardbound monograph. (This is a format which we also call a "DocuSerial.")

"Separates" are published because specialized libraries or professionals may wish to purchase a specific thematic issue by itself in a format which can be separately cataloged and shelved, as opposed to purchasing the journal on an on-going basis. Faculty members may also more easily consider a "separate" for classroom adoption.

"Separates" are carefully classified separately with the major book jobbers so that the journal tie-in can be noted on new book order slips to avoid duplicate purchasing.

You may wish to visit Haworth's website at . . .

http://www.haworthpressinc.com

. . . to search our online catalog for complete tables of contents of these separates and related publications.

You may also call 1-800-HAWORTH (outside US/Canada: 607-722-5857), or Fax 1-800-895-0582 (outside US/Canada: 607-771-0012), or e-mail at:

getinfo@haworthpressinc.com

Computer Applications in Mental Health: Education and Evaluation, edited by Marvin J. Miller, MD* (Vol. 8, No. 3/4, 1992). *"Describes computer programs designed specifically for mental health clinicians and their work in both private practice and institutional treatment settings." (SciTech Book News)*

Computers for Social Change and Community Organizing, edited by John Downing, PhD, Robert Fasano, MSW, Patricia Friedland, MLS, Michael McCullough, AM, Terry Mizrahi, PhD, and Jeremy Shapiro, PhD* (Vol. 8, No. 1, 1991). *This landmark volume presents an original and–until now–unavailable perspective on the uses of computers for community- and social-change-based organizations.*

Computer Literacy in Human Services Education, edited by Richard L. Reinoehl and B. Jeanne Mueller* (Vol. 7, No. 1/2/3/4, 1990). *This volume provides a unique and notable contribution to the investigation and exemplification of computer literacy in human services education.*

Computer Literacy in Human Services, edited by Richard L. Reinoehl and Thomas Hanna* (Vol. 6, No. 1/2/3/4, 1990) *"Includes a diversity of articles on many of the most important practical and conceptual issues associated with the use of computer technology in the human services." (Adult Residential Care)*

The Impact of Information Technology on Social Work Practice, edited by Ram A. Cnaan, PhD, and Phyllida Parsloe, PhD* (Vol. 5, No. 1/2, 1989). *International experts confront the urgent need for social work practice to move into the computer age.*

A Casebook of Computer Applications in the Social and Human Services, edited by Walter LaMendola, PhD, Bryan Glastonbury, and Stuart Toole* (Vol. 4, No. 1/2/3/4, 1989). *"Makes for engaging and enlightening reading in the rapidly expanding field of information technology in the human services." (Wallace Gingerich, PhD, Associate Professor, School of Social Welfare, University of Wisconsin-Milwaukee)*

Technology and Human Service Delivery: Challenges and a Critical Perspective, edited by John W. Murphy, PhD, and John T. Pardeck, PhD, MSW* (Vol. 3, No. 1/2, 1988). *"A much-needed, critical examination of whether and how computers can improve social services . . . Essential reading for social workers in the field and for scholars interested in how computers alter social systems." (Charles Ess, PhD, Assistant Professor of Philosophy, Morningside College)*

Research in Mental Health Computing: The Next Five Years, edited by John H. Greist, MD, Judith A. Carroll, PhD, Harold P. Erdman, PhD, Marjorie H. Klein, PhD, and Cecil R. Wurster, MA* (Vol. 2, No. 3/4, 1988). *"Provides a clear and lucid perspective on the state of research in mental health computing." (David Servan-Schreiber, MD, Western Psychiatric Institute & Clinic and Department of Computer Science, Carnegie Mellon University)*

Computers
and Information Technology
in Social Work:
Education, Training,
and Practice

Jo Ann R. Coe
Goutham M. Menon
Editors

Computers and Information Technology in Social Work: Education, Training, and Practice has been co-published simultaneously as *Journal of Technology in Human Services*, Volume 16, Numbers 2/3 1999.

The Haworth Press, Inc.
New York • London • Oxford

Computers and Information Technology in Social Work: Education, Training, and Practice has been co-published simultaneously as *Journal of Technology in Human Services*, Volume 16, Numbers 2/3 1999.

Cover design by Thomas J. Mayshock Jr.

The Haworth Press, Inc., 10 Alice Street, Binghamton, NY 13904-1580 USA

Library of Congress Cataloging-in-Publication Data

Computers and information technology in social work : education, training, and practice / Jo Ann R. Coe, Goutham M. Menon, eds.
    p. cm.
    Includes bibliographical references and index.
    ISBN 0-7890-0841-6 (alk. paper)–ISBN 0-7890-0952-8 (alk. paper)
    1. Human services–Computer network resources–Congresses. 2. Social services–Computer network resources–Congresses. I. Coe, Jo Ann R. II. Menon, Goutham M.

HV29.2 .C68 2000
361'.00285–dc21
                                                   99-058925

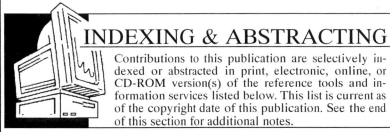

INDEXING & ABSTRACTING

Contributions to this publication are selectively indexed or abstracted in print, electronic, online, or CD-ROM version(s) of the reference tools and information services listed below. This list is current as of the copyright date of this publication. See the end of this section for additional notes.

- *Abstracts of Research in Pastoral Care & Counseling*

- *ACM Guide to Computer Literature*

- *Applied Social Sciences Index & Abstracts (ASSIA) (Online: ASSI via Data-Star) (CDRom: ASSIA Plus)*

- *Behavioral Medicine Abstracts*

- *BUBL Information Service, an Internet-based Information Service for the UK higher education community: <URL:http://bubl.ac.uk/>*

- *caredata CD: the social and community care database*

- *CNPIEC Reference Guide: Chinese National Directory of Foreign Periodicals*

- *Computer Abstracts*

- *Computer Literature Index*

- *Computing Reviews*

- *Current Contents: Clinical Medicine/Life Sciences (CC:CM/LS) (weekly Table of Contents Service), and Social Science Citation Index. Articles also searchable through Social SciSearch, ISI's online database and in ISI's Research Alert current awareness service*

- *Engineering Information (PAGE ONE)*

- *IBZ International Bibliography of Periodical Literature*

- *Information Science Abstracts*

- *INSPEC*

- *Library & Information Science Abstracts (LISA)*

(continued)

- *Microcomputer Abstracts*

- *National Clearinghouse on Child Abuse & Neglect*

- *Periodica Islamica*

- *Psychological Abstracts (PsycINFO)*

- *Referativnyi Zhurnal (Abstracts Journal of the All-Russian Institute of Scientific and Technical Information)*

- *Sage Public Administration Abstracts (SPAA)*

- *Social Services Abstracts*

- *Social Work Abstracts*

- *Sociological Abstracts (SA)*

Special Bibliographic Notes related to special journal issues (separates) and indexing/abstracting:

- indexing/abstracting services in this list will also cover material in any "separate" that is co-published simultaneously with Haworth's special thematic journal issue or DocuSerial. Indexing/abstracting usually covers material at the article/chapter level.
- monographic co-editions are intended for either non-subscribers or libraries which intend to purchase a second copy for their circulating collections.
- monographic co-editions are reported to all jobbers/wholesalers/approval plans. The source journal is listed as the "series" to assist the prevention of duplicate purchasing in the same manner utilized for books-in-series.
- to facilitate user/access services all indexing/abstracting services are encouraged to utilize the co-indexing entry note indicated at the bottom of the first page of each article/chapter/contribution.
- this is intended to assist a library user of any reference tool (whether print, electronic, online, or CD-ROM) to locate the monographic version if the library has purchased this version but not a subscription to the source journal.
- individual articles/chapters in any Haworth publication are also available through the Haworth Document Delivery Services (HDDS).

Computers and Information Technology in Social Work: Education, Training, and Practice

CONTENTS

ABOUT THE EDITORS

Jo Ann R. Coe, PhD, is Assistant Professor and Technology Coordinator for the University of South Carolina College of Social Work in Columbia, South Carolina. She received her PhD degree in Social Work from The University of Texas at Arlington in August 1999. She also has a master's degree in Social Work from Our Lady of the Lake University and a bachelor of arts in Religion from Trinity University. She has practiced as a social worker in Texas with Child Protective Services and as a therapist with sexually abused children. Her interest in distance education and technology evolved while pursuing a doctoral degree, and she now focuses her work and research in this area. She co-chaired the 1998 Information Technologies Conference where these papers were presented.

Goutham M. Menon, PhD, is Assistant Professor at the University of South Carolina College of Social Work. He received his PhD from the School of Social Work, University of Illinois at Urbana–Champaign. His research area focuses on the utilization of technology for human services, mainly looking at on-line counseling and electronic advocacy issues. Dr. Menon serves on the editorial board of the *Journal of Technology in Human Services* and is also actively involved with the Inter-University Consortium for International Social Development.

Introduction

Jo Ann R. Coe
Goutham M. Menon

Recent technological advances have had a significant impact on social work practice and education. These advances have resulted in a paradigm shift in the way social work is being practiced as well as how education is delivered. In the summer of 1998, the University of South Carolina College of Social Work hosted a week-long conference that focused on the impact of information technologies for social work education and practice. Over 200 people from 34 states and three countries attended the conference throughout the week. Participants included social work practitioners in agencies and private practices, administrators, staff development specialists, information systems specialists as well as graduate and undergraduate social work educators from over 100 schools and universities. The conference workshops covered a wide variety of topics including distance education (particularly education via the World Wide Web and interactive television), technology teaching applications, networking and on-line resources for social workers, corporate and business partnerships for technology, research studies on the use of technology and applications of technology to enhance social work practice and education.

This special issue is a selection of the ideas and projects presented at the conference and their impact on social work practice and education. The first half of the issue discusses the impact of information technologies on social work practice. Each of the articles selected discuss different aspects of technology applied to assist those in helping professions to impact the communities, clients and organizations they serve.

Jo Ann R. Coe, PhD, is Assistant Professor and Technology Coordinator, and Goutham M. Menon, PhD, is Assistant Professor, University of South Carolina, College of Social Work, Columbia, SC 29208.

[Haworth co-indexing entry note]: "Introduction." Coe, Jo Ann R., and Goutham M. Menon. Co-published simultaneously in *Journal of Technology in Human Services* (The Haworth Press, Inc.) Vol. 16, No. 2/3, 1999, pp. 1-3; and: *Computers and Information Technology in Social Work: Education, Training, and Practice* (ed: Jo Ann R. Coe, and Goutham M. Menon) The Haworth Press, Inc., 1999, pp. 1-3. Single or multiple copies of this article are available for a fee from The Haworth Document Delivery Service [1-800-342-9678, 9:00 a.m. - 5:00 p.m. (EST). E-mail address: getinfo@haworthpressinc.com].

Ray Carlson discusses how computers can be used to develop case-reasoning in child protective cases in order to practice more effectively.

Paul Freddolino and Abraham Seonghee Han discuss the use of videoconferencing technology for delivery of social services in Korea and the United States. Their article highlights the tremendous impact this technology can have on rural populations and in undeveloped areas of the world. The use of videoconferencing to conduct a breast cancer support group and coordinate social services for clients is an innovative project that directly impacts the lives of isolated and vulnerable persons.

C. David Hollister and Chandra Mehrotra discuss the use of interactive television for delivering leadership training to volunteers located in rural communities. Their study is a formative evaluation of this project that gives important feedback on how this technology can be used for training in rural areas.

David A. Patterson and Richard Cloud present an exciting and innovative application of artificial neural networks (ANN's) for predicting psychiatric rehospitalization in mentally ill outpatients. Their study supports the use of decision support tools for mental health workers as the use of ANN's achieved correct prediction rates ranging from 75%-93%.

These articles represent some of the ways that information technology is being used to impact clients directly. The final two articles were selected as they impact the larger systems of communities and organizations.

Kristine Tower discusses the use of television as a tool for impacting communities. Her article examines the role television can have on social work practice and gives practical ideas and suggestions for those in helping professions to utilize.

The final article in this section is by Brenda Kunkel, a social worker, in the corporate/private sector. Her article presents ideas on how to develop successful technology projects in social service agencies. Her perspectives combine business strategies along with human needs to ensure that organizations can make successful investments in technology to impact the clients they serve.

The second half of the issue discusses the impact of information technologies on social work higher education. As the emergence of new technologies develops at a remarkable speed, a shifting educational paradigm is occurring in which instruction is expanding from the traditional paradigm of faculty-student interaction in fixed locations at specified times to a new paradigm in which students can access the same instructional resources, regardless of location and at their own convenience. Administrators and faculty in higher education institutions are exploring cost-effective technology solutions aimed at improving productivity for students, reducing labor intensity, and providing new ways to deliver professional education and better services to students while enhancing the quality of instruction. Each of the articles selected apply different aspects of technology to help accomplish these goals.

Philip Ouellette provides an excellent discussion of how Web-based instruction can be used as pedagogical strategy for impacting human service practice. His article gives teaching strategies that support the use of moving towards a "virtual classroom."

Jerome R. Kolbo and Earlie M. Washington also support the use of Web-based instruction in developing an orientation course for educational and human service settings. They present their experience in designing and developing a course that is useful to a variety of settings.

Diane S. Falk discusses the use of a Web-based conferencing program to augment her courses. Her article presents evidence that the use of a conferencing program greatly expands opportunities for teaching, learning and communication.

Debra Gohagan discusses the use of WebQuests, a computer-facilitated instructional strategy, that is another excellent application for expanding learning opportunities.

With the increasing use of these tools in higher education, more emphasis is being placed on evaluating the use and experiences of those students involved in these applications. The final articles selected focus on this area.

Jo Ann R. Coe and John Gandy present a review of the literature on students' experiences with distance education and make recommendations for future evaluation research.

Ronald Rooney, Elena Izaksonas, and Jane Macy discuss an interesting phenomena known as site bias that occurs in distance education courses. Their article presents ideas on how to reframe this bias to site identity in order to promote goals of teaching social justice and diversity.

The articles selected for this issue present some of the exciting and innovative ideas and projects presented at the technology conference. As we move into the new millennium, it is expected that technology will continue to impact the way we practice and educate. As you read the following articles, it is hoped that you will be excited and motivated by the ideas presented and develop your own thoughts for how technology can impact communities, clients and organizations in the 21st century.

IMPACT
OF INFORMATION TECHNOLOGIES
ON SOCIAL WORK PRACTICE

Using Case-Based Reasoning to Develop Computerized Guidance for Effective Practice

Ray Carlson

SUMMARY. Research on expertise suggests that several years of extensive practice should lead to the development of good insights into effective practice. This paper describes this research and what it suggests about ways to capture and utilize such expertise in a computerized training simulator. Case-based reasoning is looked at as a way to interpret this research and its utilization. The paper also summarizes a project that is collecting such experience-based insights in the child welfare field. Particular attention is directed at ways to validate the experiential insights collected. *[Article copies available for a fee from The Haworth Document Delivery Service: 1-800-342-9678. E-mail address: getinfo@ haworthpressinc.com <Website: http://www.haworthpressinc.com>]*

Ray Carlson is Professor, Maritime School of Social Work, Dalhousie University, 6414 Coburg Road, Halifax, NS, B3H2A7, Canada (E-mail: ray.carlson@dal.ca).

[Haworth co-indexing entry note]: "Using Case-Based Reasoning to Develop Computerized Guidance for Effective Practice." Carlson, Ray. Co-published simultaneously in *Journal of Technology in Human Services* (The Haworth Press, Inc.) Vol. 16, No. 2/3, 1999, pp. 5-18; and: *Computers and Information Technology in Social Work: Education, Training, and Practice* (ed: Jo Ann R. Coe, and Goutham M. Menon) The Haworth Press, Inc., 1999, pp. 5-18. Single or multiple copies of this article are available for a fee from The Haworth Document Delivery Service [1-800-342-9678, 9:00 a.m. - 5:00 p.m. (EST). E-mail address: getinfo@haworthpressinc.com].

KEYWORDS. Expertise, experience, case-based reasoning, child welfare training

INTRODUCTION

Out of the corner of my eye, I noticed that the religious elder from the Aboriginal Community was leaving the room. The elder was one of the representatives of the Aboriginal Community on the Board of a Project to assist Aboriginal people involved in the Justice System. The meeting was assessing whether funding for the Project should be continued, and the elder had not said anything during the discussion. As the independent evaluator for the Project, I was concerned that the elder might be leaving because he was reluctant to express his concerns about the operation of the program. I decided to follow him and ask if he wanted to share his views in private.

I caught up to the elder at the refreshment table in the adjoining room. He handed me the coffee he had just poured and poured himself another. I asked how he thought the meeting was going. His eyes twinkled. Referring to the Director of the Project by name, he responded that he was a smart old rabbit. The Director was an Aboriginal person who had worked for over 15 years in the Justice System. He was very dedicated but also very serious. He seemed a little uncomfortable in meetings like this where he had to answer questions from senior administrators in various Justice and government agencies.

I asked if he thought the Director would be upset at being called a rabbit. "Not if he has spent much time in the woods," the Elder replied. "Rabbits are favorite prey for foxes, hawks, people. The majority of young rabbits are eventually caught. Rabbits that survive learn from experience about slippery spots, obstructions that will deter a larger animal, places that offer a good view, the shortest routes to a hole. The rabbits who survive to an old age are the ones who learn their territory and stay in the area they know." He noted how the Project Director avoided responding to questions outside his area of expertise. When asked about problems Aboriginal people had with some of the Justice agencies present, he described cases rather than attribute blame. "He knows this territory and how to avoid traps."

In this analogy, the elder offered an insight into the nature of effectiveness but also into his own role of elder. The Aboriginal Community has traditionally valued elders as problem solvers. Others might be more effective as spokespersons, politicians, land claim analysts, and the like. But the Community needs individuals who have developed insights into how to respond to complex problems or tasks. It is important that such individuals extrapolate from their own experiences to new problems as this individual did in using his hunting experience to recognize how to be successful in a complex bureaucratic meeting. A key Aboriginal value is to respect such individuals who have learned from extensive life experience.

EXPERIENTIAL EXPERTISE

The rapid development of computers lead to interest in how to generate artificial intelligence, that is, how to get computers to equal or surpass human expertise. Initial attempts to create computer programs that would beat chess grand masters, diagnose complex internal diseases, identify likely geological locations for oil deposits, and the like were less successful than their human counterparts. Such lack of success promoted research on expertise.

A few decades of research have yielded some remarkable insights. To become an expert a person needs some natural ability and extensive experience, but the most essential factor is intense practice (Ericsson and Lehmann 1996). Practice involves not just repetition but planned activity with appropriate feedback to assess results. Applying this concept to social work, such practice would involve detailed assessment, identifying concrete goals, developing and implementing a plan of action, and monitoring the results to see if the goals were attained. The term "practice" is used to refer to repetition and gradual refinement through deliberate monitoring of results (Ericsson et al. 1993). After years of such practice, the expert develops extensive memories as to connections between attributes of a situation, interventions and expected results.

In fact, such individuals seem to enhance their memory capacity through efficient organization in their area of expertise. The expert does not develop a better memory. Instead, the enhancement applies only to the area in which there is extensive practice, a pattern that might explain the concept of the absent-minded professor. Boshuizen and Schmidt (1992) studied medical experts who were identified as reflecting unusual diagnostic expertise. They found that instead of the biomedical reasoning normally presented in a medical school, such individuals used concepts that directly related consumer symptoms and test results to diagnostic alternatives. Because such experts do not have to work their way through normal reasoning, they can more quickly identify a range of alternatives and eliminate those that do not fit with the information in the current case. Their thoughts are sufficiently efficient to allow handling a large amount of information. Regular memory does not have the capacity to fully analyze complex situations (Holyoak, 1990).

A key idea is that these concepts evolve through experience. Ericsson and Kintsch (1995) describe how medical experts efficiently focus on key information rather than detail. They do not recall details, only the key information that influenced what action was most appropriate. The memory recognizes these key factors and suggests what steps to take to verify the nature of the problem. The risk is that such an individual will impose memories that do not fit the new situation. The person with extensive experience is less likely to do this because their memory includes a large number of alternatives and their features. If any of those features do not fit, the memories jump to other alternatives. These memories also suggest a sequence of actions that have been helpful with such situations and what has happened after each such action. Memory will recognize if the response does not fit what happened before when such actions were helpful. As a result, the expert is more likely to recognize the need to reconsider other alternatives. In the long run, if the case proves to be unique, the expert will return to trial and error like the less experienced person.

This cognitive process occurs in a natural sequence, each response evokes a sense as to what is happening and what to ask or do next. Gilhooly (1996) notes that studies that compare experts and novices find that the expert spends more time than the novice trying to recognize the nature of the problem. Once experts recognize the key features of the problem they seem to know what to expect and work through a sequence that leads to a solution. The novice tends to focus on the goal and attempt to work back trying to identify the steps needed to get there.

Experiential Expertise in Social Work

A child protection worker investigates a case where a teacher suggests that the father of one of her students is physically abusing the wife and children. She contacts the school and asks about the boy's behaviour. She is told that the boy is nervous but continually engages in physical fights with the other children.

The social worker visits the family and finds the mother home alone. She denies that any abuse is occurring, but the worker notices certain attributes of the situation that seem to fit cases where abuse did occur. The mother's response evokes an expectation that the mother will be likely to take action if she thinks about her son becoming violent like his father. She discusses this with the mother and notices the mother reacting the way she expects. She notes that it is important for boys not to see their mothers as passive victims since they will expect their girl friends to respond in the same way. Her memory suggests that it is more effective to let the mother give this issue some thought. She hands the mother her card and asks her to call if she wants any help.

A few days later the woman calls and leaves a message for the worker. The worker calls back and, when the mother seems uncomfortable, immediately asks if the husband is at home. The woman says yes, so the worker suggests that the woman act like it is a telephone survey. She then arranges an appointment by using questions that can be answered by yes or no. At that interview, the mother notes that she like the father had been physically abusing the boy. The social worker had not expected this response, but immediately asks if alcohol or drug use is involved. The mother admits that both she and her husband have drinking problems.

The social worker is reflecting a complex set of assumptions about patterns and actions and expected outcomes. She has developed an efficient method for jumping over less important features and concentrating on actions that will clarify the situation. When she receives information that does not fit her expectations it evokes another possibility.

For social work, a key advantage for this approach is that it recognizes variations according to context. Traditional research emphasizes direct co-variations in controlled environments. If someone lacks social skills, that person will be likely to lack social support and will experience more stress. Therefore, the appropriate intervention is to increase social skills. In practice, however, the social worker needs to consider context. A victim of sexual abuse might appear to reflect poor social skills which are actually a protective response to the abuse. Such a person needs protection more than improvement of social skills. The type of memories associated with expertise include such contextual variations because they have been tested by reality rather than developed for their theoretical relevance.

Implicit Learning

The above discussion emphasizes explicit learning that including thinking about goals and whether they are achieved. Holyoak and Spellman (1993) describe how this learning can also occur in an implicit manner. Implicit learning results directly from covariance. The person does not think consciously about the connection. In the same way we learn not to touch a hot stove, we learn to avoid anything that brings an upsetting result and to do those things that get us through a problematic situation.

Clients with a history of violence can be a danger to a social worker who needs to deal with these clients when they are under stress. A humorous or supportive comment can reduce the stress, and experienced workers tend to make such comments in such situations. When asked why, they have difficulty providing an explanation. They have implicitly learned that such comments help ease the tension.

Such learning is a component of the development of experience-based expertise but is more limited in value. First, implicit learning will incorporate those connections that do not include much separation in time or attention. It is most useful in developing assumptions in situations that include immediate feedback such as modifying crises. If one wants to look beyond the immediate crisis to longer-term outcomes, implicit learning will not recognize such connections. Learning what leads to later results requires some conscious attention in which the person monitors longer-term outcomes and thinks about whether they fit what was expected.

A child placement worker was taking a class in graduate school. She was writing a paper on how to reduce violence in children who have been victims of abuse. She fell behind in her work and ended up working on the assignment in her office. She got a call from a foster parent saying that they no longer could put up with this violent boy who had been placed with them. She knew that trying to find a new placement would keep her from finishing her paper. She tried a variety of techniques that sometimes convince a foster family to keep trying, but she immediately felt that this was a situation where the child had to be moved.

As she began searching for another family, she suddenly recognized the connection between this case and her paper. She realized that in this case she had never tried any of the interventions she was discussing in the paper. She recognized that her natural inclination was to think about how to get a family to accept a child, not how to create a placement that would be successful over the lone term or how to help the child resolve her or his needs. She was reflecting implicit knowledge, what worked with immediate goals. She did not think about how her immediate assumptions and actions fit with longer-term outcomes. The latter is what is normally associated with expertise.

A second limitation to implicit learning is that it is not likely to be adapted to new situations. Memory will bring to mind the connection only if the new situation looks like those previously encountered. A third limitation is the fact that implicit learning is restricted to emotionally charged situations. The learning occurs when an immediate upsetting result is avoided or an emotionally satisfying response is evoked. Explicit learning is often dependent on internal thoughts such as surprise that an expected result did not occur.

In this sense, implicit learning is helpful in resolving immediate pressures, explicit learning is more useful in achieving longer-term goals. The challenge is to capture such explicit learning and make it available to those with less experience. Otherwise a series of consumers must serve as guinea pigs while the latter develop their own insights.

CASE-BASED REASONING

If it takes years of practice for an expert to develop these complex insights, how can they be quickly transmitted to new staff? This question has prompted research on new methods of training (see Gallagher, 1994 or Carlson, 1992). Case-based reasoning was a phrase that seemed to capture the nature of this experiential learning. Gradually, the term was also used by those who wished to emulate such thinking in developing computerized knowledge bases that would give advise to the inexperienced (Kolodner, 1993).

A case-based reasoning computer program follows the following structure: A database is composed of a large number of cases reflecting how relevant problems are solved. A retrieval system is established based on the key characteristics that distinguish cases that require different actions. When a problem is presented to the system, the retrieval system uses the characteristics of the new case to locate those cases in the database which are most similar. The program then indicates how in those cases the problems were approached and the resultant success or failure. The program may include guidance as to whether distinctive features with the new problem might require adapting the responses to the similar ones in the database. Each new problem encountered can be added to the case database once it is clear whether the actions taken were successful or harmful. The database shows which prior errors to avoid and which successes to repeat (Dhar & Stein, 1997).

Kolodner (1993) notes that the quality of a case-based reasoning programs is based on

- the number of related cases that are included;
- the ability of the retrieval system to compare new cases to those in the database;
- adeptness at adapting existing case data to the variations in the new case; and
- capability to obtain feedback on success with new cases and to correct existing information accordingly.

Dhar and Stein (1997), though, note that it is the quality of the cases that is most important. The more cases that cover situations that necessitate different responses, the easier it is to find one that fits the current situation.

For a number of years, efforts have been made to develop expert systems that mirror human experts. Most have relied on setting up rules in the form of "if . . ., then . . . ." The if part of the statement specifies when the rule applies, and the then part specifies the action to take. In human services, such rules are called practice guidelines: if a client threatens to attack another person, then you must seek to warn that other person as well as deter the client. In practice, such rules become overly complex as they attempt to cover varying situations. In situations that include a variety of alternatives, case-based reasoning becomes a more feasible approach (Medsker, 1995). If the context changes, the response should change. This feature makes case-based reasoning approach particularly appropriate for social work, a field that is concerned with the complex interactions between people and their environments.

A variety of computer program shells that support case-based reasoning are now available through a special website at www.ai-cbr.com. The prior task, though, is to capture the case examples and identify how they can be classified to allow rapid recognition.

CAPTURING EXPERIENCE-BASED EXPERTISE

Recognizing that some experienced practitioners have developed insightful case memories does not mean that those memories can be easily captured and passed on to others.

The first challenge is that such memories are too complex to be easily explained by the expert. The memories are remembered as patterns that are stored according to the key attributes. To capture such insights, the person possessing such memories needs to consider typical cases. As they hear details of the case, they will remember the connections between those details and appropriate actions. Recording the responses to several similar but distinct cases clarifies which case characteristics lead to recognition of particular problems and which situations seem appropriate for which actions.

Secondly, the expert needs to be asked to respond to cases that fit that individual's memories. As a result, the cases presented need to include realistic details, address typical decisions, and fit the respondent's particular responsibilities. For example, a person who works in an office where another staff person is designated as an adolescent specialist is less likely to have developed insights related to cases involving adolescent consumers. An individual who develops such expertise is no better than a novice in responding to situations that do not fit their experience. Cases that strike the experienced person as unusual should not be assessed.

Thirdly, it is necessary to locate staff who formulate assumptions about longer-term outcomes rather than immediate pressures. This feature will be reflected by their comfort in projecting assumptions about problems and discussing progress and outcomes. Concrete, case-specific questions and assumptions suggest that the respondent has formulated memories in this area. Suppose an experienced person is asked about long-term progress for a sexual abuse victim who avoids talking about the abuse, and she replies that the victim will become more open during therapy. This respondent's views are of less value since their perception of "long-term" does not seem to extend beyond interaction with a therapist. There is no indication as to whether that person's approach was adapted to maximize consumer functioning in other roles.

VALIDITY

Experience-based insights can easily be misleading. Staff may get misleading progress reports from children who want to return home, from foster parents who want to be "nice," from social workers who want to appear to be successful, etc. Staff may convince themselves that progress has occurred because of a strong personal desire to be successful. Other staff may be frustrated with their job or supervisor or agency and find something wrong with situations that are working out well.

As a result, it is necessary to establish procedures that verify that consumer behaviour and life satisfaction are greater when the experience-based information is applied. The traditional approach is to see if multiple experts agree (Shaw and Woodward, 1990). It is assumed that experienced staff who do not interact a lot are not likely to develop the same misconceptions.

A second approach is to assess construct validity based on whether the responses of assumed experts reflect the patterns research suggests will be associated with explicit experience-based insights. Greater confidence in a person's response is evoked if the person seems to recognize the case and how to respond, responds differently to different problems, and seems comfortable in describing specific results.

Assessing service outcomes offers a third possibility. Regular collection of outcome information is probably the best means of recognizing whether those with experience-based expertise are more effective. It is also possible to consider whether newer staff achieve better results after being trained to use the insights acquired from the experts.

TRAINING

Schank (1996) notes that for decades educators have discussed the importance of learning by doing. The work on case-based reasoning now provides a sense as to what that phrase means. Learning by doing can be viewed as the accumulation and indexing of cases. When a person encounters a situation that requires decision-making, the person draws to mind the most similar prior situation. The person responds to the current situation based on what worked or did not work in that prior situation. The person develops a system for indexing such prior experiences in order to quickly identify which experiences are closest to the current one.

Critical to learning is the process of expectation failure and explanation. Case memories suggest what to expect. If a new situation does not fit these expectations, the person seeks an explanation for this lack of fit and adds a new case memory. Schank notes that learning by doing is based on:

- exposing the learner to cases;
- allowing the learner to use experience to make decisions about these cases;
- giving feedback of the effectiveness of those decisions;
- encouraging the person to develop an explanation for their successes and failures;
- repeating the process so that the person can test that explanation.

Supervised practice is a common way to support such learning for tasks where errors do not lead to a high risk. For example, a person learning how to drive can learn by experience by driving a car in a mall parking lot on a day when the stores are closed. When poor practice entails high risk such as flying an airplane, doing surgery, or a police officer responding to gun shots, learning can best occur in a simulator or virtual environment. Such a learning environment will be most effective if it has a realistic appearance and if success or failure occurs in the same way as in real life–the simulator indicates that the plane crashes, an artery is cut, and so on.

A CASE-BASED REASONING PROJECT FOR CHILD WELFARE

The question of the decade is how to reduce the costs of providing human services while maintaining or increasing the expected benefit to the consumer. The best response to that question is to replace ineffective or harmful service with services that yield better results. Such a response relies on a knowledge base reflecting effective ways to prevent and resolve problems and achieve specified goals, eliminate ineffective services, avoid service-created problems and maximize use of self-help and natural supports.

At this point, most social work domains lack such a knowledge base. The discussion of expertise suggests a way such a knowledge base might be developed. If social workers who have developed expertise can be identified, it may be possible to capture their insights and pass them along to other practitioners and trainees.

Such a task is the focus of a project developed by the Maritime School of Social Work at Dalhousie University and the Child Welfare Services Section of the Nova Scotia Department of Community Services. The goal of this project is to develop a training simulator like those used by pilots or the police. The simulator will present case situations to trainees who will be asked to develop intervention plans. Immediate feedback will be given as to how their plans differ from those reflected by experienced staff experts. The simulator will present hundreds of cases to the trainee, who will be asked to formulate insights into how to recognize situations that require different interventions. As a result, the trainee will gradually develop limited expertise without requiring consumers to be the guinea pigs during such a learning phase.

The first step in this project involved identification of and interviews with those social workers who were likely to have developed such experience-based expertise. Two or three case situations were presented to each potential respondent. Questions asked for their plan and prognosis for each case. Some questions were intended to assess the likelihood that their responses reflected expertise while the majority of the questions sought detailed intervention assumptions.

The cases and questions were formulated to take advantage of what is understood about case-based reasoning. The cases are varied in planned ways to assess what factors influence staff to utilize different responses. Each case includes five phases designed to reflect time periods in which distinct decisions must be faced.

For the first round of this project, 14 graduate students have interviewed 59 experienced staff. These staff worked in fifteen different offices throughout the Province including rural, small town and urban areas. In a related project, 2 other students interviewed ten family counselors who worked with child welfare clients.

Each respondent assesses two or three cases [a third case was presented if the respondent gave a brief response to one of the first two]. Combining these projects, the initial 69 respondents have yielded 162 case assessments. On average, each case is presented to six respondents so that 29 cases have been assessed. Initial assessments have sought to identify which staff appear to best fit the patterns associated with expertise as noted above. The next assessment have identified agreements among those who responded to the same case and factors that may have influenced such agreement.

As a supplemental test, a few respondents were re-interviewed using webcams, that is, small video cameras that are attached to a computer. Using internet connections, the interviews can be completed with the interviewer and respondent seeing each other even though they are not in the same location. In this test, respondents were asked to occasionally give intentionally inaccurate responses. The interviewer was asked to identify when they felt the respondent was being inaccurate. A comparison was made between web-cam interviews, in-person interviews and phone interviews. Results for the in-person interviews were best, but those for the web-cams were almost as good and twice as good as those for the phone. The sample sizes were small but suggest that it is reasonable to use web-cams to interview experienced staff who are not located near the University.

Preliminary Analysis

Analysis is focused on identifying:

1. the respondents who more clearly reflected the patterns associated with explicit experiential learning, that is,
   a. Formed appropriate assumptions about the situation and then asked questions which would test those assumptions;
   b. Concentrated on case variations that have relevance for action;

    c. Focused on case-relevant consumer goals in contrast to general goals or those that were relevant to the service provider rather than the consumer.

2. the actions that were recommended for each case by the respondents identified by step 1 emphasizing those actions that are recommended by more than one such respondent and were assumed to achieve significant benefit;

3. the case/situational features that seem to suggest the need for different interventions.

This analysis provides specific rather than dramatic information. Practice research typically tries to offer general conclusions such as Type X therapy is more effective than Type Y for a certain general problem. In this project, the information collected is much more complex.

The results suggest what type of actions were taken as different phases of each case.

For example, about twenty percent of the cases presented were viewed as inappropriate for involvement of a child welfare service. Most of these cases reflected poor parental attitudes but no actual harm or obvious risk for the child involved. Responses indicated which type of information would be adequate to suggest that a case could be opened in such situations. As a result, the information gives clues as to what can be assessed in a variety of situations.

Of the cases that justified intervention, staff expressed optimism for achieving reasonable progress in 41 percent, had mixed views about 24 percent, and expressed doubts about making progress in 35 percent.

- All of the last group involved cases where both parents reflected problems that had been present for an extended period of time such as addiction, violent behaviour or low self-esteem.
- This last group also lacked external support that helped with child care.

Cases that do not evoke any optimism offer less training value since the interventions identified are assumed to be inadequate. The exception is when the respondents indicated actions that lead to harmful results.

In discussing progress, respondents are likely to define case-specific goals related to resolvable problems that led to the reasons the case was opened. Child protection is the general goal, but staff need more specific goals that guide action. For example, in one case, a single mother became involved with a new boy friend and began leaving a young child alone for a few hours at a time. The boy friend liked to do things spontaneously without leaving the mother time to arrange baby sitting. The boy friend also objected to spending money on medications the child needed. Progress was focused on whether the mother consistently over an extended time carried through on plans to arrange baby sitting and maintain the medication. In other words, the respondents suggested appropriate interventions and effective ways to monitor outcomes.

Next Steps

More extensive analysis will be done to assess what case characteristics influenced case responses.

After analysis of the current results, individuals who demonstrated explicit experience-based insights will be asked to review additional cases. These cases will be selected to reflect situational variations relative to the cases already reviewed. Response to these cases will aid with the third task noted above.

During the next phase, the results will be used to create an educational computer program. That program will present the same cases to trainees and ask for their assessments. The computer will provide immediate feedback indicating how their responses differ and/or agree with those provided by staff with experiential expertise. The trainee will be asked to reflect on the reason for such discrepancies. They will repeat the assessments until they are generally able to replicate the expert responses.

The next phase will add videos of actors who will reflect consumer responses. These videos will be incorporated into the computerized training program. The final phase will add a case-based reasoning program that can be assessed by all staff if they wish advise on responding to a case. Collection of outcome information is also anticipated as a concurrent activity that will be used to validate the effectiveness of the practice of the identified experts. This information will also allow assessment of the impact of the training programs.

This summary presents these steps as a natural progression. Each one is actually a complex task that will require the same amount of developmental activity as the work summarized above. The long-run expectation, though, is a self-improving system that should lead to equalize consumer benefit throughout the child welfare service system.

REFERENCES

Boshuizen, H.P.A. & Schmidt, H.G. 1992. On the role of biomedical knowledge in clinical reasoning by experts, immediates and novices. *Cognitive Science.* 16: 153-84.

Carlson, R.W. 1992. From rules to prototypes: Adapting expert systems to the nature of expertise in clinical information processing, *Computers in Human Service.* 9: 339-350.

Dhar, V. & Stein, R. 1997. Solving problems by analogy: Case-based reasoning. *Seven Methods for Transforming Corporate Data Into Business Intelligence.* pp. 149-166. Upper Saddle River, NJ Prentice Hall.

Ericsson, K.A. & Kintsch, W. 1995. Long-term working memory. *Psychological Review.* 102: 211-45.

Ericsson, K.A., Krampe, R.T. & Tesch-Romer, C. 1993. The role of deliberate practice in the acquisition of expert performance. *Psychological Review.* 100: 363-406.

Ericsson, K.A. & Lehmann, A.C. 1996. Expert and exceptional performance: Evidence of maximal adaptation to task constraints, *Annual. Review of Psychology.* 47: 273-305.

Gallagher, J.J. 1994. Teaching and learning: New models. *Annual. Review of Psychology.* 45: 171-195.

Gilhooly, K.J. 1996. *Thinking: Directed, Undirected and Creative.* London: Academic Press, See particularly chapter 4, Expertise 2: Non-adversary problems.

Holyoak, K.J. 1990. Problem solving, *Thinking: An Invitation to Cognitive Science,* Vol. 3, ed. D.N. Osherson & E.E. Smith, pp. 117-146. Cambridge, MA: The MIT Press.

Holyoak, K.J. & Spellman, B.A. 1993. Thinking. *Annual Review of Psychology.* 44: 265-315.

Klein, M.R. & Methlie, L.R. 1995. *Knowledge-Based Decision Support Systems with Applications in Business.* New York: John Wiley & Sons.

Kolodner, J. 1993. *Case-Based Reasoning.* San Mateo, CA: Morgan Kaufmann Publishers, Inc.

Medsker, L.R. 1995. Case-based reasoning, *Hybrid Intelligent Systems.* Boston: Kluwer Academic Publishers.

Schank, Roger C. 1996. Goal-based scenarios: Case-based reasoning meets learning by doing. *Case-Based Reasoning: Experiences, Lessons & Future Directions.* Ed. D. Leake. Cambridge, MA: AAAI Press/The MIT Press, pp. 295-347.

Shaw, M.L.G. & Woodward, J.B. 1990. Validation in a knowledge support system: Construing and consistency with multiple experts. *The Foundations of Knowledge Acquisition.* Eds. J.H. Boose & B.R. Gaines. San Diego: Academic Press, pp. 39-60.

Direct Service Applications of Videoconferencing Technologies: Case Examples from Korea and the United States

Paul P. Freddolino
Abraham Seonghee Han

SUMMARY. This paper describes practice applications of videoconferencing technologies in two settings. In Korea, people who live in areas which lack social welfare expertise receive services such as education, counseling, diagnostic assessment, and therapy through a system linking the central site with three service agencies in three different cities. In the United States, an interactive video breast cancer support group links women in three distant communities monthly. Evaluative feedback concerning these applications from professional and lay users will be reviewed in detail. Implications for the use of videoconferencing in social work practice will be discussed. *[Article copies available for a fee from The Haworth Document Delivery Service: 1-800-342-9678. E-mail address: getinfo@haworthpressinc.com <Website: http://www.haworthpressinc.com>]*

KEYWORDS. Videoconferencing, social welfare, breast cancer support

Paul P. Freddolino, PhD, is Professor and Coordinator of Distance Education, Michigan State University School of Social Work, 254 Baker Hall, East Lansing, MI 48824.

Abraham Seonghee Han is Professor, Department of Special Education, and Director, Education & Welfare Technology, National Research Center, Kongju National University, Kongju, Korea.

[Haworth co-indexing entry note]: "Direct Service Applications of Videoconferencing Technologies: Case Examples from Korea and the United States." Freddolino, Paul P., and Abraham Seonghee Han. Co-published simultaneously in *Journal of Technology in Human Services* (The Haworth Press, Inc.) Vol. 16, No. 2/3, 1999, pp. 19-33; and: *Computers and Information Technology in Social Work: Education, Training, and Practice* (ed: Jo Ann R. Coe, and Goutham M. Menon) The Haworth Press, Inc., 1999, pp. 19-33. Single or multiple copies of this article are available for a fee from The Haworth Document Delivery Service [1-800-342-9678, 9:00 a.m. - 5:00 p.m. (EST). E-mail address: getinfo@haworthpressinc.com].

19

Although interactive video/videoconferencing technology is becoming more widespread in universities, hospitals, and other settings, practitioners are only now beginning to develop practical, reasonably efficient applications which have as their main goal the delivery of quality services to clients who might not otherwise find these services accessible. This paper will provide examples of such applications–in two very different cultural contexts–for diagnosis, direct service, consultations and support groups. The first case study, from South Korea, will describe the use of a videoconferencing system to link people who live in areas lacking social welfare expertise with special education personnel and other professional consultants located at Kongju National University. The second case study, from the United States, involves a real-time interactive breast cancer support group based at Marquette (MI) General Hospital, involving members in three different communities who meet once per month on the interactive system. Assessments of these systems by professional and lay users will be reviewed. The possibilities and limitations of this technology will then be discussed, along with the implications for social work practice.

THE SOUTH KOREAN TELE-SOCIAL WELFARE SYSTEM

The Tele-Social Welfare System (TSWS), a high-speed information and communication infrastructure pilot project, was operationalized at Kongju National University (KNU) in 1996. The Education & Welfare Technology National Research Center at KNU was established as the service-providing organization for other organizations located at Kwangju, Kunsan, and Taejon, which are linked via T1 communication channels. In addition to high-speed communication channels, the system consists of Tele Video Systems (TVS) and the Social Welfare Database System (SWDS) which support real-time face-to-face interaction. The demonstration system was prototyped as a national pilot project through December, 1997, and then transferred to KNU for management and operation in a live environment. The TSWS demonstration project is of great significance in the application of interactive superhighway communications to various social welfare programs because in Korea, a nation pursuing welfare socialization, people who live in areas which lack social welfare expertise need to receive services such as education, counseling, diagnostic assessment, and therapy at various times and places.

Brief History and Structure

In 1996, Kongju National University and the Korean National Computerization Agency developed jointly the Tele Social Welfare Systems (TSWS) under the auspices of the Ministry of Education and the Ministry of Information and Communication as one of the information infrastructure pilot projects. These national projects of South Korea, which aim to interconnect every segment of government as well as social welfare and educational systems by the year 2015, require major increases in communications channel capacity in order to provide centralized control and coordination (National Computerization Agency, 1977). The Tele-Social Welfare System project offers educational opportunities to upgrade practical skills and qualifications of social welfare employees who otherwise cannot receive this service because of distance from universities, colleges, and training sites (Han & Choi, 1977).

TSWS aims to ensure equal and expanded benefits of social services for needy people throughout the nation regardless of whether they are urban dwellers or remote villagers, and to accelerate improvement in the quality of services. Kongju National University, which is the central site of TSWS, is currently connected to three service agencies in three different cities via dedicated ultra high speed communications links. The agencies include a youth center, multi-social service center, and public health center, all of which are geographically located several hundred miles apart from each other.

TSWS is designed to enhance the quality of social services for diverse groups of people, particularly for people with disabilities, youth, housewives, and the elderly who have limited time and no means of transportation. This system aims to speed up the development of new models of social service delivery systems with the application of computer technology and multimedia. TSWS will enable people to receive education, counseling services, diagnostic assessment, and therapeutic interventions via multimedia and teleconferencing communications.

TSWS is comprised of two subordinate systems–the Tele Video System (TVS) and the Social Welfare Database System (SWDS). TVS, which is designed for education and counseling purposes, provides diagnoses, therapeutic interventions, and counseling services for people with disabilities, youth, women, and the elderly. This system also offers various classes for introducing cultural and educational activities. SWDS, a database containing information related to social welfare programs and services, is intended to be available to help anybody get access to and make use of assistive and adaptive devices.

Tele-Video System (TVS)

TVS, which connects four agencies at remote sites, consists of audio/video equipment and transmission devices and is designed to provide social education and counseling services via telecommunication to people with disabilities, youths, housewives, and the elderly. People served by this system are believed to have limited access to existing services or tend to underutilize the services that are available due to various reasons.

TVS provides computer assisted diagnoses and therapy for people with disabilities. This program also introduces about 120 types of assistive and adaptive devices for people with disabilities and provides related educational services. For instance, at Taejon Public Health Center, which is one of four satellite sites connected to the TVS, preschool-aged children with disabilities are provided with diagnostic assessment services. These children receive various therapies, such as visual functioning therapy, audiology training, play therapy, physical therapy, and occupational therapy. People with disabilities are taught how to use the Tele-Social Welfare Database System (TSWDS) that contains information related to social services. In order to better serve children with disabilities, the Center offers counseling services for parents and school teachers.

At another satellite site, the Multi-Social Service Center, TVS provides multimedia information on social welfare programs and services through TSWDS. In addition, the Center offers career education and counseling services for youth, and classes on hobbies, child rearing and parenting, and home economics for women. Programs for the elderly include education and counseling services for health management and mental hygiene.

Tele-Social Welfare Database System (TSWDS)

TSWDS is a database containing information on the laws and policies related to social welfare, social service organizations, rehabilitation technology, social education, and employment opportunities. This system can be accessed from remote computer terminals. People with disabilities are taught how to use the system without help from others. Those with disabilities are able to obtain the information that they need by using assistive and adaptive devices, such as paperless braille, voice synthesizer, on-screen keyboard, and pointing devices.

Analysis of the TSWS Pilot Project

Analysis of the data provided by Han (1998) shows that a total of 4,407 people (512 sessions, 796 hours) utilized the TSWS system between October 11, 1996 and May 31, 1998. Among these, the most frequently used service was the use of the TVS for purposes such as education, counseling, diagnostic assessment, and therapy. The service utilization of SWDS totalled 106 sessions, 193 hours, and 106 people. The videoconferencing formats applied to service offering and meetings among utilization-related personnel totaled 116 sessions, 157 hours, and 657 people. The service utilization through

TVS, such as education, counseling, diagnostic assessment, and therapy, is divided into welfare programs for housewives, people with disabilities, children, youth, the elderly, and others. Among these, utilization related to welfare for housewives was most frequent, with that related to disabled people second.

Tele-social welfare involves a broad range of services in addition to welfare for individuals with disabilities. An analysis of the results of the Tele-Social Welfare System pilot project and suggestions pertaining to the development plan are provided below with special attention to services related to welfare for people with disabilities and families of children with disabilities.

One hundred and fifty users of welfare programs for individuals with disabilities were selected at random and invited to participate in this research. Of these, 142 (94.7 percent) responded to the survey. Of those who responded, 83 percent expressed their satisfaction with the services provided and 8 percent indicated dissatisfaction. The reasons for their satisfaction, categorized by type in descending order of frequency, were able to meet with experts, convenient to utilize, able to save time, and easy to understand. Those who responded "able to meet with experts" indicated that assistance in dealing with their problems was sought from experts at KNU using the Tele-Social Welfare System, primarily due to the lack of relevant experts in their regions. Those who responded "convenient to utilize" or "able to save time" expressed that this system helped them save time, solved transportation problems caused by physical disabilities, reduced their financial burdens, and allowed them to get comfortable psychologically since they were already familiar with the surroundings. Some people responded that they were able to get great help from the system when considering the fact that they had not been able to travel long distance to get services for their children due to their children's disabilities.

Those who responded "easy to understand" pointed out that on the telephone, they had no choice but to rely on verbal communication in talking about their problems with experts; however, the TSWS system overcame this limitation and helped them show their problematic physical parts, particular behaviors, movements of mouths, and other attributes through direct observation on the video screen. In addition, it was noted that experts were able to use not only verbal explanation but also audio/visual materials to communicate with one another face-to-face, which played a key role in problem-solving interactions. Respondents said they were also able to understand the experts' explanations because they could ask questions.

Among those who responded dissatisfied, the majority indicated that they felt awkward and uncomfortable in communicating with a person appearing on a screen. In some cases, there were people who complained that mechanical problems prevented them from making full use of the system.

All seventeen experts who offered services related to welfare for individuals with disabilities responded to the questionnaire. Most of these respondents recognized the efficiency of the Tele-Social Welfare System. However, only 53 percent expressed their satisfaction with the use of the system, a far cry from the support reported by users. The reasons for service-provider satisfaction, categorized by type in descending order of frequencies, were not necessary to take a long trip, able to make real-time face-to-face interactions, and able to use audio/visual materials. These reasons are similar to those given by users.

The reasons for the service-providers' dissatisfaction with the system were spend too much time and effort in preparation, compared to ordinary classroom teaching; the use of teaching tools such as the data viewer or control panel is burdensome; unable to see participants' emotional conditions or behavioral changes; and not easy to get acquainted with participants. These responses show that rendering services through this system is more difficult than in an ordinary classroom or office.

As a result of the survey, it was determined that it would be desirable to enhance the presentation environment by providing various teaching tools such as a briefing system, data viewer, electronic/white board and computer, so that experts can offer necessary service by utilizing a broad range of materials and media. In the course of their work, professors may now choose additional equipment to effectively communicate teaching content by pushing buttons on a keypad. According to the user's abilities, these advanced teaching media may be regarded as useful and convenient equipment–or as awkward and troublesome. Thus, familiarization with the technological tools is a prerequisite for the effective and successful operation of this system.

The problem of the difficulty in getting acquainted with participants pointed out by both recipients and providers may be an unsolvable limitation of the Tele-Social Welfare System and other electronic media-based systems. Various countermeasures need to be implemented to resolve this shortcoming. One countermeasure may be for an expert to visit users in remote areas in order to improve mutual understanding and acquaintance. Other countermeasures include sharing of provider and users' background information prior to the initial tele-service, and the frequent display of names.

To understand better the problems associated with this social welfare system and to identify potential improvements, in-depth follow-up interviews were completed with seventeen experts who provided direct services. The interviews indicated that the majority of experts were satisfied with interactions with disabled people and their families. However, they expressed dissatisfaction with the teaching strategies and counseling strategies available to be used for their services. On the basis of their overall viewpoints, it may be noted that a wide variety of strategies suitable to three main fields–education, counseling, and diagnostic assessment or treatment–need to be established in advance, and experts offering services require well-integrated training programs designed for the application of those strategies. In addition to this, it is necessary to augment manpower support for manufacturing various supplementary materials used to increase the effectiveness of service delivery.

Malfunctioning of the system, as indicated earlier, is one reason why users expressed dissatisfaction. This is in line with the research result that the most important factor affecting the quality and effectiveness of telecommunication teaching is the integrity of equipment and sound communication (Mason, 1994; Mason & Bacsich, 1994). This fundamental requirement was reiterated in follow-up interviews with the personnel who operate the TSWS system. For this reason, it is necessary to strengthen the stable operation and management of equipment and communication networks through the establishment of regular maintenance programs. In doing this, all personnel developing supplementary materials and operating the system are required to obtain at least a certain level of professional capabilities. As such, they should be adequately supported in terms of position and salary. For training to be effective, the following is recommended: the establishment of professional and systematic educational training, the support of regular training programs, and the expansion of training fields (not only manipulation of the system, but also basic design, operation and management of the system, basic design of communication networks connected with local training centers, structure and function of MCU or CODEC, basic knowledge of PD, and various screen arrangements with the technique of data transmission and reception).

With respect to improvement of the Tele-Social Welfare Database System, the results of the interviews indicated a strong interest in connecting the system to the Internet and making it an "open system" with connectivity beyond the boundary of the current ultra high-speed communication network. Other interests include developing user interfaces for individuals with disabilities (for the disabled as well as the blind) to have access to the database, expanding the database, and replacing the database management system with one that is more advanced.

Discussion

One of the characteristics of social welfare is that the supply and utilization of services are carried out through interactions among mutually exclusive organizations. An array of already-developed information technology and the development of the information superhighway made it possible to conduct interactive activities between the supply of service and its utilization even within the framework of a Tele-Social Welfare System devoid of direct contacts among service providers and users. There turned out to be some problems in relation to the utilization of the Tele-Social Welfare System (Han et al., 1998). However, both suppliers and users share the recognition that this system will sustain its positive effects. Consequently, the resolution of a number of problems confirmed here will lay the foundation for a new social welfare service transmission system required in this era of information technology.

THE BREAST CANCER SUPPORT GROUP IN MICHIGAN'S UPPER PENINSULA

The Breast Cancer Support Group (BCSG) at Marquette (MI) General Hospital started in 1989 as a face-to-face monthly support group for women diagnosed with breast cancer at any stage in the treatment process. The group met monthly at Marquette General Hospital (MGH), which is the location of the Regional Cancer Center for the Upper Peninsula of Michigan. Although women may come to Marquette from many miles away for their initial diagnosis and treatment, the large distances and bad weather–especially in the winter–make it impossible for many women who might benefit to attend the monthly meetings.

In 1995, the nurse who facilitated the BCSG decided to use the interactive videoconferencing system already located at MGH as a means to bring women into the main group from outlying areas who were unable to make the trip into Marquette for the monthly meetings. Although the video network was linked to ten other hospitals in the Upper Peninsula, based on the number of people who had indicated an interest in being part of the group the decision was made to establish satellite groups at Baraga (75 miles) and Iron River (90 miles) from Marquette. The group went interactive with three-way meetings in September, 1995. Although attendance does vary, the meetings generally have ten to twelve women in Marquette, five or six women in Baraga, and zero to two people in Iron River.

Methods

The information about the BCSG reported here comes from interviews with members of the group completed early in 1997. The interviews were conducted by one of the group's members, and most were done by phone although a few were in person. Letters of introduction were sent to all women on the BCSG mailing list at Marquette General Hospital, and they were followed by phone calls to set a time for an interview. The response rate was very high. Among the 38 women who had actually attended at least one session using the ITV system, 31 (81.6 percent) agreed to complete the interview. The interviews generally lasted between thirty and sixty minutes.

All interviews were audio tape-recorded and transcribed verbatim. The texts of the interviews were then systematically reviewed and coded by two different staff people, with discussions held about differences in coding until they were resolved.

Results

Most of the women attended their first meeting of the group because they were looking for answers to their specific questions from women who had "been there" already, and because they wanted general information about coping with cancer. In addition to this informational dimension, the women also reported the desire for support from others who were going through the same experiences. The women were encouraged to attend the meetings by their friends or other group members. Those members who kept coming back also reported the desire to help other women by their own experiences the way they themselves had been helped earlier.

In general women in Marquette had learned about the BCSG from MGH staff or through publications—listing in bulletins or a copy of the group's informational flyer. At times, a friend or family member who had experience with the group encouraged them to attend. The women in Baraga generally learned about the group when nurses at Baraga Memorial Hospital sent them information promoting the group. Iron River women were informed about the group by the nurses and technicians at Iron County General Hospital. Although some of the women were in remission, when they began attending the BCSG most of the women were in various stages of treatment including chemotherapy regimens, radiation therapy, surgery, and post-surgery.

When asked to recall their initial impressions about what a cancer support group would be like most women reported that they were curious and thought the group would involve other women talking about their problems with cancer. Some said they frankly did not know what to expect. Most of the women were surprised to find that the group wasn't sad, that it wasn't always talk about problems with cancer and treatments. They were pleasantly surprised to find that there was much humor and laughter shared within the group, and that the group was small enough to be personal and intimate at times.

Although the women in Baraga and Iron River knew right from the beginning that there groups were going to be linked electronically to Marquette, most of the women in Marquette learned about the interactive connection by going to the meetings. When asked to recall their thoughts about being part of an interactive TV group linked with women in other places, the responses were quite varied, and mostly positive. It was regarded by respondents as interesting, amazing, fantastic, a worthy opportunity, and as providing a larger group to draw information from. Some concerns included uncomfortable feelings about being on display when televised, concerns that the group interaction was a little awkward at first, and that some of the technical problems interfered with the group dynamics.

Most of the respondents–regardless of where they were located–felt that the interactive connection was a greater benefit to the people at the remote sites, but they were willing to participate in the interactive group for the opportunity to support others. Some respondents reported the idea that the support group would be more effective by reaching more women through the ITV connection, and because they were focused on helping others this was a good thing. Women at the remote sites felt that they always could choose whether or not to sign on for the monthly meeting.

Once the interactive group had some experience, the facilitator found that there was some advantage to alternating the monthly meetings with a formal presenter at every other meeting, with the alternative meetings being devoted exclusively to informal discussion nights. Even on nights that a presenter was scheduled, the presentations were only supposed to last 30 minutes of the 90 minute meeting to allow members the choice of staying on the topic of the presentation or moving on to their own interpersonal agenda.

The members of the group–especially the women in Baraga and Iron River–reported great appreciation for the opportunity to have questions answered by the physicians and medical staff of MGH. Other interesting topics included medications and their side effects; make-overs; diet and nutrition; yoga, massage therapy, and therapeutic touch; and stress management. Many women in the Marquette group commented that they look forward to informal discussion on the nights when there was no formal speaker scheduled.

Most respondents noted that they would make a special effort to attend a presentation that was of interest to them, yet they continue to attend meetings regularly because of their desire to "be there for the others." Some of them stated openly that it is important for new people to see survivors. Women in the remote sites commented that they sometimes did not have advance knowledge of the speakers or programs, but many were nevertheless committed to attending each meeting regardless of the agenda.

A picture of a typical meeting emerges from the responses to the question: "If a visitor from outside the group were to attend a typical meeting, what would she see happening?" She would see women of varying ages, introducing themselves to women in the remote sites and to the newcomers at their own site, sharing their common experiences, sharing information, talking openly and honestly, asking questions, and sometimes joking with each other. She would see the participants offering much support and showing a lot of interest in each other. She would see the women interacting within a comfortable interpersonal atmosphere.

A visitor would see women at all sites sitting around tables looking at television monitors. Most respondents commented that they did not notice much about the other meeting rooms except that they appear to be very much alike. A visitor would be able to see the faces of the women at the other sites, and she would be able to distinguish the person who is talking.

A visitor to the group would observe that the number of participants varies, with the largest group being in Marquette, then Baraga, and the smallest in Iron River. She would notice that sometimes the interaction is difficult because the transmission is not clearly focused, and the delay in transmission is somewhat distracting. She would see that most of the interaction is initiated by the Marquette group. Finally, she would see that a social element is present as the participants enjoy refreshments provided by the MGH kitchen and occasionally at the remote sites when a group member elects to bring in refreshments.

Despite the difficulties sometimes created by the technology, a visitor would be able to see and interact with women in the remote sites. She would be able to see movement in the rooms, and she would see that sometimes there are discussions among the women in their own sites. Overall the atmosphere would strike the visitor as informal and friendly, with women at each of the sites to be like the rest–friendly, interesting and interested, albeit far away.

When asked to indicate what they like best about the BCSG in general, not focusing on the ITV aspect, most respondents said they liked being able to share their feelings with others who have been through the same things. They liked the information that is available to them, the support they receive from each other, the friendliness of others in the group, and the chance to meet new people. Many looked forward to the evening as an opportunity for socializing. Some respondents commented that the group is there if you need it, so they felt free to decide whether or not they attended.

As for the ITV aspect, most respondents commented that the interactive part provides an opportunity for people in remote sites to get support, and to have an opportunity for speakers and presentations that they would not otherwise have access to. They felt that responses were spontaneous, and that group members can obtain information immediately from other members. The groups are seen as being responsive to each other, willing to share their experiences for the benefit of others. Because of the larger, more diverse group made possible by means of the interactive connection, discussions about the various stages of the illness generate more sharing of information from a broader range of perspectives and experiences. Simultaneously this provides an opportunity to help more people.

On the negative side, some respondents commented on seating arrangements that make it difficult to see everyone at the same time because the television monitors have to be part of the group. Some reported that the interactive television format was inhibiting to the group discussion. Others reported that sometimes when there wasn't a speaker, a separate conversation would begin in each of the sites, and the conversations among women at each site was distracting to the interaction across the sites. Problems were noted with the delay in transmission and the occasional difficulties with the picture and sound. Most respondents commented that they would prefer to meet the people from the remote sites in person rather than on television, and they agreed that the ITV arrangement is more beneficial to the remote sites than to the Marquette group.

In general, the women supported the notion that the technology can bring people with a common bond together across some geographic barriers. They agreed that setting up an interactive BCSG in other communities would be a good and worthwhile thing to do because it could really benefit women in small communities by allowing the women to share information and expertise with greater numbers of people.

Discussion

Based on these interviews it appears that members find both informational and emotional support from their participation in the group, regardless of their location. While the members are clearly not completely satisfied with various audio and video distractions, in general they report that the overall impact of being "on television" becomes relatively innocuous after the first couple of sessions. Finally, although the ITV structure is not perfect, the members see lots of possibilities for other groups. While acknowledging that the remote sites have more to gain from the ITV arrangement than the Marquette group, nevertheless most members see value in more people being linked and thus more people gaining the informational and social support highly valued by all of the members.

IMPLICATIONS FOR USING VIDEOCONFERENCING APPLICATIONS IN SOCIAL WORK

Both professional and lay users of the systems described above seem to be in general agreement about several aspects of the use of videoconferencing applications to bring needed services to people who otherwise would not have access to them. Specifically six points can be drawn from these two case studies.

Access

Videoconferencing does indeed permit end users to have access to resources and services that otherwise would simply not be available to them.

Families in rural areas in Korea where professionals were in short supply were able to receive consultations directly from experts at Kongju National University. Women in rural Michigan, isolated by geography and weather, were able to link up with an important source of emotional and informational support from Marquette General Hospital. These are realities, and they suggest great possibilities for other applications to people and communities in need.

Relationships

While end users will be grateful for having access to services that would otherwise not be possible, they will generally express a preference for receiving the services and supports face-to-face. It should not come as a surprise to anyone in this field that in *most* cases–although there are exceptions–people would prefer to have at least *some* contact with the professional or with other users, even on an occasional basis. Anecdotal evidence seems to support the idea that the closer the locations are geographically, the more intense is this feeling that some personal contact should be present. Certainly the experiences in both case studies support the importance of developing and maintaining the highest possible level of *relationships* possible given the distance and the technology involved (Freddolino, 1996).

Technology

There is no way to avoid the reality that the effectiveness of any videoconferencing applications, and user satisfaction with these application, is very closely tied to the quality of the technology and how well it functions on any given day. Visual and audio problems can turn a simple conversation into an annoying experience for everyone involved. Most participants come to videoconferencing applications with the expectation that they will be as transparent as telephone conversations, while those who provide the service realize that this standard of performance is still some years away. In the interim, service providers have to recognize that this is the level of expectation, and they must maximize their efforts to insure the highest level of technological performance possible–given all of the constraints under which they must operate.

Convenience and Cost

Two of the most important benefits of videoconferencing applications are the convenience factors for users–shorter distances to drive, less time on the road through inclement weather, etc.–and cost savings for some of the out-ofpocket expenses as well–transportation costs, fees for hours spent on the road by professionals, and so forth. What are often not considered are the tremendous start-up capitalization costs for videoconferencing systems. Viewed from a broad service delivery system perspective, the generally low level of actual utilization–especially in the United States (Allen & Scarbrough, 1996)–makes videoconferencing an expensive proposition at present, and heightens the need for more applications using systems in which considerable investments have already been made.

Need for Training

To make videoconferencing applications more effective and to satisfy end users, more advanced and more functional hardware, accessories, and applications would probably be of some use. At the same time, such advances add to the financial costs of videoconferencing systems, and if they are to be used well they will require additional training on the part of those developing the applications. Such training, of course, requires more time, which then counteracts one of the perceived advantages of using videoconferencing! The resolution of this dilemma linking effectiveness to technology and training will ultimately determine for each system how its operations will be perceived by all of the key stakeholders involved, from policy makers to payers to professional and lay users.

Policy

In the final analysis, the future of applications of videoconferencing in social work and social welfare services will be determined by key policy decisions that must be made by governments and third party payers, influenced by professional and lay users. How much are we willing to spend to have high quality technology and well-trained users providing services needed by people in areas with historically little or no access to various services? Where will the funds come from initially, and who will pay for the ongoing costs of training, maintenance, and replacement? While there are other issues, such as the willingness of professionals to consider the possibilities of videoconferencing as a tool to reach underserved clients, it is difficult to avoid the cost issues if one is committed to the development of videoconferencing applications that are as effective as they might be. In this regard it will be important to observe the development of videoconferencing systems using the Internet and eventually Internet 2 because these would certainly reduce the costs of the hardware involved, placing more of the burden on training and the development of user-friendly applications.

CONCLUSION

These two case studies illustrate some of the wide range of possibilities in the application of videoconferencing technology in its current form. They have highlighted some of the positive aspects of the use of videoconferencing, and pointed out some of the challenges that must be addressed. This is an exciting field of development for social work and social welfare, and it will be fascinating to view the changes that may come as these challenges are addressed in the new era of information technology. Ultimately, the people and communities we serve should be the beneficiaries.

REFERENCES

Allen, A. & Scarbrough, M.L. (1996). 3rd annual program review. *Telemedicine Today, 4 (4)*, 10-17, 34-38.

Freddolino, P. (1996). The importance of relationships in creating a quality learning environment in an interactive TV classroom. *Journal of Education for Business, 71*, 205-208.

Freddolino, P., Nordling, C., & Olsen, L. (1998). The Breast Cancer Support Group: A demonstration of the value of interactive television (ITV) for students taking ITV courses on campus. Paper presented at the Council on Social Work Education Annual Program Meeting, Orlando, FL, March.

Han, A.S. (1998). Tele-Lifelong Learning System Using Information Superhighway. In Internet Forum Korea (Ed.), Proceedings of the SchoolNet'98 Conference on Internet for All Schools (in Korean). Seoul: Youngjin Press.

Han, A.S. & Choi, G. (1997). A televideo system for distance education and social work training. Paper presented at Conference on the 1997 Information Technologies for Social Work Education: Using to Teach Teaching to Use, Charleston, SC, August.

Han, A.S. et al. (1998). Management of Tele Social Welfare System and Future Directions (in Korean). Kongju: The Education & Welfare Technology National Research Center.

Mason, R. (1994). The education value of ISDN. In R. Mason & P. Bacsich (Eds.), ISDN Application in Education and Training. London: Institution of Electronical Engineers.

Mason, R. & Bacsich, P. (1994). Conclusion. In R. Mason & P. Bacsich (Eds.), ISDN Application in Education and Training. London: Institution of Electronical Engineers

National Computerization Agency. (Ed.). (1997). Informatization white paper (in Korean). Youngin: Author.

Utilizing and Evaluating ITV Workshops for Rural Community Leadership Training

C. David Hollister
Chandra M. N. Mehrotra

SUMMARY. Interactive television has potential merit as a medium for reaching rural audiences. The Blandin Foundation has recently explored the use of ITV for its workshops for leadership training in rural Minnesota communities. This paper presents the findings of a formative evaluation of a pilot ITV workshop on "Attracting and Sustaining Community Volunteers," in terms of its technical aspects, acceptability to participants, learning impacts, and accessibility. Criteria for selecting distance learning modalities and ITV networks and providers are suggested. *[Article copies available for a fee from The Haworth Document Delivery Service: 1-800-342-9678. E-mail address: getinfo@haworthpressinc.com <Website: http://www.haworthpressinc.com>]*

KEYWORDS. Distance learning, volunteer and leadership training

The rapid expansion in recent years of the infrastructure for interactive television and other modes of distance learning has created many new oppor-

C. David Hollister is Professor, School of Social Work, Univeristy of Minnesota, 105 Peters Hall, 1404 Gortner Avenue, St. Paul, MN 55108 (E-mail: dhollist@ che1.che.umn.edu).

Chandra M. N. Mehrotra is Professor and Dean of Graduate Studies, The College of Saint Scholastica, 1200 Kenwood Avenue, Duluth, MN 55811 (E-mail: cmehrotr@ css.edu).

[Haworth co-indexing entry note]: "Utilizing and Evaluating ITV Workshops for Rural Community Leadership Training." Hollister, C. David, and Chandra M. N. Mehrotra. Co-published simultaneously in *Journal of Technology in Human Services* (The Haworth Press, Inc.) Vol. 16, No. 2/3, 1999, pp. 35-45; and: *Computers and Information Technology in Social Work: Education, Training, and Practice* (ed: Jo Ann R. Coe, and Goutham M. Menon) The Haworth Press, Inc., 1999, pp. 35-45. Single or multiple copies of this article are available for a fee from The Haworth Document Delivery Service [1-800-342-9678, 9:00 a.m. - 5:00 p.m. (EST). E-mail address: getinfo@haworthpressinc.com].

tunities for organizations to reach out to their constituencies. The new technologies are of special interest to organizations which serve rural constituencies, because of the potential savings in travel time and expenses (Miller, 1991; Sheridan, 1992). This paper will discuss and evaluate the use of interactive television by the Blandin Foundation, a Minnesota foundation whose mission is to strengthen rural communities throughout the state.

The Blandin Foundation Community Leadership Program (BCLP) since 1985 has provided leadership training to over 2,300 Minnesotans from more than 180 communities. Program goals include both the development of participants' leadership skills and the development of networks aimed at fostering healthy, viable communities. The typical BCLP experience consists of three components: a six-day leadership retreat, a two-day workshop, and a one-day workshop. The program also seeks to develop additional continuing education opportunities for its alumni and other members of rural communities (Blandin Foundation, 1996).

The Foundation is exploring whether some of the newer communication technologies could provide a suitable training vehicle to address the continuing education needs of BCLP alumni. In fall 1997 it developed a new training module and delivered it simultaneously via interactive television (ITV) to BCLP alumni in three rural Minnesota communities.

The topic selected for this pilot project was "Attracting and Sustaining Community Volunteers," a topic that has been frequently requested by BCLP alumni. The Foundation considered it important that a systematic evaluation of this initial ITV project be undertaken. The underlying rationale was that information gained from it would be very helpful to the staff in deciding whether or not to continue distance training, and if so, how to improve the training. This report describes the formative evaluation we conducted to monitor this first ITV effort, to assess its acceptance by the program's alumni and to determine its impact upon the participants.

An instructional design team was constituted in spring 1997 to develop the learning module on volunteerism, including instructional objectives, the specific content and sequence of their presentation, and the media to be utilized (Blandin Foundation, 1997).

Interactive television was selected as the trial means of delivery, because its two-way audio and video features were thought to be more conducive than other distance learning media to the highly participatory, active learning style (MacKinnon, Walshe, Cummings & Volonis, 1995; Johnson, Johnson & Smith, 1991; Christensen, Garvin & Sweet, 1991) characteristic of BCLP workshops. The content was delivered through a mixture of strategies: presentation by the trainer, slides, small group discussions, reports back to the larger group, and large group discussions.

A test run of the workshop held in July 1997 provided useful feedback about aspects of the workshop needing adjustment. It also provided the evaluators with an opportunity to pre-test and revise two of the evaluation instruments.

The actual event was scheduled for October 1997 at three Minnesota sites: Brainerd, Alexandria, and Winona. Invitations to participate were mailed to 110 BCLP alumni. Of the 110, 28 accepted the invitation. Of the 28 accepting, 20 actually came to the event: 7 at Brainerd, 4 at Alexandria, and 9 at Winona. The small numbers are a concern, in that at the Alexandria site the small size of the group may have affected the quality of the interaction, although there is also some evidence that smaller group size has a positive impact (Biner, Welsh, Barone, Summers & Dean, 1997).

EVALUATION METHODS

The evaluation of the pilot project was designed as a *formative* evaluation (Patton, 1997). Its main purpose was to provide members of the foundation staff with information they can use to make programmatic changes aimed at strengthening future offerings in this series (Hollister, 1998).

The questions to be addressed in the evaluation were developed from issues noted in the literature on distance education and in consultation with foundation staff. Four main dimensions were identified for analysis: (1) the performance and reliability of the technology and support systems (Moskal, Martin & Foshee, 1997; Biner, 1993); (2) the acceptability of ITV delivery to the audience (Fulford & Zhang, 1993; Biner, Dean & Mellinger, 1994; Wilkes & Burnham, 1991); (3) the extent to which the workshop content was communicated and retained (Blakely, 1992; Cyrs, 1997); and (4) the participation rates and accessibility of the workshop (Spencer, 1995).

The specific questions within each of these categories were as follows:

- Technology and support systems. Were the TV images clear? Was the sound audible? Were there delays due to technical problems? Was technical support easily available to solve problems? How well could the trainer interact with participants at each site? How well could participants at one site interact with those at another site? What changes would improve the quality of the experience?
- Acceptability of ITV. Did BCLP alumni *perceive* this medium to be effective? Did they think it has any advantages over on-site training? Did BCLP alumni find anything missing? Would they recommend ITV workshops to others?
- Communication and retention of workshop content. Was the content on "attracting and sustaining community volunteers" communicated and understood? Was the content interesting? What elements of the content

did participants consider most important? To what extent was the content useful for individuals' own work with volunteers in their communities? To what extent did participants in fact later make use of it?
- Participation rates and accessibility of the workshop. Was the workshop scheduled at a convenient time? Was parking a problem? Was it difficult to find the classroom? Were the room arrangements and the seating comfortable?

Data-collection instruments were developed to secure feedback on these questions from several different sources:

- An evaluation questionnaire was given to all twenty participants immediately following the workshop.
- A telephone interview* was conducted with all twenty participants six to eight weeks after the workshop.
- A brief phone interview* was conducted with a 50% random sample of the non-participating invitees.
- A evaluation questionnaire was given to the presenter shortly after the workshop.
- Phone interviews were conducted with the site facilitators following the workshop.
- Field notes were taken at the Winona site by the evaluator, who also served as the facilitator at that site.
- The entire workshop was videotaped to inform other aspects of the evaluation.

FINDINGS

Technology and Support Systems

In general, the ITV system performed adequately, but there were some problems:

- Images and sound were mostly legible and audible, once the system was brought into electronic balance. However, four participants (20%) indicated consistent difficulty in reading some of the words on the monitor, and nine participants (45%) expressed some difficulty in clearly hearing what was being said over the TV.

---

*The authors acknowledge the able assistance of Ms. Danette Buscovick, MSW, who assisted with these interviews and with data compilation.

- There was an eight minute delay in the starting time, due to an echo problem and to the initial dimness of the image transmitted from one of the sites.
- There was also the usual one-second delay in receiving the appropriate image when a participant spoke at a site that was not already on the monitors at the other sites. Although this is characteristic of voice-activated microphones, some participants were not used to this and commented about it on their feedback forms.
- It was not possible to view the instructor and the three groups of participants simultaneously, even though there was a bank of four television monitors at each site, due to a limitation of the network when these particular regions of the state are involved. This limitation may have reduced somewhat participants' feelings of connection to the other sites. (Three participants, as well as the trainer, commented that it would have been better to see all groups at the same time.) The trainer, in particular, regretted that she could see one of the sites less than 25% of the time. She expressed concern that this situation may have reduced her ability to establish rapport with that site.
- Likewise, it was not possible at the originating site to show simultaneously both the trainer and a graphic, such as a diagram or table. Some electronic classrooms permit both to occur at once. The consequence in this instance, according to the trainer, is that she reduced the use of print overheads, which are static, and increased the use of didactic presentation, which has the potential for more dynamism.
- There was a problem of distracting conversation and noise from the other sites during the periods when participants at each site were working in small groups. (This can easily be solved by turning on the "mute" controls at each site, assuming each site facilitator has been shown where the control is located.)
- The trainer noted on her feedback form that she was unable to adjust the zoom feature on the camera that focused on herself. Her screen image was smaller than desired.
- A related concern is that site facilitators need to know ahead of time how to operate the zoom control and camera-aiming control, so that participants at other sites can have a larger image of the person speaking. It took each site facilitator a while to learn how to use the these controls, with the result that the images of speakers at some sites were initially smaller than they needed to be. Making the face image larger enables participants to "read" speakers' facial expressions better and thereby receive additional, non-verbal information. It probably also increases somewhat participants' perceptions that they are more fully interacting with the other sites.

- Name placards were sometimes not legible due to the small size of the lettering, even when the camera zoomed in. This can be addressed by having larger placards made up by the site facilitator ahead of time, so that the letters are uniformly large. Just as important, participants need to be instructed ahead of time to sit in the front rows of the classroom as much as possible, so that their images appear larger both to the trainer and to the other sites.

Acceptability of ITV Technology to BCLP Alumni

In the data collected from participants both immediately after the workshop and through phone interviews 6-8 weeks later, several trends can be noted. Thirteen (65%) of the participants indicated that the ITV format was "quite effective" or "very effective" in delivering the content on volunteerism to them. Seven (35%) indicated it was "somewhat effective" or "only slightly effective." On the one hand, many participants expressed a preference for training that is on-site, with the presenter physically present and interacting with participants. "Loss of personal touch" was a phrase given by several participants when describing the ITV workshop. One half of the 18 respondents said that they did *not* learn as well through this workshop's distance/ITV format as through the in-person format used in previous BCLP workshops they had attended. On the other hand, the other nine participants *did* think they learned as well through the distance/ITV format, and some participants saw some advantages to ITV training: several participants noted the reduction in participants' travel time that ITV workshops could provide and some noted the potential of multi-site ITV workshops for facilitating the sharing and exchange of ideas among groups from different communities. It is significant that fully 15 of the 18 persons interviewed 6-8 weeks later say that they would recommend ITV training to others in their communities. Thus, even though ITV training may not be many participants' first choice, most still see sufficient merit in this medium to warrant recommending it to others.

Communication and Impact of the Workshop Content

Despite some problems with the ITV technology, in general the content on volunteerism seems to have been communicated well and to have had some impact on participants' understanding of how to work with volunteers. None of the eight components of the training module (recruiting volunteers, orienting volunteers, sustaining volunteers, etc.) received an average (mean) rating of less than 4 on a 5-point scale (when rounded to the nearest whole number) on both *understandability* and *usefulness* to participants' own work with volunteers. The same was true of the participants' ratings of other dimensions concerning the presentation: the clarity of concepts, the extent to which it was interesting, encouragement to actively participate in discussions, the degree of rapport with presenter, and the relevance of the content for both the community and one's own community work (with the exception of "the extent to which you felt connected with participants at the other sites," which received a somewhat lower mean rating of 3.25).

A more direct measure of what was learned lies in the open-ended items, in both the questionnaire given immediately after the workshop and in the phone survey taken 6-8 weeks after the event, which asked participants questions as to what they considered most important and what has been most helpful in their work with volunteers. In the responses to both instruments a majority of participants cited at least one concept that was considered key by the team designing the workshop.

Some of the participants indicated that the content of the workshop was quite basic. These respondents noted that much of the workshop provided a good review of what they already knew, and was useful in that regard, but there is some indication that the material was not as new or as fully challenging as they may have expected.

Access to the Workshop

Twenty of the 110 persons invited to the workshop attended it. This participation rate was considerably lower than is the case for the BCLP's in-person workshops, where a 50% rate is more common. However, day of week, time of day, and the shorter advance notice could all have affected the participation rate as much or more as the use of an ITV format. More advance notice may be required for a larger turnout. Fully 40% of the sample of 45 non-attenders reached after the workshop cited "prior commitments" as the reason for not attending. A plurality of those phoned who did not attend (30% or 13 people) expressed a preference for a workshop during the day (except Mondays), rather than in the evening or on weekends.

Participants at both the Alexandria and Brainerd sites expressed some disappointment that a larger cohort of BCLP alumni from their communities was not present. Smaller numbers (four in the case of Alexandria) seemed to reduce morale somewhat, judging by the comments made.

One participant suggested that it would have been good to have included a more detailed agenda for the workshop, and another noted the need to include in the letter of invitation a floor plan showing the room number and location in large buildings like the Winona Technical Institute.

DISCUSSION

ITV technology has both strengths and limitations as a medium for delivering workshops. One strength is its potential to deliver training to several sites simultaneously and interactively. A second strength is its multi-media aspect–its capacity to deliver graphics, video clips, music, and so on, not just the image and voice of a presenter. It also has the advantages of saving travel time and expense for participants (thereby increasing access for some); of delivering the same content to potentially greater numbers of participants than a single on-site workshop; and–of special importance to organizations like the Blandin Foundation–of facilitating the sharing of ideas across communities. ITV will not necessarily save money compared to traditional workshops; this depends on a variety of factors. In fact, for some configurations the opposite could be true, if one adds in the user fees, site charges, and time of the technicians and site facilitators.

ITV may also be of interest to organizations such as the Blandin Foundation for other purposes, such as providing consultation to communities and facilitating inter-community meetings.

ITV's disadvantages include sporadic problems in technical performance, limitations in camera and monitor versatility at many sites, and diminution of some dimensions of engagement of trainer and participants and participants with each other, resulting in a somewhat lower degree of acceptance by participants, compared to on-site training. It is not at all surprising that the overall response of participants in this workshop was to still prefer on-site training, even though most said they *would* recommend ITV training to others. This finding is parallel to the experience of educational institutions using ITV for classroom courses. Most students still prefer in-person instruction to ITV, probably because it seems more lively, but many evaluations of classroom learning show approximately the same gain in learning with both modalities. In the meantime, ITV reaches additional educational audiences–people who for various reasons can not come to the campus to take a course (Hobbs and Christianson, 1997).

Some of the problems encountered in this pilot ITV project can be solved quite easily, such as ensuring that the sites selected will have technicians available, asking technicians to provide site facilitators with a small amount of on-the-spot training in camera and sound control, and adjusting some of the details in the preliminary information provided to participants. Other problems are built into certain sites and/or connections, such as the inability in this instance for the trainer and the participants to see all three sites plus the trainer simultaneously, and the inaccessibility to the trainer (at the originating site) of the zoom control for the camera that focuses on the trainer.

There are also now available in Minnesota and many other states several public and commercial ITV systems and providers, giving organizations such as the Blandin Foundation greater choice. Based on the experience of this pilot project, the criteria influencing choice of ITV sites and providers should include:

- ability to connect with the target community sites,
- system readiness for one-time events such as workshops ("user friend-liness"),
- versatility of camera controls,
- ability of the monitor clusters at each site to simultaneously show the instructor and all of the participating sites,
- availability of technical support prior to and during the event,
- total cost of instructional delivery,
- low number of gateways (switching points between one network and another), and
- similarity of signal type.

The last two considerations are important in that technical problems tend to increase as the number of gateways increase and/or there is conversion from analog to digital signals or vice versa.

Organizations such as the Blandin Foundation who are seeking new means for outreach may wish to consider some other distance learning options. Each of them has advantages and limitations, as also does traditional, on-site train-ing (Smith, 1998; Wood & Parham, 1996). The choice, which could vary by workshop, should depend in part on what the organization seeks to maximize:

- If it is deemed important to maximize direct interpersonal engagement, traditional training on site may still be the best choice.
- If it is desired to maximize the number of participants reached in group settings, satellite broadcast may be the best choice.
- If it is desired to maximize convenience to individuals, videotape pro-duction and distribution may be the best choice.
- If it is desired to maximize the learner's choice of topic and control of pace, web-based training may be the best choice.
- If it is desired to optimize both interpersonal interaction *and* the number of participants reached, while also maximizing inter-community com-munication, ITV may be the best choice.

It would be useful to undertake additional trials of ITV workshops to see what improvements can be accomplished in light of what has been learned through this project. In the evaluators' judgment there was in this pilot proj-ect sufficient technical efficiency, sufficient evidence of educational impacts, and sufficient acceptance by BCLP alumni of both technology and content to warrant additional trials of ITV for training purposes.

A recommended next step is to implement both an ITV workshop on volunteerism and a traditional on-site workshop on volunteerism, using the same trainer and content for both. Follow-up data could be collected for both workshops, using measures similar to the ones employed in this study. If this step is followed, there will be a sounder basis on which to compare the strengths and limitations of ITV training with on-site training.

CONCLUSION

The pilot project has been somewhat analogous to the shakedown cruise given to new ships, which typically reveals some aspects that need adjustment (loose rivets, unexpected vibrations, etc.). Much has been learned through its evaluation about ways to improve ITV delivery of community workshops.

The Blandin Foundation has taken an important and innovative step in trying out a new mode for reaching out to rural communities. It is important to remember, however, that this experience has involved only one mode of distance learning (ITV) over one network (MNET), using one set of classroom facilities, with one topic (volunteerism), using one set of instructional techniques in one alumni workshop. Other distance modalities and other ITV networks, studios, topics, instructional techniques, and communities should also be tried in order to gain a fuller understanding of ITV's potential for community workshops. These trials should be accompanied whenever possible by a formative evaluation, similar in scope and methods to the one described here, so that a sound empirical basis for choosing the most appropriate outreach modality can be developed.

REFERENCES

Biner, P.M. (1993). The development of an instrument to measure student attitudes toward televised courses. *American Journal of Distance Education, 7 (1)*, 62-73.

Biner, P.M., Dean, R.S. & Mellinger, A.E. (1994). Factors underlying distance learner satisfaction with televised college-level courses. *American Journal of Distance Education, 8 (1)*, 60-71.

Biner, P.M., Welsh, K.D., Barone, N.M., Summers, M., & Dean, R.S. (1997). The impact of remote-site group size on student satisfaction and relative performance in interactive telecourses. *American Journal of Distance Education, 11 (1)*, 23-33.

Blakely, T.J. (1992). A model for distance education delivery. *Journal of Social Work Education, 28 (2)*, 214-221.

Blandin Foundation. (1996). *Working with the Blandin Foundation: Building healthy communities throughout rural Minnesota.* [Brochure]. Grand Rapids, MN: Author.

Blandin Foundation. (1997). *Attracting and sustaining community volunteers.* Unpublished training manual.

Christensen, C.R., Garvin, D.A. & Sweet, K.A. (1991). *Education for judgement.* Boston, MA: Harvard Business School Press.

Cyrs, T.E. (1997). *Teaching and learning at a distance: what it takes to effectively design, deliver, and evaluate programs.* San Francisco, CA: Jossey-Bass Publishers.

Fulford, C.P. & Zhang, S. (1993). Perceptions of interaction: The critical predictor in distance education. *American Journal of Distance Education, 7 (3),* 8-21.

Hobbs, V.M. & Christianson, J.S. (1997). *Virtual classrooms: educational opportunity through two-way interactive television.* Lancaster, PA: Technomic.

Hollister, C.D. (1998). *Evaluation of the distance learning workshop 'Attracting and sustaining community volunteers.'* Unpublished manuscript.

Johnson, D.W., Johnson, R.T. & Smith, K.A. (1991) *Active learning: cooperation in the college classroom.* Edina, MN: Interaction Book Co.

MacKinnon, A. Walshe, B. Cummings, M. & Velonis, U. (1995). An inventory of pedagogical considerations for interactive television. *Journal of Distance Education, 10 (1),* 75-94.

Miller, D. (1991). Trim travel budgets with distance learning. *Training & Development, 45(9),* 71-74.

Moskal, P., Martin, B., & Foshee, N. (1997). Educational technology and distance education in central Florida: An assessment of capabilities. *American Journal of Distance Education, 11 (1),* 6-22.

Patton, M.P. (1997). *Utilization focused evaluation: the new century text.* (3rd ed.). Thousand Oaks, CA: Sage.

Sheridan, D. (1992). Off the road again: Training through teleconferencing. *Training, 29(2),* 63-68.

Smith, T.W. (1998). Distance education is a strategy: What is the objective? *American Journal of Distance Education, 12 (2),* 63-72.

Spencer, B. (1995). Removing barriers and enhancing openness: distance education as social adult education. *Journal of Distance Education, 10 (2),* 87-104.

Wilkes, C.W. & Burnham, B.R. (1991). Adult learner motivations and electronic distance education. *American Journal of Distance Education, 5 (1),* 43-50.

Wood, J.B. & Parham, I.A. (1996). Distance learning: Video conferences as vehicles for faculty development in gerontology/geriatrics. *Educational Gerontology, 22,* 105-115.

The Application
of Artificial Neural Networks
for Outcome Prediction in a Cohort
of Severely Mentally Ill Outpatients

David A. Patterson
Richard N. Cloud

SUMMARY. Social workers and other mental health workers lack clinical decision support tools to predict which clients are at greatest risk of psychiatric rehospitalization. Artificial neural networks (ANNs), are computer decision support tools that make prediction and classification decisions based on accumulated experience and information contained in successfully solved cases (correct decisions). This study evaluates the use of ANNs in predicting rehospitalization of severely mentally ill outpatients. Eight Bayesian ANN models achieved correct prediction rates ranging from 75% to 93% for two prediction conditions. These results support the utility of Bayesian ANN models in the development of clinical decision support tools. *[Article copies available for a fee from The Haworth Document Delivery Service: 1-800-342-9678. E-mail address: getinfo@haworthpressinc.com <Website: http://www.haworthpressinc.com>]*

KEYWORDS. Artificial neural networks, mental health

David A. Patterson is Associate Professor, and Richard N. Cloud is a Doctoral Candidate, University of Tennessee-Knoxville, College of Social Work.

Address correspondence to: David A. Patterson, University of Tennessee-Knoxville, College of Social Work, 109 Henson Hall, Knoxville, TN 37996-3333.

[Haworth co-indexing entry note]: "The Application of Artificial Neural Networks for Outcome Prediction in a Cohort of Severely Mentally Ill Outpatients." Patterson, David A., and Richard N. Cloud. Co-published simultaneously in *Journal of Technology in Human Services* (The Haworth Press, Inc.) Vol. 16, No. 2/3, 1999, pp. 47-61; and: *Computers and Information Technology in Social Work: Education, Training, and Practice* (ed: Jo Ann R. Coe, and Goutham M. Menon) The Haworth Press, Inc., 1999, pp. 47-61. Single or multiple copies of this article are available for a fee from The Haworth Document Delivery Service [1-800-342-9678, 9:00 a.m. - 5:00 p.m. (EST). E-mail address: getinfo@haworthpressinc.com].

Rehospitalization of severely and persistently mental ill clients is a common and expensive problem faced by social workers in community mental health settings. Social workers are often engaged in efforts to maximize the functioning of clients in the least restrictive community setting. Rehospitalization disrupts ties to community support systems and families and creates multiple problems and stressors for clients (Kent & Yellowlees, 1994). Re-admission to inpatient psychiatric facilities creates additional cost demands on already financially stressed public mental health systems (Rice, Kelman, & Miller, 1992).

Kent and Yellowlees (1994) have identified four categories of predictors of psychiatric hospitalization: (a) client characteristics such as social functioning, diagnosis, and symptomatology; (b) demographic variables including gender, ethnicity, age, and employment status; (c) system and organizational factors such as admissions criteria and alternative placement options; and (d) admitting personal characteristics such as years of clinical experience. Psychosocial factors found to be associated with rehospitalization include substance abuse (Carpenter, Mulligan, Bosler et al., 1985; Gorelick, Irwin, Schmidt-Ladener et al., 1990, Sullivan, Wells, Morgenstern, & Leake, 1995), repeated prior admissions (Carpenter, Mulligan, Bosler et al., 1985; Patterson & Lee, 1998; Postrado & Lehman, 1995), inadequate social support and low social functioning (Mezzich and Coffman, 1985), medication non-compliance (Carpenter, Mulligan, Bosler et al., 1985; Casper & Pastva, 1990; Sullivan et al., 1995), living with family of origin (Mesch & Fishman, 1994), age of mental illness onset and first admission (Abramowitz, Tupin, & Berger, 1984; Carpenter, Mulligan, Bosler et al., 1985), and the use of intensive case management services (Patterson & Lee, 1998). Sullivan et al. (1995) have pointed to the need for more information on rehospitalization risk factors which are responsive to community-based interventions.

DECISION SUPPORT TOOLS

In our review of the literature, we found no attempts to develop systematic rehospitalization prediction methods. Despite the abundance of identified risk factors, at present, social workers and other mental health workers lack decision support tools to successfully predict which clients are at greatest risk of rehospitalization. In the absence of decision support tools, clinicians are left to rely on clinical judgement to attempt to determine the risk of rehospitalization faced by their clients. Dawes, Faust, and Meehl (1989) reviewed nearly a 100 studies that compared actuarial judgements (statistically derived decisions) to clinical judgements in decisions of diagnosis and outcome prediction. They concluded that evidence clearly demonstrated the superiority of actuarial judgements over clinical judgement. The saliency of this finding adds further impetus to research to develop decision support tools for the prediction of rehospitalization.

Learning Systems

Weiss and Kulikowski (1991) suggest that learning systems, computer programs that make prediction and classification decisions based on the accumulated experience and information contained in successfully solved cases (correct decisions) can be viable decision support tools. The primary goal of learning systems is to solve complex real-world decision making problems by making correct conclusions. Like humans, learning systems use the information in existing data on prior cases to make future decisions. These new statistical pattern recognition techniques tend to be nonlinear and nonparametric methods. Error rate estimation techniques are used to compare the degree of fit of various distributions to the sample data and optimize new data performance (SPSSa, 1997; Weiss & Kulikowshi, 1991). In other words, learning systems are capable of heuristically recognizing the patterns or relationships between variables and outcomes. In this process, learning systems do not attempt to imitate human cognitive processes; but instead capitalize on the computational capacity of the computer. In the past, inefficient statistical techniques and the limitation in personal computer hardware and software packages have limited the practicality of learning system applications. Computationally intense methods of computer learning have become practical with the advent of faster computer processors.

Artificial Neural Networks

ANNs are computer-based learning system that have demonstrated capacity in complex pattern recognition tasks, including prediction, classification, and decision making (Cross, Harrison, & Kennedy, 1995; Galletly, Clark, & McFarlane, 1996; Zou, Shen, Shu, Wang, Feng, Xu, Qu, Song, Zhong, Wang & Liu, 1996). There are numerous types of neural network designs including radial bias function, multi-layer perceptron, Bayesian network, Hopfield network, and Kohonen networks (Cheng & Titterington, 1994; Sarle, 1997; SPSS, 1997b). This discussion will be limited to widely used and empirically tested multi-layer perceptron networks and Bayesian networks which show considerable promise as a network design, particularly with limited data sets (Cross, Harrison, & Kennedy, 1995; Sarle, 1997; SPSS, 1997b).

Multi-layer perceptron networks are the computer-learning descendants of simple perceptrons (Gallant, 1993; Jubak, 1992). Simple perceptrons are devices or computational procedures that linearly discriminate whether an input pattern belongs to one of two categories (Cheng & Titterington, 1994;

Weiss & Kulikowshi, 1991). Unfortunately, many real-world problems, such as which client is most at risk of rehospitalization during a given time period, do not have simple linearly divisible solutions (Cross, Harrison, & Kennedy, 1995). The multi-layer perceptron networks described below, have an additional hidden layer of computational units or nodes, and a learning algorithm, that allow them to find nonlinear solutions to complex problems.

The layers of nodes in artificial neural networks are analogous to brain neurons and are linked by a set of weighted connections (e.g., synapses). Figure 1 depicts a 6-4-1 neural network in which there are six input nodes (representing the six variables in the model), four nodes in the hidden layer (middle), and one output node. ANNs identify patterns between input (criterion) and target (predictor) variables in successive cases. In this iterative process, the model improves its predictive ability by adjusting the connection weights between nodes with each successive case. This process results in the parallel (simultaneous) distribution of computation across the network in much the same way the brain learns by strengthening synaptic connections (Galletly, Clark, & McFarlane, 1996, Jubak, 1992). Like humans, ANNs utilize experience in the form of input data and continue to perfect learning, improving decisions and predictions regarding future cases (Haykin, 1994).

The development of a neural network is an iterative, experimental process that requires adjustments in the design of the network as training and testing of models' performance are evaluated. Sample data are divided into cases used for training, validation, and model testing. In SPSS's Neural Connection (1997a), a single spreadsheet or SPSS file containing the sample data set can be opened, the relative size of each subset specified, and cases can then be randomly assigned to one of the three uses.

To begin the training of the neural network, the linkages between nodes in the network initially are assigned random weights (Sarle, 1997; SPSS, 1997a;

FIGURE 1. 6-4-1 Artificial Neural Network Model.

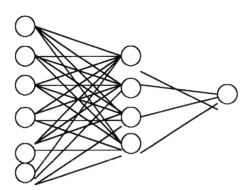

Weiss & Kulikowshi, 1991). Networks are typically composed of input nodes, one for each independent or predictor variable, a hidden layer of nodes, and one or more output nodes. With each successive case presented to the model, the weights linking the nodes are recalculated and summed. Each node in the hidden layer uses a nonlinear function to convert the weighted sum of its inputs into an output signal. The output signals from the nodes in the hidden layer are again summed and nonlinearly transformed into the model's predicted output, which is then compared to the actual output. If the predicted output is within a predetermined error range, it is considered by the network as correct, and the pattern therefore learned. If the predicted output is outside this acceptable error range, it is then "back propagated." Back-propagation means that the linkage weights in the network are then re-calculated based on the error between the network's predicted output and the actual output (Sarle, 1997; SPSS, 1997a). This process is repeated until the error is reduced to a predetermined acceptable level. At this point, the network has learned the optimal pattern of association between the input data and output data and it is considered trained (Collins & Clark, 1993).

Concurrent with the model's training, a validation data set is used to adjust the weights or parameters of the model. In this validation process, new cases are introduced to the model created in the training stage in order to adjust the weights of the connections (model calculations). This is done to correct for any overspecification of the model that may occur in the training process (Cross, Harrison, & Kennedy, 1996). Overspecification, which is also called "overtraining" in the neural network literature, results from noise or error in the training data. Unfortunately, the ANN model learns this noise during its training, reducing the model's ability to generalize to new data. To prevent this a validation data set is introduced to correct for overspecification during the training (SPSS, 1997a).

The number of hidden layers in the model (Collins & Clark, 1993) affects the ability of a neural network to converge or find an optimal solution. SPSS's Neural Connection software allows the user to specify the use of one or two hidden layers, though the manual cautions that a second layer generally does not improve network performance (SPSS, 1997b). Sarle (1997) provides a more detailed discussion beyond the purposes of this introduction of the relative merits for the selection of more than one hidden layer for a range of types of neural networks.

The number of nodes in a hidden layer is another decision point in the development of a neural network model. An increase in the number of nodes in a hidden layer increases the number of overall linkages in the model and therefore the complexity of the model (Collins & Clark, 1993; SPSS, 1997b). While more nodes in a hidden layer may dramatically improve the performance of the model with the training data, it can produce a network that is over-specified and unable to generalize to the cases in the validation data set.

The predictive utility of an ANN model is evaluated following its training and validation with test data (Collins & Clark, 1993; Cross, Harrison, & Kennedy, 1995; Sarle, 1997). The test data set is composed of new cases on which the ANN model has not been trained. This test data set is introduced to the model and prediction accuracy can be measured with the correlation between the predicted and actual outputs or with a simple percentage correct. The research literature contains reports of correct predictions in excess of 90 percent found in the evaluation of test data sets (Bart, 1991; Pritchard, Duke, Coburn, Moore, Tucker, Jann, & Hostetler, 1994; Zou, Shen, Shu, Wang, Feng, Xu, Qu, Song, Zhong, Wang & Liu, 1996). For instance, Brodzinski, Crable, and Scherer (1994) developed an ANN model that achieved 99 percent correct classification of juvenile recidivism compared to 63 percent achieved with discriminant analysis classification. If the test data set does not achieve the desired level of discriminative or predictive ability, the model is reconfigured through the addition or removal of variables, nodes, or hidden layers and retrained and validated in an iterative, experimental process (Collins & Clark, 1993).

ANNs are applicable to four types of problems, classification, prediction, time series forecasting, and data segmentation (Brodzinski, Crable, & Scherer, 1994; SPSS, 1997a; Steyaert, 1994). Classification involves the assignment of cases into two or more categories, such as diagnostic classification. Prediction refers to determining the probability of some event, such as out of home placement. Time series forecasting uses time ordered information to predict future occurrences, such as facility occupancy rates. Data segmentation uses large databases to create profiles or clusters, such as profiling clients who are likely to require high levels of services.

A recently developed variant of the multi-layer perceptron networks described above are Bayesian networks (Neal, 1997, SPSS, 1997b). Bayesian networks are architecturally similar to multi-layer perceptron networks and can be used for classification and prediction problems, but unlike multi-layer perceptron networks, do not need a validation data set. Consequently, Bayesian networks are useful with smaller data sets, a methodological constraint not uncommon to many social service settings. Multi-layer perceptron networks require a validation data set to prevent overtraining or learning the error/noise in the data. Bayesian networks achieve their computational efficiency by adding an additional term to the learning algorithm that corrects for the effect of error/noise on the resultant network. This additional term in the algorithm is derived from the application of Bayesian statistics. Simply stated, Bayesian statistics examine how prior and posterior knowledge of events impact probability distributions and the subsequent prediction of error.

Consequently, Bayesian networks are able to control for the affect of error/noise in the training data set while learning to recognize the relationship between inputs and outputs. The utility of Bayesian networks in the prediction of rehospitalization is tested in this study.

ANNs have been applied to predict psychiatric hospital length of stay (David, Lowell, & Davis, 1993), recidivism patterns of juveniles (Brodzinski, Crable, & Scherer, 1994), injury severity and survival in trauma patients (Rutledge, 1995), severity of illness and use of hospital resources (Lawrence, 1991), diagnostic pattern recognition in acute toxoplasmosis cases (Afifi, Hammad, Gavr, Elshinawi, Khalifa, & Azab, 1995), workplace behavior (Collins & Clark, 1993), graduate student success (Wilson & Hardgrave, 1995), and prediction of international conflict (Schrodt, 1991). The strength of artificial neural networks lie in their potential to exceed the performance of experts (Schrodt, 1991), are robust in the face of nonlinear and nonparametric data (Galletly, Clark, & McGarlane, 1996), and they are able to remain robust in the face of missing and noisy data.

Brodzinski, Crable, and Scherer (1994) found that the ANN model they developed was 51 percent more accurate than a discriminant analysis model in the prediction of juvenile recidivism. Zou, Shen, Shu, Wang, Feng, Xu, Qu, Song, Zhong, Wang, and Liu (1996) report their development of ANN models that exceed the ability of an expert system in making psychiatric diagnoses using the Composite International Diagnostic Interview (CIDI) (Robins, Wing, Wittchen et al., 1988). Collins and Clark (1993) compared ANN models with discriminant regression models by (a) using a small sample (N = 81) and a large sample (N = 649) and (b) using a purposefully degraded data in which 33 percent and 100 percent of values in one of four independent variables were replaced with a missing value indicator. They found that their ANN models out performed the discriminant regression models in cross-validation multivariate correlations and correct classifications, especially with larger samples. Collins and Clark reported that their ANN model with 33 percent missing data achieved an 85 percent correct classification. Surprisingly, even when the ANN model's data, in one of four variables, was degraded 100 percent, it correctly classified 78 percent of cases. The implications are significant for social work settings, where missing data can be a significant problem.

The purpose of this study was to evaluate the utility of Bayesian ANNs in the prediction of rehospitalization for a cohort of severely and persistently mentally ill individuals. The goal was to develop and test the performance of Bayesian ANN models at predicting rehospitalization under two conditions. One condition required prediction of rehospitalization as a dichotomous event, rehospitalization or no rehospitalization. The second condition required prediction of an ordinal measure of rehospitalization frequency, (a) clients not likely to be rehospitalized (no rehospitalization episodes during the test period), (b) those who will likely have infrequent rehospitalizations (1 or 2 episodes), and (3) those clients who are at risk of frequent rehospitalizations (>2 episodes). Our intention was to lay the empirical foundation for the development of a more systematic means of assessing risk of rehospitalization. The development and deployment of systematic risk assessment decision support tools can alert social workers to modifiable risk factors and guide intervention. Greater discrimination of rehospitalization risk allows for differential application of intervention and social resources. Moreover, lowered rehospitalization rates resulting from selective interventions based on ANN decision support tools could result in significant cost savings to financially stressed mental health organizations. In sum, the capacity to identify clients who are at risk of experiencing frequent rehospitalizations is critical for both clinical and fiscal reasons.

METHOD

Subjects

Subjects were 196 outpatients receiving mental health services at a community mental health center in Knoxville, Tennessee. The Helen Ross McNabb Mental Health Center's interdisciplinary treatment teams provided a range of services to these clients, all diagnosed with a major mental illness and a prior history of hospitalization in a state psychiatric hospital. The racial and ethnic composition of the subjects was 153 Caucasian (78%), 41 African American (21%), and 2 of other racial origin (1%). There were 107 males (55%) and 89 females (45%). The mean age was 45.8 (S.D. 12.9) and the mean monthly income was $477 (S.D. 189). The diagnostic profile of the subjects on first Axis I diagnostic category was as follows: schizophrenia 131 (66%), affective disorder 43 (22%), organic disorder 8 (4.1%), other 14 (7%). Thirty-two of the subjects had an Axis II personality disorder (16%). One hundred and eight of the subjects were receiving intensive case management (ICM) services while the remaining 88 subjects, though eligible for intensive case management services did not receive the services due to a lack of fiscal resources in the mental health center.

Prevention of rehospitalization and extension of community tenure was one of the expected outcomes of the ICM program. Case managers providing services to the ICM subjects (a) could provide more frequent contact with clients due to reduced case loads, (b) had additional fiscal resources to use when warranted to attempt to prevent rehospitalization, and (c) were mandated to use aggressive outreach as the preferred mode of intervention (Waters, Womack, Hinton, 1991, p. 1). The two primary objectives of the ICM program were to (a) facilitate independent functioning by assessment of client strengths, linkage to resources, and the provision of support, and (b) increase the continuity of service provision to clients. The non-ICM subjects received medication evaluations, occasional visits to the day hospital program, and intermittent contact with a psychiatric nurse or psychiatrist.

Data Sources/Instrument

This study used three data sources. The Tennessee Department of Mental Health and Mental Retardation provided admission and discharge dates for all prior hospitalizations in Tennessee State Hospital facilities. The mental health center's management information system made possible the ready extraction of demographic, diagnostic, and outpatient services data. Finally, the subject's current case manager or primary therapist used a standardized instrument in a chart review to measure each subject's current and historical functioning across a number of dimensions. This chart review instrument is described elsewhere (Patterson & Lee, 1998).

Design

This study used a retrospective, analytic exploratory design to examine the frequency and duration of rehospitalization of subjects over a 30-month period from July 1990 to December 1992. Bayesian artificial neural network (ANN) algorithms were developed for the two rehospitalization prediction conditions using SPSS Neural Connection (1997b). SPSS Neural Connection employs icons and a graphical user interface to depict an array of tools available for construction of an ANN. Each of the resultant ANNs in this study were comprised of four components, (a) a spreadsheet input tool, (b) a data filter, (c) Bayesian network tool, and (d) a text output tool. The spreadsheet input tool contained the data set, which was imported as an SPSS file. The data filter allows ANN developers to select variables for inclusion in the model, to visually examine each variables distribution and descriptive statistics, and trim distributions as needed. The Bayesian network tool trains on the data set using either default parameters or those specified by the researchers in order to calculate weights for the final model. The text output tool allowed for the testing of the final model on cases not previously analyzed. The results yield information on the percentage of correct prediction, model error, and the actual values and predicted weights all test cases.

Two data sets with the same six input variables were used in this study. These six variables were selected from the original 34 variables of the data set based on theory and empirical findings (Patterson & Lee, 1995; 1998). The input variables included length of case management prior to hospitalization, number of mental health services provided, number of hospitalizations prior to the study period, number of days of hospitalization prior to the study period, the presence or absence of intensive case management, and total days in community prior to first rehospitalization. The two data sets are differentiated only by their target variables. The target (outcome) variable for the ANN predicting a dichotomous outcome (no rehospitalization) was 0 or 1 indicating whether the client experienced psychiatric rehospitalization during the 30-month period of the study. The target variable for the ANN predicting frequency (ordinal outcome) of rehospitalization was derived from data indicating the number of hospitalizations for clients during the 30 months of the study.

ANNs are generally developed in an experimental manner in which variables are added and removed, distributions of variables are trimmed to maximize homogeneity across distributions, variables are standardized, and analytic tools are tested for their ability to increase predictive ability and reduce error (SPSS, 1995). Such an experimental procedure was followed in this study. We systematically tested the effect of removing variables and trimming variable distributions over repeated trials. The goal in this process was to maximize the percentage of cases for which the ANN models could correctly predict rehospitalization for both the dichotomous and ordinal prediction conditions.

Unlike other ANN models that require assigning portions of the data set for training, validation, and testing, the Bayesian network tool only requires allotting data for training and testing. We experimented with assigning different proportions of the data set to training and testing in order to find a proportional assignment level that optimized the models predictive ability. The ability to develop highly predictive models with limited cases allotted for training is important in situations where a small number of subjects are present.

RESULTS

To establish the differential frequency of rehospitalization and estimate the cost of clients most at risk, we divided the cohort into three groups, clients with no rehospitalizations, those with 1 or 2 ($M = 1.3$), and those with 3 or more ($M = 4.1$). Table 1 displays the respective number of hospitalizations, lengths of stay and estimated costs for the three groups. The $350 per day figure used in cost estimates in Table 1 is based on the current acute inpatient per diem charge at Lakeshore Mental Health, the state psychiatric facility in which these subjects were hospitalized. The 26 subjects with three or more hospitalizations accounted for 46 percent of the estimated hospitalization costs in the study period. The average length of stay for subjects with 1 or 2 hospitalizations was 47 days, while for subjects with 3 or more hospitalizations had an average length of stay was 48 days. The mean total hospitalization cost per subject during the study period was $21,307 for subjects with 1 or 2 hospitalizations compared to $69,112 for subjects in the frequent hospitalization group. As is evident in the lower half of Table 1, treating rehospitalization as a dichotomous event causes the loss of discrimination of the subgroup of subjects who account for a disproportional number of hospitalizations and resultant costs.

We conducted multiple trials to arrive at eight Bayesian ANN models that maximized the prediction of rehospitalization across the two prediction conditions (dichotomous and ordinal target variables). The predictive ability of the models is presented in Table 2, along with the varying allocations of cases

TABLE 1. Rehospitalization Cost and Utilization (Days)

Ordinal Rehospitalization Analysis:

Group:	0 Episodes (n = 72)	1 or 2 Episodes (n = 98)	Over 2 Episodes (n = 26)	Total (n = 196)
Hospitalizations	0	127	107	234
Length of Stay in Days	0	5,966	5,134	11,100
Cost of Stay Assuming $350/Day	$0	$2,088,100	$1,796,900	$3,885,000

Dichotomous Rehospitalization Analysis

Group:	0 Episodes (n = 72)	1 or More Episodes (n = 124)	Total (n = 196)
Hospitalizations	0	234	234
Length of Stay in Days	0	11,100	11,100
Cost of Stay Assuming $350/Day	$0	$3,885,000	$3,885,000

TABLE 2. Predictions of Rehospitalization

Training vs. Testing Case Allocation	Training Cases	Test Cases	Dichotomous % Correct	Ordinal % Correct
70% training and 30% testing	138	58	93	80
60% training and 40% testing	118	78	89	75
50% training and 50% testing	98	98	89	81
40% training and 60% testing	78	118	89	80
Mean	108	88	90	79
Standard deviation			2.0	2.7

between training vs. testing. The mean predictive accuracy for the dichotomous models was 90% compared to 79% for the ordinal models. Surprisingly, the effect of increasing the number of training cases had little or no effect on the level of predictive ability as reflected in Table 2. Varying the number of training cases between n = 78 to 138, resulted in small and unpredictable variation in predictive accuracy ranging from 89% to 93% (M = 90%; SD = 2.0%) in the dichotomous condition, and from 75% to 81% (M = 79%; SD = 2.7%) in the ordinal condition.

DISCUSSION

The results of this study demonstrate the capacity of Bayesian artificial neural networks to predict correctly rehospitalization in a longitudinal data set drawn from a cohort of severely and persistently mentally ill subjects. In both prediction conditions, dichotomous and ordinal, ANN models produced correct predictions with 80 percent or greater accuracy in seven out of eight models. The accuracy of the dichotomous rehospitalization prediction models ranged from 93% to 89%, while the ordinal rehospitalization prediction models ranged from 81% to 75%. The greater predictive ability of the dichotomous models is likely due to the fact that ordinal models were required to make a more discrete differentiation and therefore more likely to produce error. However, the capacity of the ordinal models to detect subjects at risk of frequent rehospitalization is important given the fact that while these subjects represented only 13 percent of the cohort, they accounted for 46 percent of the days of hospitalization and resultant costs.

The Bayesian models in both prediction conditions were composed of only six variables. The goal of producing accurate and reliable ANN prediction models, which operate on a minimal number of variables, is significant as one considers the development of systematic risk assessment systems. If ANN models are to have clinical utility in decision support, parsimonious models that require less data collection across fewer variables will need to be developed. Parsimonious ANN models are less cost intense as they require less clinician time for data entry. A distinct advantage of an ANN over other statistical methods is that ANNs can be trained by continuing data flow. That is, ANNs learn from the entry of new cases into the model. This feature allows the model to adapt to emerging changes in social work practice populations. For instance, alterations in practice patterns by case workers responding to ANN predictions of clients at risk could be detected by an ANN and subsequent prediction of risk altered by the changed practice behavior.

ANN researchers (Brodzinski, Crable, & Scherer, 1994; Collins & Clark, 1993; Schrodt, 1991) have pointed out that one of the strength of ANNs over other analytic procedures is their ability to use data with missing and erroneous values. This robustness in the face of data noise is because information processing is diffused across numerous weightings within the network. Single errant or missing values are not likely to result in miss classification (Schrodt, 1991). This feature of ANNs is important to social work researchers, administrators, and practitioners who often have to work with incomplete information.

On the other hand, regression models have the advantage of providing information on the relative contribution and importance of each variable in the prediction model, which aids in theory generation. At present, ANNs lack a convenient or readily interpretable means to determine the effect of a single variable on the outcome of interest. This limitation suggests that ANNs are presently not the tool of choice for theory building. New ANN software packages may make the model weights and network parameters available (Collins & Clark, 1993; SPSS, 1997b).

A clear limitation of this study is that we have used retrospective information. Further research should be designed to build ANN models on existing data and test their predictive or classification utility and efficacy on prospective data. Rehospitalization risk assessment is presently a matter of clinical judgment. Our research suggests that systematic risk assessment and decision support tools available with ANNs may significantly improve clinical decisions.

REFERENCES

Abramowitz, S., Tupin, J. & Berger, A. (1984). Multivariate prediction of hospital readmission. *Comprehensive Psychiatry. 25*, 71-76.

Afifi, M.A., Hammad, T.A., Gabr, N.S., Elshinawi, S.F.S., Khalifa, R.M., Azab, M. E. (1995). Acute toxoplasmic infection in immunocompetent patients. *Clinical Infectious Diseases. 21 (6)*, 1411-1416.

Agresti, A. (1996). *An Introduction to Categorical Data Analysis*. New York, NY: John Wiley & Sons.

Bart, W.G. (1991). Use of an artificial neural network for diagnosis of myocardial infarction. *Annals of Internal Medicine. 115*, 843-848.

Brodzinski, J.D., Crable, E.A. & Scherer, R.F. (1994). Using artificial intelligence to model juvenile recidivism patterns, *Computers in Human Services. 10 (4)*, 1-18.

Carpenter, Mulligan, Bosler, et al. (1985). Multiple admissions to an urban psychiatric center: A comparison study. *Hospital and Community Psychiatry. 36*, 1305-1308.

Casper, E.S. & Pastva, G. (1990). Admission history, patterns, and subgroups of heavy users of a state psychiatric hospital. *Psychiatric Quarterly. 61*, 121-135.

Cheng, B. & Titterington, D.M. (1994). Neural networks: A review from a statistical perspective. *Statistical Science. 9 (1)*, 2-54.

Collins, J.M. & Clark, M.R. (1993). An application of the theory of neural computation to the prediction of workplace behavior: An illustration and assessment of network analysis. *Personnel Psychology. 46 (3)*, 503-524.

Cross, S.S., Harrison, R.F. & Kennedy, R.L. (1995). Introduction to neural networks. *The Lancet. 346*, October 21, 1075-1079.

David, G.E., Lowell, W.E., & Davis, G.L. (1993). A neural network that predicts psychiatric length of stay. *MD Computing. 25 (2)*, 87-92.

Dawes, R.M., Faust, D. & Meehl, P.E. (1989). Clinical versus actuarial judgement. *Science*. 24, 1668-1674.

Gallant, S.I. (1992). *Neural Network Learning and Expert Systems*. MIT Press: Cambridge, MA.

Galletly, C.A., Clark, C.R. & McFarlane, A.C. (1996). Artificial neural networks: A prospective tool for the analysis of psychiatric disorders. *Journal of Psychiatry and Neuroscience. 21*(4), 239-247.

Gorelick, D., Irwin, M., Schmidt-Ladener, S. et al. (1990). Alcoholism among male schizophrenic inpatients. *Annals of Clinical Psychiatry. 2*, 19-22.

Haykin, S. (1994). *Neural Networks: A Comprehensive Foundation*, NY: Macmillan, p. 2.

Jubak, J. (1992). *In the Image of the Brain*, Boston: Little, Brown and Company.

Kent, S. & Yellowlees, P. (1994). Psychiatric and social reasons for frequent rehospitalization. *Hospital and Community Psychiatry. 45 (4)*, 347-350.

Mesch, G.S. & Fishman, G. (1994). First readmission of the mentally ill: An event history analysis. *Social Science Research*. 23, 295-314.

Mezzich, J.S. & Coffman, G.A. (1985). Factors influencing length of hospital stay. *Hospital and Community Psychiatry. 36*, 1262-1270.

Neal, R. (1997). What is Bayesian learning? *Neural Network FAQ*. Sarle, W.S. (Ed). Introduction periodic posting to the Usenet newsgroup comp.ai.neural-nets, URL: ftp://ftp.sas.com/pub/neural/FAQ.html.

Patterson, D.A. & Lee, M.S. (1998). Intensive case management and rehospitalization: A survival analysis. *Research on Social Work Practice. 8 (2)*, 152-171.

Patterson, D.A. & Lee, M.S. (1995). Field trial of the global assessment of functioning scale-modified. *American Journal of Psychiatry. 151 (9)*, 1386-1388.

Postrado, L.T. & Lehman, A.F. (1995). Quality of life and clinical predictors of rehospitalization of persons with severe mental illness. *Psychiatric Services. 46 (11)*, 1161-1165.

Pritchard, W.S., Duke, D.W., Coburn, K.L., Moore, N.C., Tucker, K.A., Jann, M.W. & Hostetler, R.M. (1994). EEG-based, neural-net predictive classification of Alzheimer's disease verses control subjects is augmented by non-linear EEG measures. *Electroencephalography and clinical Neurophysiology. 91*, 118-130.

Rice, D.P., Kelman, S. & Miller, S. (1992). The economic burden of mental illness. *Hospital and Community Psychiatry. 43*, 1227-1232.

Robins, N.L., Wing, J., Wittchen, H.U., Helzer, J.E., Babor, T.F., Burke, J., Farmer, A., Jablenski, A., Pickens, R. & Regier, D.A. (1988). The Composite International Diagnostic Interview. A epidemiologic instrument suitable for use in conjunction with different diagnostic systems and in different cultures. *Archives of General Psychiatric. 45 (12)*, 1069-1077.

Rutledge, R. (1995). Injury severity and probability of survival assessment in trauma patients using a predictive hierarchical network model derived from ICD-9 codes. *Journal of Trauma. 38 (4)*, 590-597.

Sarle, W.S., ed. (1997). Neural Network FAQ, part 1 of 7: Introduction periodic posting to the Usenet newsgroup comp.ai.neural-nets, URL: ftp://ftp.sas.com/pub/neural/FAQ.html

Schrodt, P.A. (1991). Prediction of interstate conflict outcomes using a neural network. *Social Science Computer Review. 9 (3)*, 359-380.

SPSS Inc. (1997a). *Neural Connection 2.0 Application Guide.* SPSS: Chicago.

SPSS Inc. (1997b). *Neural Connection 2.0 User's Guide.* SPSS: Chicago.

SPSS Inc. (1996). Build better models faster with the new feature-packed Neural Connection 2.0. *Keyword. 62,* 3.

SPSS Inc. (1995). *Neural Connection 1.0 User's Guide.* SPSS: Chicago.

Steyaert, J. (1994). Soft computing of soft technologies: Artificial neural networks and fuzzy set theory for human services. *Computers in Human Services. 10 (4)*, 55-67.

Sullivan, G., Wells, K.B., Morgenstern, H. & Leake, B., (1995). Identifying modifiable risk factors for rehospitalization: A case-controlled study of seriously mentally ill persons in Mississippi. *American Journal of Psychiatry. 152 (12)*, 1749-1756.

Waters, R.M., Womack, P. & Hinton, J. (1991). *The Tennessee Case Management Program: Status Report on Implementation.* (Report). Nashville, TN: Office of Planning and Evaluation, Division of Mental Health Services, Tennessee Department of Mental Health and Mental Retardation.

Weiss, S. M. & Kulikowski, C.A. (1991). *Computer Systems That Learn: Classification, and Prediction Methods from Statistics, Neural Nets, Machine Learning, and Expert Systems.* San Mateo, CA: Morgan Kaufmann Publishers.

Wilson, R.L. & Hardgrave, B.C. (1995). Predicting graduate student success in an MBA program: Regression versus classification. *Education and Psychological Measurement. 55 (2)*, 186-195.

Zou, Y., Shen, Y., Shu, L., Wang, Y., Feng, F., Xu, K., Qu, Y., Song, Y., Zhong, Y., Wang, M. & Liu, W. (1996). Artificial neural network to assist psychiatric diagnosis. *British Journal of Psychiatry. 169, (1)*, 64-67.

Fashionably Late?
Social Work and Television Production

Kristine D. Tower

SUMMARY. In the enthusiasm for faster and more efficient technology for practice and education, social workers should not deny the obvious. Television has been, and will continue to be, the most influential tool of communication in American society. This article examines the role of social workers in broadcast television and describes the mechanics of TV production for novice social worker/producers. *[Article copies available for a fee from The Haworth Document Delivery Service: 1-800-342-9678. E-mail address: getinfo@haworthpressinc.com <Website: http://www.haworthpressinc.com>]*

KEYWORDS. Television, social work practice

For nearly 50 years, television has been the predominant form of information technology. Despite competition from personal computers over the past two decades, broadcast television remains the most successful medium for the transmission of ideas and images to the largest audience. Cable television, telephone, and on-line computer services are already converging. The TV set, with its higher resolution and larger screen, is certain to endure as the primary hardware in American homes well into the new century. It is important for

Kristine D. Tower, EdD, MSW, is Assistant Professor, University of Nevada, Reno.

Address correspondence to: Kristine D. Tower, University of Nevada at Reno, Reno, NV 89557-0068 (E-mail: rjtower@aol.com).

[Haworth co-indexing entry note]: "Fashionably Late? Social Work and Television Production." Tower, Kristine D. Co-published simultaneously in *Journal of Technology in Human Services* (The Haworth Press, Inc.) Vol. 16, No. 2/3, 1999, pp. 63-79; and: *Computers and Information Technology in Social Work: Education, Training, and Practice* (ed: Jo Ann R. Coe, and Goutham M. Menon) The Haworth Press, Inc., 1999, pp. 63-79. Single or multiple copies of this article are available for a fee from The Haworth Document Delivery Service [1-800-342-9678, 9:00 a.m. - 5:00 p.m. (EST). E-mail address: getinfo@haworthpressinc. com].

social workers to understand and employ the power of this technology to foster the goals of the profession.

Television viewing has contributed to the positive public image of many types of human service professions, including medicine and law. Unfortunately, this has not been true for social work. Only a handful of worthwhile programs for broadcast television have ever been produced with social workers as central characters (Andrews, 1987). Too often, media images about social workers and their clients have been demeaning or inaccurate (Kaufman & Raymond, 1995/1996). Given the lack of positive media attention, it is no wonder that social work is "not uniformly known and endorsed by the public" (Brawley, 1995, p. 1676).

The most certain approach to improving the public's perception of the profession is for social workers to actively participate in shaping their image. Although it may be awkward for practitioners and educators to seek recognition for their accomplishments, it is necessary to invite the media's attention. Moreover, social workers have a duty to set the record straight when the public is misinformed about professional issues. Brawley and Martinez-Brawley stated:

> If social workers do not take the initiative and make the effort to present an accurate picture of themselves, their work, their clients, and community resources and problems on a routine basis when things are going relatively well and the press is not looking for blood, they will continue to find themselves in a defensive posture in relation to the media because the only time the media will be aware of them will be when they are in trouble. (1982, p. 77)

This admonition to social workers may be justified, but consider the reasons for the silence. There is a shortage of social work articles or books about producing for broadcast television or other media. Few schools of social work offer content on the subject within their curriculum.

During the period between 1990-1997, this author served as the producer on five documentaries made for broadcast on commercial and public television. New concepts were learned, techniques were refined, and understanding about technology increased with each video project. More important, the benefits of TV production were realized. The knowledge gained from those experiences has been synthesized in this article to share with colleagues. The author had two goals in mind: (1) to encourage and facilitate new social worker/producers, and (2) to promote critical thinking and scholarly discussion about using broadcast television as a means for shaping the image of social work.

The utility of video technology for social work practitioners and educators is increasingly evident for a myriad of other applications, including computer-based training (CBT), distance education, video conferencing, and Web site development. The basic production steps described in this paper are suitable for any of the media used for such purposes (e.g., videotape, CD-ROM, ZIP/JAZZ discs, DVD). Although this article is primarily concerned with social workers using broadcast television to communicate effectively with the public, suggestions are introduced which may also be used to create interesting classroom or agency presentations.

WHY HAS IT TAKEN SO LONG FOR SOCIAL WORKERS TO UTILIZE THIS TECHNOLOGY?

Historically, social workers may have avoided television due to their objections about the medium's influence, particularly on children. On average, youngsters witness at least 8,000 murders and over 100,000 other assorted violent acts on television by the time they finish grade school (Huston, Donnerstein, Fairchild, Feshbach, Katz, Murray, Rubenstein, Wilcox, & Zuckerman, 1992). Sadly, despite decades of efforts by researchers and policy makers to decrease TV violence, just the opposite has occurred (Lazar, 1994). Disdain for this phenomenon is understandable, but how can social workers hope to counteract the negative impact of television if they have no voice within the medium?

It is possible that some social workers shun involvement with television out of general mistrust of the media. Fear is a reasonable response given the potential for damage to an individual's or an agency's reputation caused by erroneous reporting. How many times have social workers been embarrassed by comments that were misquoted or were taken out of context by the print media? The advantage of producing one's own TV program is the control that the social worker has over the outcome.

Practitioners may have also had legitimate concerns about ethical issues involved in producing television, such as client confidentiality. Two basic questions must be considered when utilizing this type of information technology in social work: "(1) To what extent will social work values be incorporated into this process? and (2) Will the end result promote high quality social work practice?" (Cwikel & Cnaan, 1991, p. 114). It is possible to produce interesting TV shows about sensitive issues without rejecting social work principles.

Most likely, social workers have not been more involved in TV production because they lack knowledge about the mechanics of the process. Some may have had disappointing results when attempting to use home camcorder equipment for professional purposes. Others may have participated in community access television only to be disillusioned by the limited viewership. Achieving satisfying results from broadcast television takes more effort than these simple approaches. However, producing high-quality television for commercial or public television does not require extensive technical knowledge. Professional video photographers (known as *videographers*) and editors may be hired as production partners to do the highly specialized work. Social workers are already well-trained to do the majority of tasks that are the responsibility of television producers. Producers must be able to research an issue, network with people affected by the issue and gain their cooperation/ support, find funding and other resources, make final decisions about content, and coordinate all of the entities involved until the project is complete. Television production is similar in many ways to case management.

LEARNING TO PRODUCE TELEVISION

In this era of inexpensive digital cameras (under $1,000) and desktop editing systems (under $200), it could be argued that social workers don't need professional help to create their own television programs. If the programs are created for narrow-cast purposes, such as classroom applications, in-service training, video conferencing, or community access television, this author would agree with that position. For broadcast purposes, however, the video technology is much more sophisticated and expensive than most human service agencies can manage on their own. Television cameras alone may cost over $75,000 dollars!

There is no one correct way to make a television program. There are, however, some common mistakes made by novice producers that hurt their chances of having a show aired on broadcast television. Throughout the remainder of this article, suggestions are presented to aid new producers in successfully developing their first television projects, such as documentaries. The reader may discover regional differences in terminology or TV station preferences, but most of the concepts described below are universal.

Social workers in practice or educational settings will often find commercial and public television stations receptive to collaboration on projects involving social work issues. Of course, the stations expect to receive funding to pay for production and broadcasting costs. They will, however, frequently reduce their normal rates (as a public service) or assist with matching funding (e.g., foundation grants to public television). They have the equipment that's necessary for high-quality production and they're a good resource for finding talented videographers and editors. More important, they have a mechanism to broadcast the program once it is finished.

GETTING STARTED

The first hurdle for any producer is the funding. Television stations will gladly assist social workers to develop a budget for grants or other fundraising. The money is available, if the producer is determined to find it. Many local, state, or federal grants target innovative approaches to special issues and/or populations. Television is a contemporary approach to meeting a variety of social work objectives including: providing outreach and peer support, teaching self-advocacy, empowering through information, building collaboration and cooperation, and promoting systems change. Grantwriters should include similar language when developing their proposals. Also, it helps to mention the recognition that the contributor will receive in the show's opening or closing credits.

Another challenge facing the social worker/producer is the need to define the focus of the program. The limitations of time and funding will influence this decision, of course, but it's still hard to know when enough is enough. Narrowing the focus is an ongoing necessity because, once taping begins, compelling side issues will unexpectedly emerge. The producer must be judicious in deciding which of these issues to pursue. To define the focus, consider the following suggestions. First, be reminded of the time-honored journalistic approach to getting a good story: who, what, where, when, why, and how. Who is the program about? Who is the intended audience? What is the program about? Where is this taking place? Why is this program being made? When will the program be made? How will the program be made? Next, approach the project from the social work perspective by considering the topic ecologically. Who are the people and what are the issues at micro-, meso-, and macro-system levels? What impact will the program have at each level? If done well, all three levels of systems will be addressed.

Social work projects, unlike big-budget Hollywood productions, are generally accomplished through the hard work of a very limited crew. The social worker/producer will usually work with one videographer. In some ways, one committed videographer is preferable to working with several part-timers (who may have with no real investment in the program). In small productions, the videographer is usually responsible for direction, lighting, and sound. With luck, there will be a production assistant available to help the videographer manage the equipment. The producer arranges the venues for videotaping and often serves as the interviewer. After taping, the producer organizes the raw footage and prepares for editing. If necessary, the producer also writes text and locates a competent narrator.

Early in the process, the producer needs to decide whether or not to seek out celebrity figures (called *talent*) for the program. A popular and well-respected host can lend credibility to a television show. Unfortunately, the difficulty and expense of arranging for talent may outweigh the benefits. If a celebrity donates time to host or narrate a show, the producer must have budgeted for the expense of traveling (perhaps for an entire video crew), lodging, food, and other necessities. Moreover, celebrities are bombarded with requests for donations of their time. It doesn't hurt to ask, of course, but it's better to have budgeted for talent. Occasionally, actors or musicians will reduce their rates for social causes that are compatible with their philosophical views.

GENERAL CONCEPTS

Television is a visual medium. It is essential for a program to have eye appeal in order to keep the attention of an audience. Vivid images are more powerful than lengthy, on-camera discussions or speeches (known as *talking heads*). In fact, broadcasters consider talking heads to be less desirable content than footage of action scenes. Optimally, the ratio of talking heads to action footage in a documentary should be about 30/70. Roughly 30% of the show should consist of on-camera interviews, including: discussions with consumers, social workers, and other human services professionals. The remaining 70% should be action scenes that support the topic, including: social workers making home visits; hospital, school, court, or jail scenes; or support group meetings. Included in the action footage are other generic images that are relative to the topic, but not necessarily specific to the participants, such as: a group of children at play, an unidentified mother pushing a baby stroller, a broken toy, a slamming door, a ticking clock, empty liquor bottles, traffic, and so on. This footage (called *B-roll footage*) is used to help set the tone of the scenes. The B-roll footage gives the producer an opportunity to be creative and allows the editor to select from a range of material for use to cover up problems (more about this later).

Another early consideration is the production approach. If the social worker is an expert about a particular topic, the approach is easier and more economical. A planning tool known as a *storyboard* is developed which will guide the videography and editing. The storyboard is essentially a script of all of the scenes that the producer hopes to capture to tell a story in logical order. After the footage has been taped and reviewed, the producer revisits the storyboard to determine if the scenes should remain in the same order. If not, the script may be changed before starting to edit.

If a producer isn't an expert about the chosen topic, the storyboard approach will not work. In this case, the process is investigative, similar to qualitative research. Since the producer is learning more about the issues while videotaping interviews and action footage, it's impossible to plan the entire program in advance. Rather, the unfolding story tells itself. One interview leads to another. Comments from respondents spark ideas about visual images that need to be videotaped. Eventually, enough footage is captured to exhaust the topic sufficiently. At that juncture, the producer examines all of the major points that emerged during videotaping. Those points are organized into a script containing the producer's chosen sequence of scenes. Although it's true that this approach is costly and time-consuming, it could be argued that it is more fruitful.

Regardless of the approach taken, the producer must consider the pace, or rhythm, of the show as it is pieced together. Not all of the scenes will be equally as interesting. The most engaging parts should be used at appropriate times to maximize their impact on the viewers. For instance, the opening scene needs to grab the viewers' attention so that they'll commit to watching the rest of the program. Conversely, the closing scene should be memorable, adhering to the old adage about always leaving the audience wanting more. If the show is lengthy, powerful scenes need to be placed in the middle to keep the viewers interested. Although the influence of MTV and contemporary advertising has upped the pace of some television productions, it is this author's opinion that a good story overrides the demand for rapid visual changes.

Another concept for new producers to grasp is that a TV show consists of innumerable small parts. The trick of making a production appear seamless is to string those parts together so that interviews and action scenes flow. It is not necessary to try to videotape perfect scenes from opening to close. Sometimes the participants will be articulate and sometimes they'll ramble. That's okay. The editor will take the most salient and interesting parts and piece them together to make a coherent program. One of the reasons for obtaining an abundance of B-roll footage is so that the editor can cover up the problem spots with interesting visual images.

Interviewing Techniques

Interviewing participants for television purposes is unlike the clinical interviewing techniques that are commonly used by social workers. When interviewing, the producer must be conscious of how the footage will be edited. In most cases, the interviewer will not be seen in the final version of the program. Therefore, it is necessary to maintain silence long enough before and after each question to make it possible to eliminate the interviewer's voice in editing. It's hard to refrain from responding to an interviewee's comments, especially when they're emotional. But it is worse to have to reject otherwise great footage because the producer's voice overlapped with the respondent.

To reduce anxiety, interviewees should be instructed about the taping process. It is a good idea to let them know that they can't really make any fatal mistakes. If they fumble with their answers, they may repeat them. That's one advantage of videotape over live television. Respondents should be informed that the interviewer will not be seen in the edited show, so the questions that are asked must be incorporated into their answers. To illustrate, if a respondent was asked, "How long have you worked at this agency?" and answered, "Eight years," the footage would be useless in editing. By itself, the answer doesn't make any sense. If instead, the respondent said, "I've worked at this agency for eight years," the footage would be fine. Additionally, respondents should avoid looking directly at the camera or the videographer. Instead, they should talk to the interviewer (who is strategically positioned to the side of the camera) as though they were having a one-on-one conversation.

One complication of interviewing for videotape is the need to control the sound. Extraneous noise can ruin good footage when it's too loud or dissonant. Airplanes flying overhead, loud traffic noises, ringing telephones, even the humming of refrigerators and air conditioners, can spoil a scene. If possible, those problems should be minimized before videotaping begins. Moreover, it is important to capture a minute or so of additional natural sound (without anyone talking) at each location for use in editing. Known as *ambient* or *nat sound*, this footage enables the editor to match and smooth out the sound quality between editing cuts.

It should be mentioned that the producer is responsible for ensuring that all of the participants give written permission to be videotaped. This is true of interviewees and others who may be recognizable in the finished program. Most institutions, such as hospitals or schools, will also require permission before they'll allow videotaping to take place on their premises. In general, the generic images captured on B-roll will not be held to the same high standards. Videotaping of crowds, the backs of heads, the movement of traffic, people milling in public places (like parks), and other similar images will not require written permission from each individual.

Here's a final cautionary note about interviews: the producer should never promise to allow participants to make final decisions about the edited video. It is common for the interviewees to complain about how they appear on tape (e.g., their hair, weight, mannerisms). The final decision about using selected footage cannot rest with the respondent who might rescind permission simply because of a bad hair day!

Videography

Novice producers will have to rely heavily on the skills of the videographer to capture good footage for the program. It is advisable to meet early in the process to establish rapport and to discuss the goals of the project. The producer may want to ask to see samples of the videographer's previous work. In order to communicate effectively with this important production partner, it's useful to understand some of the terminology used in videography. A brief glossary of additional terms is presented in Appendix A.

As producers gain confidence, they may use their own creativity to request specific types of camera shots. Recently, for instance, this author asked the videographer to open a scene at a homeless shelter by shooting a close-up of a ragged teddy bear then pulling out slowly to reveal the dismal conditions of the shelter. Producers may also borrow ideas from favorite movie or TV scenes. For example, after watching an Alfred Hitchcock movie, this author asked the videographer to open on a scene of a woman in a wheelchair by taping her shadow on the sidewalk before she gradually rolled into the camera's view.

Most important, the producer needs to be sure that the videographer has taken plenty of footage at each location, far more than will actually be used. A general rule of thumb is to shoot ten times the amount of footage needed (e.g., 10 hours for a one-hour show). It is expensive and time-consuming to return for additional footage. Look around for images that are relevant to the theme of the program at each location (e.g., still photos, the landscape, religious or cultural symbols, toys, books, medical equipment) and insist on taping B-roll footage. While most videographers know the importance of capturing extra footage, sometimes the producer must remind them. In the end, the editor will be grateful for the variety of choices.

Editing

Editing, like videography, is truly an art form. It has changed considerably during the last decade as new technology has emerged. Most commercial and larger public television stations now have *digital* equipment for editing. This is a major advancement from the old days of *analog* technology. With analog, a production had to be edited in sequence from beginning to end, like recording an audio cassette tape at home. If a mistake was discovered in the middle of a program, the show would have to be re-edited from the point of the error to the end. Through digital technology, editing systems (e.g., AVID) make it possible to load all of the chosen footage into a computer before beginning to edit. Producers and their editors can try out ideas and move scenes around without negative consequences.

After the first segments of videotaping are captured, the producer begins to prepare for editing. Each tape should be numbered as it is finished. At the end of each taping session, the videographer will take the original tapes (known as *source tapes*) back to the studio. Copies (called *window dubs* or *window burns*) will be made for the producer by converting the source tapes, which are usually recorded on BETA, to a VHS format. The window dubs are identical to the source tapes except that they have a running *time code* at the bottom of the screen. With each tape uniquely numbered, the time codes can help the editor find specific points within the source tapes.

An important editing concept for novice producers to understand is the layering process involved in making a finished TV show. When the videographer is taping, at least two *channels* (audio and video) are being recorded at the same time. In editing, those channels may be used together or separately. Additional audio and video channels may be added, such as music, narration, or subtitles. Because it is possible to separate the channels, there will be times when footage that seems unusable (e.g., poor lighting, bad sound, out of focus) is salvageable, at least on one channel. Making a video is like baking a cake; it's put together in layers, and sometimes problems can be covered up with a little frosting!

Preparing the Footage

Before editing can take place, the most tedious job in the production process must be done. This job is known as *cataloging the footage*. All of the raw footage on the source tapes must be described in detail with time codes, so that editing decisions can be made. In the process of cataloging all of the tapes, the producer becomes intimately familiar with the footage. In order to write everything down, it is necessary to go back and forth in the tape, over and over again. While it is painfully monotonous, this is how the producer comes to really know his or her footage. There will not be time to look for the best parts once editing begins. Editing is the most expensive phase of the project, so the producer must be prepared before heading to the studio. This is an example of the format that this author uses to catalog the source tapes.

Identify: Interview with Mary P.   Pg.: 2 of 6
                                                                     Tape #:8

Time	Type	Description
	Q	Tell us about the type of work that you do at this agency.
03:40	MS	(M.) "Here at the Community Center, we offer a variety of services. An
		intake worker meets with new clients to discuss the problems that
		brought them into the center. Then, we can set up counseling, either
		individually or in groups. (M. smiles) We also offer advocacy to people
03:55		who are having a hard time getting through the court system." ***
	Q	What is the eligibility criteria?

Notice that the tape is identified by a description of the content (an interview with Mary) and a unique page number (2 of 6) and tape number (#8). The first entry described on this page is a record of the question that was posed to Mary. Note the "Q" written under "Type." Since the questions will not be appearing in the show, there's no need to record their time codes. A beginning and an ending time code is recorded for Mary's statement. The type of camera shot is identified, in this case a medium shot (MS). The (M.) under "Description" is a reminder that Mary is speaking. Within the description there is a notation about a change in her affect. The three stars at the end of the statement indicate that this is a very good piece of footage, in terms of quality and content. The producer can use a system of stars to rate the footage so that the best clips are used in the final show.

Rough Editing

After cataloging the footage, the producer is ready to begin compiling a rough edit on paper. Guided by the window dubs, catalog, and system of identifying the best footage, a draft of the scenes can be assembled. The draft will be used by the editor to load the computer with all of the footage that the producer hopes to use. When developing the draft, it is necessary to remember the concept about layering. This is an excerpt from a draft for a recent video produced by this author:

Tape(s): <u>4</u>   Scene: <u>Matt the social worker/coach</u>

8:48 Matt	9:50 Girl shoots ball	9:21 Matt shoots, fingers wiggle
9:04	10:07	9:32

8:48	Ambient sound of Matt talking and playing B-ball
9:32	

4:48 Feet	14:04 Baskets	18:16 Matt interview	3:04 CU ball
4:58	14:11	18:26	3:12

4:48 Amb.	14:04	18:13 Matt interview
4:58	Amb. 14:08	18:34

Initially this example seems complex, but it is really quite simple. Note the "V" and "A," which signify video and audio channels. The time codes identify the location of the footage on the source tapes. The scene opens with the camera on Matt, while he is talking and playing basketball. The audio channel will stay the same throughout the first few scenes. The video channel will change to include footage of a girl throwing a ball, as Matt's voice continues to be heard on the audio channel. Then, the video returns to Matt, matching up to the audio channel. The next scene will be a shot of jumping feet using both video and audio channels. A scene of the ball falling into the basket follows. The ambient sound will match the video for the first few seconds, then Matt's voice will be heard. The video will match up to Matt for 10 seconds, then leave him again for a close up of a basketball. Note that his audio continues until the end of the last scene.

Additional Editing Concepts

The novice producer should not panic if unable to develop a draft as sophisticated as the one previously described. The editor will help, as long as the producer has prepared a list of time codes and can give directions about how the scenes should go together (remember the *storyboard*). One difficulty is having the terminology to be able to describe the effects that the producer is trying to achieve. Terms to aid in communicating with the editor are presented in Appendix B.

One of the final stages in the editing process involves embellishing or *garnishing* the appearance of the program. This is done through the use of transitions, special effects, titles, or other overlays. Music and narration may be added. Sometimes additional environmental sounds, like birds chirping or water flowing, will enhance sound quality. Once again, it's important to realize when enough is enough. Too many special effects can be a distraction and will lower the caliber of the production.

After all of the editing is done, the resulting product is a *program master* which contains the final version of the show. The studio will use the master to broadcast the show and to make VHS copies for distribution. It is impossible to describe the producer's satisfaction when receiving that finalized copy of the program. Unlike so many interminable tasks in social work, here's one that ends well. The producer has truly created something of value both personally and professionally.

Implications of Television Production for Social Work

The benefits of television production become apparent during and after the making of the show. Some of the most significant gains are those experienced by the program's participants. The following examples are just a sampling from the author's collection of production anecdotes. One young man began dating for the first time since his traumatic brain injury. He said that he felt more self-confident since appearing on TV. Another interviewee entered into treatment after seeing himself on one of the source tapes. He recognized that his problem drinking was evident and he wanted to do something about it. His portion of the show was retaped after he began his sobriety. A female respondent became interested in social work and returned to college to pursue her degree. An estranged father and daughter began speaking to each other again, after he saw the TV interview in which she declared that she wanted to be an architect. . . . just like her father! In one case, a viewer from a distant state became intrigued with the artwork of a participant and commissioned him to do a highly-paid project.

The most obvious benefit of TV production is the impact it has on the viewing audience. Viewers from some of the most remote areas in the country have called or written to express gratitude about addressing an issue that affected their lives. The production clearly served as a means of providing peer support and outreach to distant rural communities. Some people called to request copies of the shows; others had suggestions for future programs.

One of the most exciting outcomes for this author has been the effect that TV production has on social work students. During several projects, students assisted with production tasks ranging from carrying equipment to cataloging footage. The most recent production, *Faces of Change*, was a class project that was carried out almost entirely by students in a social work media course at the University of Nevada, Reno. Students report increased awareness of their duty to work with the media and greater confidence about their ability to do so.

Finally, television production has profound effects on the producer. The networking and collaboration that occurs in planning and carrying out the project builds lasting relationships. The social worker's knowledge about the topic of the show grows expansively. There is no denying that TV production is arduous, but it is also just plain fun. The work is not as lonely as writing journal articles or textbooks. It is exhilarating to be out on location with a video crew and to experience the camaraderie. Moreover, the bond that the producer and participants experience when watching the finished program together is unparalled.

FINAL COMMENTS

In this article, the author has attempted to provide novice producers with sufficient basic information to begin their first broadcast television projects. Television production offers social workers an important tool for disseminating information to the public. Stoesz stated, "Developments in social welfare policy and programs of the past two decades make it imperative for social workers to exploit means for establishing a dialogue with the public" (1993, p. 367). His point is excellent, but he doesn't go far enough in his suggestions about how to accomplish the task. He encouraged social workers to write more op-ed articles for newspapers and journals. That's a good beginning, but too limited in scope. If the intended audience consists of people living in poverty, children, individuals with disabilities, aged persons, or other disenfranchised groups, shouldn't their medium of choice be the one exploited? Heaviest television usage occurs among people with low incomes and restricted leisure activities, Even when given alternative choices, television viewing accounts for the majority of media usage among children (Lazar, 1994). Social workers should consider these facts and think critically about how to harness the power of this popular medium. Television isn't all bad. In fact, some studies have demonstrated that watching selected TV programs can be therapeutic (Rubin, 1991; Stosny, 1994). More studies of this nature are needed to strengthen the validity of such claims, but social workers don't have to wait any longer to get started. One thing is certain, social workers won't be able to judge the value of the medium fairly unless they begin to utilize the technology to produce their own television programs.

REFERENCES

Andrews, J. (1987). Social work public image building: "East Side/West Side" revisited. *Social Service Review, 61 (3)*, 485-497.

Brawley, E.A. (1995). Mass media. In *Encyclopedia of Social Work*, (19th ed.). Washington, DC: NASW Press, 1674-1682.

Brawley, E.A., & Martinez-Brawley, E.E. (1982). Teaching social work students to use the news media for public education purposes. *Journal of Education for Social Work, 18*, 76-83.

Cwikel, J.G., & Cnaan, R.A., (1991). Ethical dilemmas in applying second-wave information technology to social work practice. *Social Work, 36 (2)*, 114-120.

Huston, A.C., Donnerstein, E., Fairchild, H., Feshbach, N.D., Katz, P., Murray, J.P., Rubenstein, E.A., Wilcox, B., & Zuckerman, D. (1992). *Big World, Small Screen: The Role of Television in American Society.* Nebraska: University of Nebraska Press.

Kaufman, A.V., & Raymond, G.T. (1995/1996). Public perceptions of social workers: A survey of knowledge and attitudes. *Arete, 20 (2)*, 24-35.

Lazar, B.A. (1994). Why social work should care: Television violence and children. *Child and Adolescent Social Work Journal, 11 (1)*, 3-19.

Rubin, A. (1991). Cable TV as a resource in preventative mental health programming for children. *Education Digest, 11*, 26-31.

Stoesz, D. (1993). Communicating with the public. *Social Work, 38 (4)*, 361-504.

Stosny, S. (1994). "Shadows of the Heart:" A dramatic video for the treatment resistance of spouse abusers. *Social Work, 39 (6)*, 686-694.

APPENDIX A

Glossary of videography terms

Camera Terms

Head shot: Close up of a person's face/head.

1, 2, or 3 shot: Camera is focused on one, two, or three people.

Group shot: Camera is focused on group of more than three people.

Close up: Camera focuses on close detail, such as a person's eye or hands. May also refer to a detailed shot of a part of a large object, such as a license plate on a car, or a full shot of a small object, such as a ring or photograph.

Medium shot: Camera is focused on person's head, shoulders, and upper body, or may refer to 2, 3, or group shot that is focused on more than just heads, but less than full bodies. May also refer to a shot of a large object, like a car.

Wide shot: Camera is focused on whole person/group of people with background showing. May also include shots of large objects within broader contexts, such as a car driving down the freeway.

Push in: Camera angle goes from a wider to a closer shot, such as from a medium to a close-up shot.

Pull out: Opposite of push in.

Exit-left, right, up or down: Describes the direction taken when a subject exits from camera view.

Lighting Terms

White balance: Before videotaping, cameras are color-balanced by focusing on a white paper or cloth to eliminate unwanted color.

Hot spot: An unwanted glaring light that splashes across a person or object.

Shadows: Unwanted dark spots.

Key light: The main light that's used to illuminate the subject's face or an object.

Back light: A light that's used behind a subject to eliminate shadows or hot spots.

APPENDIX A (continued)

Fill light: Fills in at about 50% of the light of a key light, used to fill in the dark shadows around the sides of a subject.

Lighting gels: Colored transparencies that are used to adjust light. A blue gel, for instance, will adjust tungsten light to look like daylight.

Sound Terms

Lavaliere mike: A microphone that is clipped to the subject's clothing, usually on the lapel. Use when interviewing individuals or couples.

Shotgun: A microphone that is attached to the camera. Doesn't provide the clarity of a lavaliere mike for capturing speech, however, may be used in outside settings or other places when lavaliere mikes aren't available or appropriate. Used to capture ambient sound.

Boom mike: A microphone that is held by a long pole hanging over the subjects. Useful for recording groups of people.

APPENDIX B

Glossary of editing terms

EDL: Edit Decision List. This list is generated on a computer. It contains all of the edit decisions for the entire program.

Transitions: These are the methods for changing from one scene to another; may include dissolves, fades, or one of numerous other techniques.

Dissolve: A commonly-used transition in which one scene gradually dissolves into the next. The length of the dissolve creates varying effects.

Fade: A dissolve to black or white. This technique is especially useful for creating the illusion of time passing or to signify the closure of a major segment of the program.

Cutaway: Refers to short clips of B-roll footage. Used to splice scenes together and cover up problems.

Upstream: Refers to the location of a point on the tape. Means that the point is found earlier in the tape.

Downstream: Opposite of upstream. The point is found later in the tape.

VO: Voice Over. Use of one source of audio sound (e.g., a person's voice) edited over a different source of video.

Straight cut: Two scenes are connected together with no transitions used.

L-cut: One channel remains constant throughout segment, but the other changes (often involving a VO) at beginning or end.

T-cut: Like an L-cut, but in this case, one channel remains constant throughout the segment, but the other channel changes in the middle (instead of the beginning or end).

Jump cut: Generally speaking, an undesirable edit, in which two similar segments of tape of a single subject are spliced together without using a transition or cutaway. Causes an abrupt "jump" between the segments. Is now finding acceptance on certain types of productions, such as music videos.

Off-line: The editing that takes place while creating an EDL.

On-line: The final editing that uses the EDL to create the finished program.

CG: Character generator. A device that is used to add text, such as subtitles and credits.

Sound mixing: The editing of sound levels within and between scenes. Also refers to adding sounds.

Technology Investment Trends

Brenda R. Kunkel

SUMMARY. Social service agencies across the country are investing in a wide range of technological, business process reengineering, and organizational change projects. These projects include:

- using technology to connect social workers to enable collaborative case management;
- building databases with sophisticated querying applications that allow quick, effective decision making at the front-line and management levels; and
- expanding the number of ways clients can access services through the use of the Internet, kiosks, electronic benefit transfers, etc.

Successful projects have a clearly identified business need and a strategy for addressing that need. This strategy includes understanding the process, organizational and technological context, evaluating alternative means of meeting the need, and developing a solid program management plan. *[E-mail address: getinfo@haworthpressinc.com <Website: http://www.haworthpressinc.com>]*

KEYWORDS. Social services, technology, states, technology investment

TECHNOLOGY INVESTMENT TRENDS

The world of people working with people to create change at the individual, family and societal levels is now continuously colliding with the world of

Brenda R. Kunkel, MSW, is Social Services Consultant, IBM Global Government Industry (E-mail: bkunkel@us.ibm.com).

Address correspondence to: Brenda R. Kunkel, 17543 Bowie Mill Road, Derwood, MD 20855.

[Haworth co-indexing entry note]: "Technology Investment Trends." Kunkel, Brenda R. Co-published simultaneously in *Journal of Technology in Human Services* (The Haworth Press, Inc.) Vol. 16, No. 2/3, 1999, pp. 81-95; and: *Computers and Information Technology in Social Work: Education, Training, and Practice* (ed: Jo Ann R. Coe, and Goutham M. Menon) The Haworth Press, Inc., 1999, pp. 81-95. [E-mail address: getinfo@haworthpressinc.com].

technology designed to speed up, replace, or enhance people's work. These collisions are often met with mistrust, frustration, or avoidance, as with any phenomena outside of our control. The desire, however, is for technology projects to be met with the anticipation, relief, or satisfaction of expectations exceeded. How social workers react to technology depends on how the change is introduced, i.e., whether they believe compelling reasons exist to employ technology or whether the project seems to be technology for technology's sake.

Many states are investing in large technology projects for a variety of reasons. Some states are setting up databases that allow front line workers and management to search for information needed for individual care plans or for budget decisions. Other states are creating virtual one stop shopping centers that allow clients to initiate contact from any location or are using advances in communication technology to allow isolated clients or social workers to connect with the people and information they need. At the same time, agencies are combining, reorganizing, or splitting up and legislation and research are pointing to new or re-focused ways of serving clients. Balance is critical to the long term success of these agency improvement efforts. Winning projects pay equally strong attention to technology implementation, process improvement, and organizational change.

Millions of dollars are spent on these initiatives in social service and education agencies, and with the recent budget windfalls, this is a better time to get funding for an initiative. In approving a project, funders believe that their investment will pay off in terms of greater efficiency, better service, or better results. Building a good business case is critical to acquiring funds and starting an investment down the path to success. To build a good business case, an agency must understand what mission critical need is being addressed, consider alternatives, and put a solid program management plan in place.

This article first surveys common activities in the technology, process, and organization arenas of social service agencies. The subsequent discussion suggests steps to be taken in evaluating technology investment options.

TECHNOLOGY AND SOCIAL SERVICES

Technology is changing the way social work is practiced and taught in many ways. Three such change agents are communications, electronic business, and databases. These three now shape the way we connect with one another, the way we interact with our clients and the public, and the way we get and use information. Choosing the appropriate technology for an agency depends on understanding how that agency needs to change in order to better serve clients, to satisfy new demands or to produces required results.

Communications

The most familiar technological change is the one which we use to connect with one another. While technology has facilitated better communication, the real work of making better connections with one another comes through changing the way we work and the way we are structured. Connectivity projects succeed when the end users have a responsibility that is made easier by the new technology, are trained on how to use the technology, and are rewarded for taking advantage of the technology.

- Voice Response technology allows potential clients to find the right re-source by choosing from automated phone menus. The advantage to this technology is that clients can receive answers 24 hours a day, 7 days a week. Call centers allow agencies to provide a human response to the client.
- Clients, students and other stakeholders can now communicate with so-cial workers whenever the need arises through the use of voice mail and electronic mail. They can tell their story without translation by a third party message taker and can be assured that the message arrived at its destination quicker than a postal letter. These mail systems when com-bined with cellular phones and pagers allow social workers to keep in constant contact.
- Groups can interact without being in the same location through the use of video and teleconferencing or through bulletin boards and discussion forums on the Internet. These discussion avenues save travel time and expense, especially for social workers in remote areas or for a small group with similar interests separated by great distance.

Many technology projects have improved communication as a goal. The underlying assumption is that if it were easier for clients to communicate with social workers or for social workers to communicate with one another, dupli-cation would decrease and collaboration would increase. This assumption becomes reality when people are prepared for its arrival and understand the advantage of using the technology.

Hawaii's ASK 2000 initiative has successfully provided information and referral services for health and human services for several years. ASK 2000 is a call center providing referral information for community services. The public tends to take advantage of the phone service, while providers tend to take advantage of the information on the Internet. Originally part of a larger project, this project succeeded because it fulfilled a need in the community, was within their current skill level to use, and was designed by a coalition of service providers tasked with ensuring current, accurate, relevant information is made available. The reason for the lack of success of the original project, as has been true for projects in other states, is that the public was unfamiliar with the technology.

Electronic Business

E-business means performing an organization's core business functions using electronic transactions. Telephony and data warehouses often accompany a move to Electronic Business, while networks provide the infrastructure. Internet sites or web pages allow current and potential clients to obtain information and conduct transactions. Kiosks provide a means for clients to exchange information with an organization in other frequently visited places, such as malls and libraries. In addition to these three, electronic benefit transfers and distance learning are becoming standard practice for some programs.

- A network traditionally allowed members of an organization to electronically connect through wiring in a building. This networking concept has been expanded to include allowing social workers to dial into the network from a remote location and work as though in their offices. More recently, organizations established intranet and Internet networks to increase the ease, speed, and number of people they wish to connect. Software applications can be placed on these networks, which saves time in updating and sharing files.
- Many organizations have their own web page that allows visitors to their Internet site to send and retrieve information with the organization. Links to related sites increases the value of the web page to clients seeking specific information. Automated forms that interact with databases allow visitors to apply for services or check their eligibility for specific programs. Security and confidentiality are often cited as the reason why social service agencies hesitate to use the Internet for other than general information sharing. However, advances in Internet security, such as digital certificates, have greatly improved confidence in transmitting sensitive information.
- Kiosks are computer stations in public places, such as malls, libraries or agency waiting areas, that allow the user to search for information by touching the screen. This technology is often used in social service agencies to increase awareness of services, to reach out to potential clients, and to allow inquiries to be made anonymously.

E-business projects, as with all technology efforts, require a strong link to an agency's strategic goals and culture. Social workers are finding that more clients are appearing in their agency because of information they received from an Internet site or kiosk. Network applications are the norm in many government and private for-profit agencies as well as most larger non-profit agencies. Electronic transfer of benefits and client information are becoming integral to social service program design.

New Hanover County, North Carolina connected all of the county case workers in order to share information between programs and to eliminate the number of agencies clients needed to visit to get needs met. This network allows case workers to screen clients for programs other than their own. The flexibility of the system's design allowed the county to continue implementation in the midst of welfare reform. The county is currently exploring ways of improving connections with the State systems.

Montana's Virtual Pavilion allows visitors to their Internet site to obtain information on many State programs. Kiosks in state offices also allow potential clients to fill out applications for some programs. The State hopes to facilitate posting of job openings and job searches. The public is also expected to benefit from reduced wait time when requesting State documents, such as birth certificates.

New Jersey's One Ease Link will establish networks of social service providers at the community level. Three state departments collaborated on this initiative with the objective of easing interaction among their currently distinct providers at the local level. A collaborative case management package will allow agencies to screen for one another's programs and to make referrals. This virtual one stop shopping concept is seen more often throughout the country.

Databases

The collection, storing, sorting, and retrieving of information in data warehouses has become a staple in many agencies and programs. Current efforts involve integrating databases from different programs and using sophisticated methods to obtain specific combinations of information. For example, several states want to link their job training and employment databases with their welfare databases and then to obtain management reports that allow them to comply with new federal reporting requirements.

- Over the last several years several states and local social service programs have moved from paper files to electronically recording client information and service provision. Current database management allows the flexible capturing, categorizing and reporting of data. The warehousing of data has been enhanced by recent business intelligence and system integration tools.
- Many health and human service programs have their own database and applications for collecting and retrieving information. When an agency decides to create a means of sharing information between programs, the

existing systems are termed "legacy systems." As we move through radical changes in welfare, education, and employment and training programs, these legacy systems are often found to be inadequate individually. Agencies initiate systems integration projects to create a means for information to be exchanged among the legacy systems of each program. There is also a trend to use systems integration projects to design a method for front line agencies to be able to generate management reports for their unique use or for workers to retrieve information about a client from different databases.

- Decision support tools allow social service agency management to query databases in such a way that allows them to obtain information and have it ordered in a useful format for immediate management decisions. Another use for business intelligence capability is the sharing of best practices among front line workers. As social workers enter information regarding their experience delivering services to a particular client or under particular circumstances, the information is categorized so that a case worker facing a similar situation or type of client can search for how this event was handled.

Financial investments in data warehouse, systems integration, and business intelligence projects are substantial. Therefore, the imperative is strong to truly understand the social work business problem to be addressed by the project. Most technology design decisions are reversible after implementation. However, the time and effort to improve processes and redesign organizational structures prior to and in conjunction with technology projects is much more cost effective than patching or buying more technology.

The State of Washington created an Automated Client Eligibility System (ACES) as an integrated, on-line, statewide system that consolidates support for Income Assistance, Food Stamp and Medicaid programs. Washington WIN, another state project, placed kiosks within the community to facilitate job searches. These kiosks are linked to State databases from multiple agencies. Current plans call for moving this capability to the Internet to further enhance the link between job seekers and appropriate agencies and with employers.

North Dakota's Department of Human Services created RESPOND to increase collaboration among staff within all of its divisions. The vision for RESPOND was one caseworker per client, one intake process applicable to all divisions, one set of rules for all divisions, and one centrally imaged case file accessible instantly by all divisions. RESPOND uses an expert system technology to determine how to assist each client. The system's artificial intelligence customizes questions based on prior responses so that clients receive support specifically tailored to each individual. The RESPOND project uses rapid application prototyping: a methodology for conducting accelerated development by breaking down the state's objectives into manageable systems and issuing new software releases every six to nine months.

CHANGING THE SERVICE DELIVERY PROCESS

A process is a series of activities that we do in carrying out our job responsibilities. Processes have distinct beginnings and endings that require inputs and produce outputs leading to outcomes. Core business processes are those that are critical to an agency's mission, while support processes enable staff to perform core business processes. "Intake client," "develop treatment plan," and "refer client" typify core business processes in social service agencies. "Procure funding" and "hire staff" are common support processes. "Manage contracts" exemplifies a process that could be core if an agency outsources its service delivery mission or support if used to augment work of the agency's staff.

Business Process Reengineering is a management trend affecting many social service agencies. The requirement to develop integrated, comprehensive care plans for clients, the move to outcome measurement, and the need to be information driven all affect processes within social service agencies and research done by social workers. Advances in technology and social work practice, in conjunction with the shifting political environment, provide social workers the means to make radical changes to the way we educate students and serve clients. Leadership grounded in reality acquired through experience can put social workers in the driver's seat for defining policy changes affecting our programs.

Integrated, Comprehensive Care Plans

Social service agencies are increasingly asked to change the way they serve clients to incorporate more services, provide life cycle services, and coordinate the delivery of services. In process improvement activities, social workers map their workflow to understand who does what, where delays and bottlenecks exist, and where mistakes or rework occurs most frequently. With this understanding they decide whether to change the order of work done, to eliminate, change or add activities, or to change who does which activities. Objectively laying out and looking at what they do, often allows social workers to see the potential for change and to feel empowered to make the change, rather than to simply adjust to it. In moving to integrated, comprehensive, or collaborative case management, social workers can use process improvement techniques to make controlled, rational changes that can be supported with technology or they can use process reengineering techniques to dramatically alter the way services are delivered.

Social service agencies are increasingly looking to packaged solutions to radically change the way they deliver services. A packaged solution is a software application plus the consulting services to implement the technology. The presumption is often that "if we build it, things will change," or, that once front line workers have the technology at their desks they will use it to deliver services more efficiently and produce the desired client outcomes. With good training and a mandate to use the technology, most front line workers adapt. However, optimal use of the technology and long term success depend on having a process improvement plan and organizational redesign plan in operation at the same time as the technology plan. With a three-pronged approach, social service providers and educators can make a paradigm shift in their approach to educating students or serving clients.

A consortium of states developed ALMIS (America's Labor Management Information System) to create a virtual one stop shopping center for employment and training services. Iowa, partnering with IBM, implemented the Common Intake System. This technology project queries legacy system databases and facilitates sharing of information among case workers through the use of groupware. All of the Service Delivery Areas (SDA) within the state will use the same tool to screen clients for program eligibility and then to refer them to the appropriate providers. Since each SDA is currently operating independently, designing the technology requires finding common ground so that the application is useful to everyone.

Montgomery County, Maryland is designing a collaborative case management system through a non-profit organization, the Network of Community Resources, established specifically for this purpose. Through the use of technology, every public and private health and human service provider throughout the county will be able to access released client information, screen for eligibility for any program, and locate the appropriate service provider mix to meet the multiple needs of clients. This project will, at a minimum, facilitate the way social workers perform their current jobs, and, if used optimally, will create a system of care that can provide for all of a client's needs in an integrated fashion.

Outcome Measurement

The emphasis on measuring performance and achieving outcomes provides social workers with an opportunity to change the way they work. The current push is away from controlling how something is done to evaluating what happens as a result of work performed. In social services, this has represented a shift from scheduling and paying for number of persons served or slots available to payment when a client maintains employment, a student achieves a specified skill level, or a family becomes self-sufficient, safe, and healthy. Program evaluators use a spectrum of measures to determine effectiveness, including: inputs to understand the resources required; outputs to calculate the number of units produced per resource consumed; outcomes to describe the impact of performance; proxy measures to approximate the impact of performance; systemic measures to look at the big picture impact of the performance of several processes; and others.

Social service agencies and educational institutions look to technology to assist in collecting data for performance measurement. Data warehouses and intelligent querying systems allow management and program evaluators to analyze on many levels the work being done and the impact on clients.

The State of Tennessee developed the ACCENT system to collect information on service delivery to clients in their welfare program, Families First. The ACCENT system was developed several years ago to provide a common eligibility screening tool for the Department of Human Services. The Department uses information collected from this and other systems to meet federal reporting requirements for the outcome measures in the Temporary Assistance to Needy Families programs and to identify trends in service delivery. More recently, DHS made a management decision to move to performance based contracting with their vendors. This change is intended to increase the competitive pool of vendors, to be an impetus for innovative service delivery, and to help clients achieve long term success in becoming safe and self-sufficient.

Information Driven

Traditionally, social workers operate according to policies established through legislative mandates and management decision making. As caseloads increase and shift between programs, one stop shopping across programs is becoming a best practice model for service delivery. To be successful, this model requires that front line workers have the ability to design a care plan that accounts for all of a client's unique needs. Good service delivery, therefore, requires that policies contain high level guidance and that information pulled from databases, such as client index and service providers, becomes the basis for deciding how to serve a client. Policies will contain desired outcomes and performance standards, but not dictate how a client is to be served.

Broward County, Florida is creating a network among its providers to allow the exchange of information. While each entity will maintain its own database, an application containing a search engine will be made available to each agency so that they can query the other systems regarding the service history of a client. Providers are concerned about confidentiality and about maintaining systems designed to meet their unique service delivery needs. However, as a service delivery system, these providers want to reduce dupli-cation of effort and maximize the benefits clients can receive from a coordinated approach to care.

New York is creating a Workforce Development System that will allow universal access for job seekers and employers to training and employment information. The system is being designed through partnerships led by the Department of Labor and the Department of Education. Service providers and employers play a dominant role in designing the system which will provide clients with three levels of care: self-service, group, and individual. The creation of job search and talent bank databases accessed via the Internet and other means, places the emphasis on providing information to clients when and how they want it. Also under consideration is a mechanism for allowing clients to schedule appointments and for case workers to receive reminders of appointments and other client events.

ORGANIZATIONAL CHANGE IN SOCIAL SERVICES

Social Service agencies are changing their structure, their staffing mixes and their management methods. Collaboration, flexibility and innovation characterize the transforming agencies. The move from a bricks and mortar, hierarchical, independent service delivery system has been needed to enable process reengineering and technology projects.

Collaboration

Legislators are increasingly requiring that programs collaborate in serving specific populations. For example, the Welfare-to-Work program requires collaboration between the organization administering the Temporary Assistance to Needy Families (TANF) program and the Private Industry Councils of the Job Training and Partnership Act (JTPA) program. The funding and regulatory barriers between programs are being whittled away through programs like the Empowerment Zones. Sometimes the programmatic systems integration leads the technological systems integration and sometimes it follows. In either case, social workers and other front line staff need the cross training required to navigate multiple programs and the incentives to do so. They also need the improved communications and team building required for building trust and paving new paths of information exchange. Collaboration provides an opportunity for social service agencies or common service areas to rethink how they collectively serve the individuals in their catchment area.

Contending with turf issues often presents a major barrier to collaboration. Some social workers are mistrustful of the methods of other agencies, others are concerned about maintaining client confidentiality, and still others fear a loss of funding or being taken over by another agency. Preparing for and contending with these issues is necessary to successful implementation of any project, i.e., to whether or not technology gets used or whether new processes are followed.

The San Diego, California Health and Human Services Agency is developing an organizational change plan to join several departments into a united agency. The purpose of the change is to enhance services to families, including prevention, self-sufficiency, and improved system access. Technology improvements, a competition program among vendors, and functional re-engineering will increase the efficiency of employees and ultimately result in the redeployment of more resources to direct service provision.

The Canadian province of Manitoba and the city of Winnepeg are merging their social service agencies. The new merged organization will enable case workers to have access to all the information on the income assistance-related services being delivered to an individual or family. The project includes obtaining integrated case management applications, a new performance measurement system, and alternative ways for clients to access the system, such as through kiosk and smart cards. The vision of the merged organization recognizes that some clients will remain more dependent than others, less able to move to self sufficiency, but through the use of re-engineered processes and innovative leading-edge information technology, such clients will also feel the benefit of the improved process.

Flexibility

Just as agencies and educational institutions are switching to more collaborative organizational relationships, so are they also switching their organizational structures to be more flexible. Virtual organizations allow social workers to change their physical location to be where clients and potential clients have easier access. Social workers in these environments are connected to their colleagues through teleconferencing and electronic networks. Social service agencies are also rethinking their definition of agency as they install technology that allows client to connect with them through kiosks at malls or networks in non-agency buildings. Organizational charts are becoming more fluid as social workers build on their initial broad training to move among programs as funding and client needs change.

Connections is a cross system service coordination model to ensure that comprehensive, seamless, prevention-oriented services are available to all families in Cabell and Wayne counties, West Virginia. This model is designed to provide single intake and cross agency family service coordination. The Cabell-Wayne Family Resource Network Agencies electronically connects organizations and community based resource centers. They developed a process to ensure community wide participation via community forums, training, public awareness campaign.

Tioga County, Pennsylvania was recognized by the Ford Foundation and Harvard University as a finalist in the "1997 Innovations in American Government Awards" competition. Their "Decategorized Human Services Delivery Program" created an internal, multi-disciplinary team to review cases. The county approached this organizational change by gaining political support, emphasizing staff training, and keeping the pace of change in line with staff needs in order to foster a sense of belonging. Turf issues were dealt with by reminding staff that they had been generically trained in their professions and were then shaped by the programs for which they worked.

The city of Oakland, California and Bridge West Oakland Housing are installing network computers into 206 apartments and linking them to an onsite, IBM-run computer training center. Residents will have access to basic computer training, specific job skills training and educational programs at the computer center from their apartments. The success of this project is attributed to grassroots leadership in the Resident's Council of the housing complex.

EVALUATING TECHNOLOGY OPTIONS IN SOCIAL SERVICE AGENCIES

The preceding sections described the possibilities in technology, process and organizational change that are taking place throughout the country. But how does a social service agency evaluate its options and what makes a good choice?

Identify the Business Need to Be Addressed

All good solutions have clearly defined problem statements. A strategic plan outlines the priority issues that an agency wishes to address in accomplishing its mission. No single project can address all of the gaps. Therefore, each project should be linked to a specific set of business (i.e., service delivery, teaching, or research) needs that can be linked to the strategic plan. A technology plan may only address part of the need and should therefore, be explicitly connected to the necessary process and organizational change plans.

Understand the Context in Which the Need Exists

In social service agencies this means understanding trends and forecasts in client utilization of services and funding patterns as they relate to the need to be addressed. It also means understanding the role the agency plays in the larger service delivery system and in meeting the full range of an individual client needs–both now and in the future. In addition, the agency should understand their current and desired technological environment, service delivery process, and organizational design.

Explore Alternative Means of Satisfying the Need

Options that should always be included when exploring alternatives are that of maintaining the status quo, of handling the solution completely internally and of completely outsourcing the function in which the business need is found. Collecting information on these extreme choices will provide good comparative data for the purchase options, and may spur creative thinking in finding a solution. Purchase options can be found by requesting information from vendors, by brainstorming with diverse groups of stakeholders, and by searching for best practices.

Develop Criteria Against Which to Evaluate Alternatives

The return on investment of any alternative should consider the full life cycle costs and benefits. For tangible items, this includes the cost of acquisition plus maintenance and labor. Intangible costs and benefits need to be considered, including the impact on client or vendor behavior and staff morale, the ability to be innovative, and the value to carrying out mission-critical tasks. A social service agency should then develop a list of criteria that the ideal alternative must meet in order to address the business need within the context of this specific agency's situation. The criteria should be weighted to reflect their relative importance to one another and then each alternative is scored against the criteria. The selected alternative can then be justified not just in terms of financial benefits, but in terms of its fit with the agency's strategic plan and operational needs.

Consider Acquisition Strategy Options

Strong competition is often held as the hallmark of a good acquisition strategy. Competition can be encouraged by using incentives, by evaluating past performance, by writing outcome instead of methodological requirements, and by many other means. In addition to encouraging competition, social service agencies may want to consider partnering relationships with vendors that would allow risk and gain sharing. These relationships often require substantial investments in time and effort by both sides during the planning stages of a project. A third acquisition strategy consideration is whether and how to break the final deliverable into modular components that can each be competed and that will each produce a deliverable that makes progress toward the ultimate goal. If the components can be competed in varying order rather than sequentially, the agency can adjust its plan for changes in funding or to coordinate better with other projects.

Evaluate Risk

Risk factors can generally be grouped into schedule risks, costs risk, technical risks, and programmatic risks. Specific factors are often identified by bringing customers, managers, suppliers, technical staff, and other key stakeholders together to provide a list of critical success factors and statements regarding the impact of not implementing the project as planned. A work breakdown schedule lists the implementation tasks in chronological order, showing which tasks are dependent upon others for initiation or successful completion. This work breakdown schedule can be tied to costs and an array of possible scenarios played out to find an acceptable schedule and cost configuration. A risk management plan needs to be put in place to not only mitigate the risks, but also to be prepared for what to do should the need arise.

Create a Change Management Plan

Change Management helps agencies minimize the depth and length of performance disruptions brought about by transformations. By addressing barriers to change, change management allows agencies to build capability and commitment to the new ways of operating. A structured communications plan is a critical component to managing change and must be based on research of target audiences, communications history, the change requirements, and collecting and measuring feedback and effectiveness. Change management plans also generally include categorization of stakeholders into the roles they will play in the change and developing a strategy for keeping the pace of change within the tolerable limits of those who must make the change happen or adapt to it.

Design a Performance Measurement Plan

Performance measurement of a vendor in implementing a project centers on the value the agency is receiving. Value is the amount of benefit received relative to the cost. Earned value tracking systems are designed so that the agency knows what benefits have been received over a given time period and for a specific price.

Develop a Program Management Plan

A Program Management Plan pulls together the acquisition strategy, risk management plan, change management plan, and performance measurement plan. The selected alternative is also evaluated on the program management options it allows and whether the desired program management approach can be used.

A good business case considers all of the above steps when justifying a particular course of action.

CONCLUSION

Why do so many technology, reengineering and reorganization projects fail?

- There is not a good and urgent reason for taking on the change
- The executive team sees this as something that the organization has to do and do not see themselves as part of the change
- People do not understand how the change will take place or they do not realize the impact it will have on them
- Inadequate attention is given to one or more of the three interdependent types of change: organizational, technological and process
- A number of change initiatives are managed in a disconnected manner
- There was not a good program management plan in place prior to initiating the change

The examples of innovation and investment provided above represent a small sample of what is happening in social services around the country. Social workers could benefit from sharing their experiences and collaborating to address mutual needs. Social service agencies are in a favorable economic time to pursue technology investments, but they will need to make a strong business case from the frame of reference of their funders and stakeholders. Partnerships among social service agencies, with vendors, and with customers/clients present the best chance of success for building credibility and momentum.

IMPACT
OF INFORMATION TECHNOLOGIES
ON SOCIAL WORK EDUCATION

Moving Toward
Technology-Supported Instruction
in Human Service Practice:
The "Virtual Classroom"

Philip M. Ouellette

SUMMARY. With the challenge for human services faculty to better integrate classroom materials to the realities of today's practice and the advent of several new communication technologies and technology-mediated instructional software, the use of Web-base instruction and the "Virtual Classroom" as a pedagogical strategy may be a viable added dimension to the learning process for human services practice

Philip M. Ouellette, PhD, ACSW, is Assistant Professor, University of South Florida, School of Social Work and Child and Family Studies, Louis de la Part Florida Mental Health Institute, 4202 East Fowler Avenue MGY 132, Tampa, FL 33620.

[Haworth co-indexing entry note]: "Moving Toward Technology-Supported Instruction in Human Service Practice: The 'Virtual Classroom.' " Ouellette, Philip M. Co-published simultaneously in *Journal of Technology in Human Services* (The Haworth Press, Inc.) Vol. 16, No. 2/3, 1999, pp. 97-111; and: *Computers and Information Technology in Social Work: Education, Training, and Practice* (ed: Jo Ann R. Coe, and Goutham M. Menon) The Haworth Press, Inc., 1999, pp. 97-111. Single or multiple copies of this article are available for a fee from The Haworth Document Delivery Service [1-800-342-9678, 9:00 a.m. - 5:00 p.m. (EST). E-mail address: getinfo@haworthpressinc.com].

97

courses with the potential to improve learning efficacy. Possible teaching strategies are discussed as well as implications for research. *[Article copies available for a fee from The Haworth Document Delivery Service: 1-800-342-9678. E-mail address: getinfo@haworthpressinc.com <Website: http://www.haworthpressinc.com>]*

KEYWORDS. Technology-supported instruction, social work education, virtual classrooms, telelearning

A paradigm shift is taking place in higher education instruction. Instruction is expanding from a mode of faculty-student interaction occurring in fixed locations at specified times to one in which students can access the same instructional resources in a variety of forms, regardless of location and at their convenience. This is becoming possible because several new technologies have matured to such an extent that instruction can be delivered to students on the campus, in their homes, or in their work places (Baker & Gloster, 1994). As a result, the traditional classroom model of instruction is increasingly being questioned as the sole viable mode of edification and learning (Chen-Lin & Kulik, 1991).

The words "distance education" and "virtual classrooms" are heard everywhere in higher education as colleges and universities grapple to do "more with less" and are attempting to reach a larger number of learners. The advent of new technologies in education has created unprecedented challenges for academic administrators and faculty to explore several cost-effective technology solutions aimed at improving learning productivity for students, reducing labor intensity, and providing new ways to deliver professional education and better services to students while enhancing the quality of instruction. Technology-based instruction, especially network-based instruction, is viewed as a means to increase faculty productivity and to accommodate more students with existing facilities (Levin, 1991; Johnstone, 1993).

This article discusses how technology-supported learning environments can contribute to the changing educational paradigms presently occurring in higher education. As new technologies continue to be integrated in the human services field, not only does the way we deliver instruction and training to human service student practitioners change, but also, how we think about how they learn changes. This article addresses how several technology-based communication instruments such as electronic mail, electronic bulletin boards, listservs, network-based discussion groups and desktop video conferencing coupled with Web-based active learning strategies can enhance the development of conceptual and practice skills in the human service field.

SHIFTING EDUCATIONAL PARADIGMS

The rapid growth of new information technology and advanced communication networks is forcing educators to reexamine pedagogical foundations. According to Barr and Tagg (1995), the educational paradigm that has governed most of our colleges and universities to date is one that defined a college or university as "an institution that exists to provide instruction." Subtly but profoundly, higher education is moving from an Instructional Paradigm to a Learning Paradigm.

This gradual shift is occurring as colleges and universities recognize that they are institutions that exist to produce learning. When a college or university views its mission from a "learning paradigm" as its educational premise, the idea of producing more with less becomes conceivable because learning outcomes and the learner's activity becomes the focus of attention and not hours of classroom instruction or sitting time. Moving from an instructional to a learning paradigm also means that the faculty member's role changes. In an "Instructional Paradigm" the faculty member's role tends to be viewed as that of an "actor" where knowledge is transferred from instructor to students. In a "Learning Paradigm," the role of the faculty member shifts from primary instructor to become more of a guide in the learning journey of students. As students interact with each other through guidance from faculty, students discover knowledge for themselves through a set of action-learning activities.

Educational productivity cannot always be easily measured with an Instructional Paradigm type of college or university. Exposure to instruction appears to be the primarily element to measure. Some university faculty have suggested that our dominant view of instruction mistakes a means for an end. That is, it takes the means or method, referred to as "instruction" or "teaching," and makes it as the college's end or purpose and assumes that exposure to instruction will produce learning (Barr & Tagg, 1995). In addition to a shift toward new educational models, some educators have adopted the constructivist view of learning. This view of learning holds that "knowing is a process of actively interpreting and constructing individual knowledge representations" (Jonassen, 1991). From a constructivist perspective, learners learn best if they are cognitively active as new information is provided to them. An example of an ideal interactive learning environment includes creating a learning context where learners summarize information in their own words, draw diagrams to describe connection between certain concepts and state their own conclusions on issues presented (Dalgarno, 1995).

When teachers design instructional materials for technology-supported instruction, active-learning and cooperative learning strategies are often the preferred pedagogical methods used. Action learning strategies are learning systems that demand active participation on the part of the learner. Some have indicated that teachers who demand active learning are likely to bring about substantially greater learning success than those who do not (Brooks, 1997). Cooperative and collaborative learning strategies engage students in constructive, reacculturative conversations with one another. What is learned is not only about what students read but what is said to one another about what they read (Bruffee, 1993; Pence, 1993). In other words, the interactional context, irrespective of the medium used, is an important factor contributing to learning outcomes. It is important to incorporate learning strategies that engage the learner interactively with others as well as seeking out sources of new information. Learning is more correctly attributed to well-orchestrated design strategies than to the inherent superiority of various delivery methods (Hannafin & Hooper, 1993).

Advanced communication networks currently available to the human service educator can permit students and faculty to "talk" electronically whenever they like or when the need arises (Baker & Gloster, 1994). Learning assignments can be given and received electronically. Faculty can hold "virtual" office hours, freeing them from rigid schedules, and enabling students to obtain information with little waste of time and without sacrificing the fundamental, close-knit quality of the student-mentor relationship. In developing an alternative educational model conducive to a technology-supported learning environment, faculty become facilitators and guides for individual learners rather than simple conduits for transmitting information (Coombs, 1992). Instead of teaching, faculty can move from being the sole information source of expertise to that of a coach. That is, the human service educator serves as coach to a student's own discovery learning process making learning a much more student driven process. The notion of student-driven learning is consistent with andragogical theory (Knowles, 1980) and is harmonious with most educational models used for the training of human service professionals. That is, most training programs for human service professionals promote the integration of theory and practice through actual practice in field placements and internships coupled with some concurrent seminar or classroom session that permit interaction between faculty, and students on some practice theme.

Learner-centered instruction that is guided by faculty and made adaptable to each student's individual learning needs can be significantly more effective, and provide more flexibility for faculty and students, than the traditional lecture-centered model of instruction (Gifford, 1996).

TEACHING PRACTICE COURSES IN THE HUMAN SERVICES

As a result of changes in educational paradigms and the evolving nature of an ever growing information society, new challenges have been created for educating human services professionals. Most human services training programs in the United States have not designed their curricula, most especially their practice curricula, to be amenable to new modes of instruction. Classroom-based instruction coupled with field experience in community agencies continues to be the primary mode of instruction for most practice courses.

The Challenge

Human Services students continue to report that their best learning experience in graduate school is associated with their field instruction or internship program. It is interesting to note, however, that if we closely look at the primary method of instruction in most internship programs, we are reminded that a student's field experience is usually individualized to both student and agency needs and active learning strategies are widely used as the primary mode of instruction. There is ample evidence that the two most important determinants of learning are time-on-task and active learning strategies (Ewell & Jones, 1996). In conjunction with field instruction, human services students are required to enhance practice knowledge and skills through required practice courses in individual, family, group and community work. Faculty are consistently faced with the dilemma of matching classroom instruction and materials with the changing needs of human service practice. Students and field instructors continue to challenge university faculty to better integrate classroom materials to the realities and needs of human service practice.

Another dilemma encountered by graduate programs in the human services field is the availability of its training program to the distant learner or student whose learning style may not always be amenable to a traditional classroom setting. At present, graduate education in the human services and the delivery of course content is well suited for the student who has easy access to campus resources. Most full-time students, employed prior to being admitted to a graduate program, must take time away from work, limit their employment activity during their training period and, must acquire sufficient financial resources to sustain the rigors of a structured graduate program. Although attempts have been made to offer graduate level education on a part-time basis to accommodate the working human service professional, some potential students are not easily reached by traditional campus-based instructional programs. Students having difficulty accessing campus resources include those who are in isolated field practice areas with limited supervisory resources, and students whose learning styles, individual personalities or whose life demands, such as working mothers, are not always conducive to a traditional classroom discussion format.

Perhaps the use of a technology-supported instructional environment may provide options for some students not well served by current instructional methods. It may also serve to bridge the gap between classroom instruction and the realities of field practice when teaching the courses in the practice sequence of a human service program.

TECHNOLOGY-SUPPORTED INSTRUCTION: THE "VIRTUAL CLASSROOM"

With the emergence of new technologies in the educational sphere, now is a good time to revisit what is our educational mission in the human services field. Learning about the efficacy of technology and its use cannot be acquired from a mechanistic or didactic instructional method but rather from a "hands on" experiential process that leads to discovery. This appears to coincide with current shifts in higher education models that lean toward a "learning paradigm."

A Viable Option

When shifting from an instructional to a learning paradigm, the educational mission is not instruction but rather that of producing learning for every student by whatever means work best. As some have indicated, it is true that a lecture-discussion classroom format, the primary means of producing instruction in North American colleges and universities today, does in fact produce a lower cost of instruction than the use of individualized active learning strategies (Chizmar & Williams, 1996). Evidence that the lecture-discussion method of instruction is ineffective at producing learning continues to increase (Chizmar & Williams, 1996; Guskin, 1994). Although it may be erroneous to suggest at this early stage that the use of technology-supported instruction would be less expensive than traditional classroom instruction, the technology-supported learning environment would permit the educator, especially the human service educator, to focus on a whole new potential audience for training as well as provide a viable option for enhancing the efficacy of learning outcomes for some students. As technology-supported learning environments increase, this does not mean that faculty and traditional classrooms will entirely be replaced, but rather new educational models conducive to a technology medium will continue to evolve. Some studies have already shown that students supported by technology-mediated learning required about one-third less teaching time than students using traditional lecture/textbook methods. Not only did college students using technology learn faster, six months after completing their studies, they tested better on the subject being taught than their peers who had been taught in traditional settings (Chen-Lin & Kulik, 1991).

USE OF TECHNOLOGY FOR HUMAN SERVICE TRAINING AND PRACTICE

Computers have already been used successfully in the training of human service professionals. For example, computers have been used to assist in the teaching of social work practice courses using computer-assisted instructional (CAI) programs and interactive videodiscs (IVD) (Seabury & Maple, 1993) as well as computer-based expert systems (Kelly, 1994). Other human service educators have found that computer-based simulation technology, when properly used, holds great potential benefits in training human service practitioners (Wodarski & Kelly, 1987; Patterson & Yaffe, 1994). In addition to the use of computers as an instructional aid, computers are increasingly being used by human service practitioners as an assessment tool such as the Clinical Assessment System (CAS) program (Nurious & Hudson, 1988) and are increasingly being integrated in actual social treatment protocols. Child Welfare agencies have introduced computer technology in the work environment of their practitioners in an attempt to bring important improvements in the quality of work life (Cahill & Feldman, 1993). With the increase computerization of professional settings, some have advocated for increase education in the proper uses of computers in human service practice (Pardeck & Schulte, 1990).

The Internet

The exponential growth of the Internet in recent years is another contributing factor for human service educators to consider moving toward the development of the "Virtual Classroom" as a learning aid for training human service practitioners. For many human service professionals, the Internet has increased access to empirical and practice knowledge and also has facilitated information exchange (Giffords, 1998). For a number of years now, the Internet's vast network of computers has offered an innovative forum where human service students, field instructors, practitioners, researchers and educators can come together and exchange information, engage in common community projects, disseminate research findings and share important discoveries with each other. An Internet site which exemplifies how researchers in the field of Children's Mental Health share findings and exchange information using this electronic medium is ResourceNet (http://lumpy.fmhi. usf.edu) developed by the Division of Children and Families at the Louis de la Parte Florida Mental Health Institute. This is but one of many human services related Web sites that exist on the Internet today. Although reports indicate that the use of the WWW continues to expand in higher education, it is primarily used for information dissemination and marketing rather than for teaching and learning (Green, 1996). With continued access to information from the WWW and increased opportunities for electronic networking capability coupled with a well-designed field experience, human services students could enhance practice knowledge and skills through Web-based teaching.

Web-Based Teaching

Improvements in communication technology and recent developments in Internet-based instructional software such as WebCT (http://www.webct.com/webct/) and Web Course in a Box (http://www.madduck.com/), facilitate the transition from classroom instruction to the "Virtual Classroom." Web-based teaching can be used not only for the enhancement of practice skills but also for introducing human service professionals to the use of computer and telecommunication technology in the work place. Support for incorporating new information technologies into existing core courses in human service professional education has long been suggested (Cnaan, 1989). Although some attempts have been made to integrate technology courses as part of the curriculum in some human service training programs (Schoech, 1990), the use of World Wide Web as a primary instructional medium in the human service field appears just to be beginning (Schutte, 1997). Although human service educators' experience with Web-based delivered courses have been limited, some initiatives show promising results (Stocks, 1998). Given that access to the Internet from a field practice or internship site is now more possible than a few years ago, the use of the "Virtual Classroom" may be a useful pedagogical strategy that could enhance the integration of theory and practice skills while students are completing internships. A unique kind of learning environment could evolve that would serve to bridge the gap between classroom content and the realities of field practice as well as bringing human service graduate education in line with today's shift toward learning paradigms.

Goals of the "Virtual Classroom"

The "Virtual Classroom" or Internet-based instruction can provide an opportunity to develop an educational model for the practice sequence of human service courses which

- allows human services students to take a more active role in integrating classroom materials in direct practice,
- allows human services faculty to express the content of a course in more than one format,
- broadens the array of resources brought to the classroom or to the human services student's internship experience,

- increases opportunities for interaction between academic faculty, field instructors and students,
- produces an individualized learning environment for every student by whatever means that works best for his/her learning and practice reality while in training,
- provides an opportunity for faculty to focus on learning outcomes of a particular practice area within particular work settings,
- allows for the development of alternative pedagogical strategies.

Possible Pedagogical Strategies

A variety of pedagogical strategies and interactive mediums to meet practice course objectives in a technology-supported learning environment could be used. The following describe but a few possibilities:

Class Bulletin Board: A class bulletin board could be created just for students enrolled in the "Virtual Classroom." The use of the bulletin board would ensure student participation through weekly postings of attendance messages. The electronic bulletin board would facilitate ongoing communication between students, field instructors, and faculty. For example, messages could be posted for help, advice, announcements, helpful tips, and for the coordination of student team assignments.

Public/Private Forums: A public forum could be developed for major topics covered in a practice course. Students, field instructors, and faculty could post replies to course content. In addition, a private forum could be established for groups of students who would come together to discuss a group project with each other without other class interference from other class members. Such a strategy could promote collaborative learning and sense of team work.

Class Listserv: A class listserv could be established to provide a more controlled learning environment. Listservs are considered a good way to implement online critiques of work where several other on-campus classes participate, or better still, where the same class on several different campuses shares work electronically. A listserv could also link discussion of many human services students enrolled in practice courses from different professional schools. This would increase student and faculty interactivity as well as provide a means for shared curriculum resources and learning activity materials. In this way, the professor of a particular practice course is just one component of the learning resources available to the student and is no longer the sole gate-keeper of the knowledge of a particular practice area. Examples of human service related listservs can be found with the Social Work Access Network (http://www.sc.edu/swan/listserv.html).

Electronic Mail: The "Virtual Classroom" for human service practice course could use electronic mail as a medium for collaboration from student-to-student, student-to-instructor, and instructor-to-student. Experience has shown that extensive use of e-mail for both students and faculty has a great social-levelling or equalizing effect. Interaction with people anywhere in the world through only text, frees the exchange of ideas and information from biases that can be caused by visual appearances. It has already been found that students are much more likely to seek help from the instructor via e-mail than to make an appointment to see him or her in an office and, in addition, students are more likely to seek help from each other or from anyone in the world through e-mail (Chizmar and Williams, 1996).

The Class Chat Room: Using the power of network connectivity and advances in cable and telephony, collaboration could take on an expanded meaning in a "Virtual Classroom." Any group of people could be brought together for a meeting at the same "time" without regard to "place." One could hold text-based conferences (online chat groups), audio conferences (phone conferencing), and full-audio and video conferencing right from our desktop through desktop video presentations. In this way tutoring could be offered remotely. Mentors or experts could be brought into the "Virtual Classroom" and in the field from anywhere in the region or the world if need be. Desktop video conferencing software, such as White Pine's CU-SeeMe or Microsoft's NetMeeting, could permit students interning in remote areas to attend class irrespective of time and place as well as receive needed supports. Through a combination of e-mail, bulletin boards, and chat room utilities, students could begin to think in terms of the learning process and the course materials being studied as a twenty-four-hour-a-day, seven-days-a-week experience, rather than a three-hours-a-day, once-a-week learning experience. Faculty, students, field instructors, professional peers and human services experts worldwide could always be within reach of each other.

Learning Assignments: Submission of learning assignments and critiques could be done through the use of electronic class drop folders rather than having to return to the campus to drop off assignments. All work could be critiqued with feedback being returned electronically to the student through e-mail. Class and private student folders could permit electronic storing of assignments and work in progress. Each student could have an online folder for their work to which only they and the instructor would have access. In this way it would be possible for the electronic posting of grades after each assignment for those students who give the instructor permission to post grades.

Minute Paper: Another pedagogical strategy which could be used in the "Virtual Classroom" in a human service practice course would be the "Minute Paper" exercise (Angelo and Cross, 1993). A typical Minute Paper asks students to respond, in the final minute or two of a virtual class session, to two questions: (a) What is the most important thing you learned today? and

(b) What is the muddiest point still remaining at the conclusion of today's session? In this way, faculty get ongoing feedback as to the learning progress of each student.

Interactive Web Pages: A series of interactive Web pages could be used to organize online course content, where materials dedicated to the course would be stored. Students could find electronic versions of handouts, course syllabi and course guides. An example of an electronic version of a course syllabus for a human service practice course can be found at the University of South Florida School of Social Work (*http://www.cas.usf.edu/social_work/family.sow.html*). The many requests that students make for another copy of a lost course guide can now be replied by the following: "just download a new copy from the class server." In the long run, this strategy alone could reduce the enormous costs associated with photocopying materials. Access to course materials would greatly be improved. Students could download class notes, reading assignments, and changes in course content instantaneously without having to wait for the next scheduled class session.

Electronic Exhibits: Electronic exhibit areas could be developed for class projects of the "Virtual Classroom." We could employ a constructionist strategy of teaching (Bednar et al., 1991) with a strong emphasis on learning projects. A key strategy for the use of class time would be to view and critique work in progress. Electronic exhibit areas could provide the student with an opportunity to acquire immediate feedback and even Internet-wide critique of work completed if he or she so wished.

Practice Consultations: With communication technology and desktop video conferencing currently available, faculty members could join supervisory sessions between field instructors and students to facilitate linkages between theory and practice. Networking opportunities between field and academic faculty would greatly be improved thereby enhancing the individual learning needs of human service students. As communication technology continues to improve with the increased use of streaming audio and video, Web base instruction will have an even greater impact on the way the human service educator provides instruction.

Principles of Good Practice

To ensure that the development of a "Virtual Classroom" meets the standards for good educational practice, certain guiding principles may be necessary. Principles for good practice for distance education advanced by Kraught (1996), in addition to Western Governors University's distance learning standards (*http://www.wiche.edu/telecom/projects/wgu distance learning standards.htm*) may serve as a useful starting point to ensure that distance learning standards are designed to ensure that courses and programs are of high quality. Based on these precepts, the "Virtual Classroom" for a practice course in the human services field would strive to maintain the following fundamental principles:

- The student and teacher would share responsibility for the quality of the learning process.
- The core motivation, for both student and teacher, should be the satisfaction that derives from improving the quality of the student's learning (Cobb, 1992).
- The electronically supported practice course would be provided by or through an institution that is accredited by a nationally recognized accrediting body.
- The course offered through technology-supported instruction would meet the same specialized accreditation requirements of classroom-based instruction courses.
- Individual schools and educational programs to train human service professionals would have the main responsibility to review the course requirements it provides via technology.
- The practice course offered via the use of technology would result in learning outcomes appropriate to the rigour and breadth of the degree being awarded.
- As with regular classroom course instruction, qualified human services faculty would provide appropriate oversight of the course offered via electronic means.

IMPLICATIONS FOR RESEARCH

Further studies are needed to ensure that technology-mediated pedagogical methods are based on sound educational principles and learning paradigms. Future research related to the use of the "Virtual Classroom" or Internet-based instruction for the enhancement of human service practice could be directed toward addressing some of the following questions:

- Will students in "virtual" learning situations feel isolated, with a reduced semblance of human contact with their faculty instructor(s) or other students attending the same course on campus?
- How can effective advising and academic support services be made available to students experiencing a "virtual" learning environment?
- How can students be sure that their learning experiences will equal those in traditional lecture-discussion classroom instruction?
- What type of learner is best suited for a "virtual" learning environment?
- Will the use of technology improve our ability to help students produce learning while reducing their cost for acquiring quality instruction?

- What is actually being learned in a "Virtual Classroom" regarding human service practice? How well is practice knowledge and skills being learned?

CONCLUSIONS

This paper addresses the possibilities for introducing a technology-supported instructional environment to enhance existing human service practice courses. Using active learning strategies in conjunction with the use of several computer-based communication instruments such as electronic mail, electronic bulletin boards, listservs, network-based discussion groups and desktop video conferencing, would provide a context for interactivity and dialogue. Students would discover conceptual knowledge about human service practice through experiential means at a pace and time convenient to the realities of their learning context. The development of both conceptual and practice skills for human service student practitioners could greatly be enhanced if their technology-supported instruction was coupled with a well-integrated field or internship experience. This will require close collaboration between human service educators and field instructors. The use of a "Virtual Classroom" may also reduce the student's down time, traveling from one learning site to another thereby providing more time for action-learning activities. In addition, a technology-supported teaching experience would provide faculty with an opportunity to explore the ethical dilemmas created by the use of technology in human service education as well as allowing for the discovery of new pedagogical strategies to enhanced learning outcomes of students.

REFERENCES

Angelo, T., Cross, P.T. (1993) *Classroom Assessment Techniques: A Handbook for College Teachers;* San Francisco: Jossey-Bass Publishers, p. 148.

Baker, W., Gloster, A. (1994) Moving Towards the Virtual University: A Vision of Technology in Higher Education; *Cause/Effect;* Volume 17, Number 2, Summer. pp. 4-11.

Barr, R., Tagg, J. (1995) From Teaching to Learning: A New Paradigm for Undergraduate Education; *Change,* November/December 1995, 13.

Bednar, A.K., Cunningham, D., Duffy, T.M., & Peery, J.D. (1991) Theory into practice: How do we link? In G.J. Anglin (Ed.) *Instructional Technology: Past, Present, and Future.* Englewood, CO: Libraries Unlimited.

Brooks, D. (1997) *Web-Teaching: A Guide to Designing Interactive Teaching for the World Wide Web;* New York: Plenum Press.

Bruffee, K.A. (1993) *Collaborative Learning: Higher Education, Interdependence, and the Authority of Knowledge,* Baltimore: Johns Hopkins University Press.

Cahill, J., Feldman, L. (1993) Computers in Child Welfare: Planing for a More Serviceable Work Environment; *Child Welfare*, Vol LXXII, Number 1, January-February, pp. 3-13.

Chen-Lin C., Kulik, J. (1991) Effectiveness of Computer-Based Instruction: An Updated Analysis; *Computers in Human Behavior*, 7 (1-2) pp. 75-94.

Chizmar, J., Williams, D. (1996) Altering time and space through network technologies to enhance learning; *Cause/Effect*, 19(3), Fall pp. 14-213, Fall 1996, pp. 14-21.

Cobb, G. (1992) Teaching Statistics, in L.A. Steen (ed.), *Heeding the Call for Change: Suggestions for Curricular Action*, MAA Notes No. 22; Washington, DC: Mathematical Association of America, 20.

Coombs, N. (1992) Teaching in the Information Age; *EDUCOM Review*, March/April, 30.

Cnaan, R.A. (1989) Social Work Education and Direct Practice in the Computer Age, *Journal of Social Work Education*, 25 (3) pp. 235-243.

Dalgarno, B. (1995) The World Wide Web as an Interactive Learning Environment: Limitations and Enhancements; http://ws114.adm.csupomona.edu/lab/articles/paper01.html (November, 1997).

Ewell, P., Jones, D. (1996) Indicators of "Good Practice" in Undergraduate Education: A Handbook for Development and Implementation; Boulder, Colorado: *National Center for Higher Education Management Systems*; pp. 19-27.

Gifford, B.R. (1996) Mediated Learning: A New Model of Technology-Mediated Instruction and Learning, *Mediated Learning Review*, Academic Systems (http://www.academic.com/mlreview/brgpaper.html) (June, 1998).

Giffords, E. (1998) Social Work on the Internet: An Introduction; *Social Work*, 43 (3), pp. 243-251.

Green, K. (1996) *1996 Campus Computing Survey.* Encino, CA: Campus Computing.

Guskin, A. (1994) Reducing Student Costs and Enhancing Student Learning, Part II: Restructuring the Role of the Faculty; *Change*, September/October, 6.

Hannafin, M.J., Hooper, S.R. (1993) Learning Principles, in Fleming, M., Levie, W. H. (Eds) *Instructional Message Design* (2nd ed.) (pp. 191-231), Englewood Cliffs, NJ: Educational Technology Publications.

Jonassen, D.H. (1991) Objectivism versus Constructivism: Do We Need a New Philosophical Paradigm? *Educational Technology Research and Development*, 39 (3).

Johnstone, B.D. (1993) Learning Productivity: A New Imperative for American Higher Education; *Studies in Public Higher Education* No. 3 (Albany, NY: Office of the Chancellor, State University of New York), pp. 1-31.

Kelly, M. (1994) Training Applications of Expert Systems; *Journal of Continuing Social Work Education*, 6 (2), pp. 15-19.

Kraught, B. (1996) Principles of Good Practice for Distance Learning Programs; *Cause/Effect*, 19 (1), Spring; pp. 6-8.

Knowles, M.S. (1980) *The Modern Practice of Adult Education*; Chicago: Associated Press.

Livin, H.M. (1991) Raising Productivity in Higher Education; *Journal of Higher Education*, 62 (3), pp. 242-262.

Nurious, P.S., Hudson, W.W. (1988) Computer-Based Practice: Future Dream or Current Technology? *Social Work*, 33(4), pp. 357-362.

Pardeck, J., Schulte, R.S. (1990) Computers in Social Intervention: Implications for Professional Social Work Practice and Education; *Family Therapy*, 17 (2), pp. 109-121.

Patterson, D., Yaffe, J. (1994) Hypermedia Computer-Based Education in Social Work Education; *Journal of Social Work Education*, 30 (2), pp. 267-277.

Pence, H.E. (1993) Combining Cooperative Learning and Multimedia in General Chemistry; *Education*, 113 (3), pp. 375-380.

Schoech, D. (1990) *Human Services Computing: Concepts and Applications*; New York: The Haworth Press, Inc.

Schutte, J.G. (1997) Virtual teaching in higher education: The new intellectual super-highway or just another traffic jam. <*http://www.csun.edu/sociology/virexp.htm*>

Seabury, B., Maple, F. (1993) Using Computers to Teach Practice Skills, *Social Work*, 38 (4), pp. 430-439.

Stocks, J.T. Freddolino, P.P. (1998) Evaluation of a World Wide Web-Based Graduate Social Work Research Methods Course; *Computers in Human Services*, 15 (2/3), pp. 51-69.

Wodarski, J., Kelly, T. (1987) Simulation Technology in Social Work Education, *Arete*, 12 (2), pp. 12-20.

Internet-Based Instruction as an Innovative Approach to Managing Prerequisite Curriculum Content in a Graduate Social Work Program

Jerome R. Kolbo
Earlie M. Washington

SUMMARY. Students admitted to graduate social work programs possess varying levels of understanding of prerequisite curriculum content. Compounding this situation is that social work educators teaching at the foundation level are now required to provide an expanded array of curriculum content in their courses. This article conceptualizes an Internet-Based orientation course as a unique tool for preparing students with prerequisite curriculum content necessary for successful integration and mastery of a graduate curriculum. Several steps are presented in the design and development of the course: obtaining support and approval, identifying and collecting data, designing and developing course components, and implementing and evaluating the course. Although course development occurs within a social work education setting, findings from this Internet-Based orientation course are applicable to other educational and human service settings. *[Article copies available for a fee from The Haworth Document Delivery Service: 1-800-342-9678. E-mail address: getinfo@haworthpressinc.com <Website: http://www.haworthpressinc.com>]*

KEYWORDS. Internet-Based instruction, graduate social work education

---

Jerome R. Kolbo and Earlie M. Washington are affiliated with the University of Southern Mississippi, School of Social Work, Box 5114, Hattiesburg, MS 39406-5114.

[Haworth co-indexing entry note]: "Internet-Based Instruction as an Innovative Approach to Managing Prerequisite Curriculum Content in a Graduate Social Work Program." Kolbo, Jerome R., and Earlie M. Washington. Co-published simultaneously in *Journal of Technology in Human Services* (The Haworth Press, Inc.) Vol. 16, No. 2/3, 1999, pp. 113-125; and: *Computers and Information Technology in Social Work: Education, Training, and Practice* (ed: Jo Ann R. Coe, and Goutham M. Menon) The Haworth Press, Inc., 1999, pp. 113-125. Single or multiple copies of this article are available for a fee from The Haworth Document Delivery Service [1-800-342-9678, 9:00 a.m. - 5:00 p.m. (EST). E-mail address: getinfo@ haworthpressinc.com].

113

Distance education in social work, in which learners are remote from the primary institution and the instructor, is still in its cultural infancy (Murphy et al., 1996). Schools of social work are now witnessing a major paradigm shift in teaching and learning. Increasingly, social work educators are teaching a majority and sometimes the entire curriculum using interactive television technology (Siegel et al., 1998). By the end of the century, social work programs are expected to incorporate information technologies as a regular part of their pedagogical approach.

Much of the research on distance education in social work has focused on the use of television and media technology as a medium of instruction (Freddolino, 1996; Raymond, 1996; Siegel et al., 1998; Thyer, Polk, & Gaudin, 1997; Thyer et al., 1998). No published studies describe or evaluate the use of Internet-Based instruction in social work education programs. In fact, to date, the Council on Social Work Education's Commission on Accreditation has not received a single proposal requesting approval of an Internet-Based social work curriculum (Leashore & Wilson, 1998). Nevertheless, as more educational institutions gain access to the Internet and technology improves, social work education programs are expected to increase their use of Internet-Based instruction.

Like other distance education technologies, Internet-Based instruction appears to offer certain advantages for students. Most notable are the opportunities for self-directed and self-paced learning, standardized assessment of learning and individualized education plans. Since the Internet allows students, instructors and subject matter to be in different, non-centralized locations, the real potential of Internet-Based teaching is that instruction and learning can occur independently of time and location (Cyrs, 1997). Despite these benefits, can the Internet provide new modes of teaching and learning in social work education that are as or more effective than the traditional classroom? Can the Internet be effectively used to assist programs in providing expanded academic support services to students?

This article describes the steps involved in the development of an innovative approach to teaching and learning, an Internet-Based orientation course, in a graduate social work curriculum. The Internet-Based orientation course as described in this paper was designed to provide students with prerequisite content to increase their level of preparedness for the first semester of graduate foundation courses. Prerequisite content is organized into two major areas in this course. First, to facilitate student understanding of the connections between and among graduate courses, the course provides a detailed overview of the graduate social work curriculum and the Curriculum Policy Statement (CPS) for Master Degree Programs in Social Work Education. Second, to enrich student understanding of the person-in-environment context of professional social work practice, the course surveys selected content from the MSW program's liberal arts foundation curriculum.

The authors' hypothesize that an Internet-Based orientation course can strengthen a graduate social work program's ability to provide academic support services, with the goals of increasing both student preparedness before matriculation and their successful mastery of curriculum. In this way the course is linked to the program's achievement of desired student outcomes. Once the course is fully implemented, evaluation studies will determine the effectiveness of the course in preparing program graduates for competent advanced social work practice with individuals, families, groups, communities and organizations.

COURSE DEVELOPMENT

The idea for an Internet-Based orientation course was both faculty- and student-driven. Midway through Fall 1997, the idea emerged in the School of Social Work's Graduate Curriculum Committee meeting. Several faculty members teaching first year students expressed concern over the range of student preparedness for the graduate curriculum. The need to cover "prerequisite" content for many students reduced time available to cover required curriculum content. At this meeting, the first author expressed interest in developing an Internet-Based course to address these issues. Later, several students approached the second author, as Director of the School, regarding their concerns over course demands and expectations. The two authors met and established a plan for developing the course.

The plan included the following steps: obtaining support and approval, identifying and collecting data, designing and developing course components, and implementing and evaluating the course. Each of these steps is discussed below.

Obtaining Support and Approval

The first step, obtaining support and approval occurred at three levels. Administrative support and approval at the first level, within the School of Social Work, was realized immediately as the Director was fully aware of the issues being presented by students and faculty and of the proposed solution. The Director addressed the full faculty to discuss the proposed course and issues concerning workload management, resources and support, and length of time needed for successful implementation.

Support and approval at the second level, within the College of Health and Human Sciences, was obtained through meetings with the Dean. Interest in the innovative nature of the course, the use of available technology and congruency with the missions of the college and school resulted in obtaining support and approval for the course at this level. Support and approval at the third level (i.e., university) was obtained through the submission of a proposal describing the course as an educational intervention designed to improve graduate instruction.

Funds to support program development were allocated at all three levels: the School, College and University. The School provided funds to cover costs for faculty development and training activities, hardware and software and program supplies. In preparation for course development, School funds were used to support the first author's participation in an intensive hands-on training conference on designing and developing web courses. Required software for image and photo editing for web graphics was also purchased using these funds.

The College provided funds to hire an Engineering and Computer Technology graduate student to provide technical assistance and development of the interactive components of the course. The graduate assistant devoted 20 hours weekly during the summer semester to create the courseware. Additionally, university funds were used to cover 100% time (three-course equivalency) of the first author's summer salary.

Identifying and Collecting Data

The second step in the development of the course included the identification and collection of course content. Data were gathered through focus groups with first year graduate students, written surveys of faculty teaching foundation courses, and a face-to-face interview with the Director and MSW Program Coordinator. All data were collected during Spring 1998.

All (n = 44) of the first-year graduate students were approached about participating in focus groups regarding their preparedness for the graduate program. Each of the students was provided with a focus group survey form. Forty students participated in the focus groups held the following week. Thirty-three of the 40 students returned the focus group survey forms. Ten students held baccalaureate degrees in social work. Twenty-three students held undergraduate degrees from different disciplines. The focus group survey consisted of questions about student preparedness for each of their first semester foundation courses (Human Behavior and Social Environment I, Social Welfare Policy, Social Work Generalist Practice I, Social Work Research I, and Field Education I). In addition, each student was asked to list and describe content that they believed would have better prepared them for these foundation courses.

Seven of the 12 full-time graduate faculty who had recently taught one or more of the foundation courses returned written surveys. Faculty members were asked questions regarding student preparedness for each course and to list and describe prerequisite curriculum content that they believe would have better prepared students for their courses. Data collected during the face-face meeting with the Director and MSW Program Coordinator, obtained through open-ended questions, centered on their vision for an Internet-Based orientation course to cover prerequisite curriculum content.

Student focus groups, faculty surveys, and face-to-face interviews yielded primarily qualitative data. All responses were recorded, summarized, and organized into themes. Seven graduate students, under the guidance and supervision of the first author, collected and analyzed the data. These students conducted the study as part of their spring semester second-level research project. Their report (Aubin et al., 1998) suggested three needs of incoming graduate students to: understand the "big picture" of the graduate curriculum, review prerequisite curriculum content, and acquire material resources.

"The Big Picture" of the Curriculum. The primary need was for students to enter the program with a sense of the "big picture." Of concern was students' lack of knowledge of the integrated and interrelated nature of the curriculum (i.e., how each of the foundation and advanced courses fit together, both horizontally and vertically). Some students compartmentalized the program, focusing only on specific courses. Consequently, the interconnectedness of courses taken the same semester or those taken the following semesters was not well understood.

These findings suggested that students were unable to see the connections despite the current approach of providing this information at the day long graduate orientation and referring students to the Student Handbook and Field Education Manual for this content. Students believed that too much information was being covered too quickly in a one-day orientation course and generally were unable to recall much of the information covered during orientation. Thus, these findings suggest that provision of this content through another mode of delivery might be more effective in helping students comprehend the "big picture" of the curriculum.

Review Prerequisite Curriculum Content. Students and faculty indicated a need for the provision of prerequisite content examining common theories, terms and concepts in the program's liberal arts curriculum. Both groups believed that the review of this information would better prepare students for each of the five foundation-level courses offered during the first semester of study. Within the graduate curriculum, courses draw heavily from a variety of related disciplines. Such an approach is ideally suited to the general systems framework of the graduate social work curriculum. Since General Systems Theory has its origins in biology, physics and mathematics, familiarizing students with concepts and terms in these disciplines is necessary. Likewise, students need prior exposure to terms and concepts undergirding the problem-solving/planned change process and ecological system perspectives.

Acquire Material Resources. A third theme was related to the need for prior knowledge of and access to potential resources. Resources most frequently identified by students included course syllabi, links or references to other sources of information about services, and information on the location and types of field placements as well as methods by which informed decisions can be made about field placement options. Students wanted access to faculty via e-mail and information on how to access other support services, including general information about the community, the campus, parking, housing, financial aid, computer labs, and libraries. Each of these was viewed as critical in planning and coordinating one's schedule around such things as employment, field placement, childcare or other professional and personal responsibilities. Students believed that prior access to these resource materials would better prepare them for all courses.

Designing and Developing Course Components

Data from faculty, students, and administration not only provided the content for the course, but directly influenced course development and design. Due to delays in obtaining content, materials, and references from faculty, the initial focus was on developing the course structure. The data suggested at least two levels to the course. The first level (Volume I) provides general information about the orientation course and the graduate program (refer to Figure 1).

Once students have reviewed the content in Volume I of this course, they must complete an online exam. The exam questions must be completed and submitted to the instructor before admission to the second level (Volume II). Admission to the second level requires a password provided by the instructor only after review of the exam.

The second level is organized into nine mandated curriculum areas. The student first reviews content regarding a specific area (refer to Figure 2 for an example of Diversity). The student may then review how this is covered in each of the five courses in the fall semester. For example, the student reviewing diversity may click on a button for HBSE. This will take the student to a screen (Figure 3) that covers diversity in the context of HBSE, and gives the student the option of reviewing the HBSE syllabus, common terms and concepts, helpful readings, and useful links. The student always has the option of returning to other texts within either Volume I, Volume II, or any option on the bookshelf.

Upon completion of the second level, students take a final exam. Exams are constructed so that if the student is unable or unprepared to complete them, they may leave the exam and return to it after further review of the

FIGURE 1. Level One of the Orientation Course

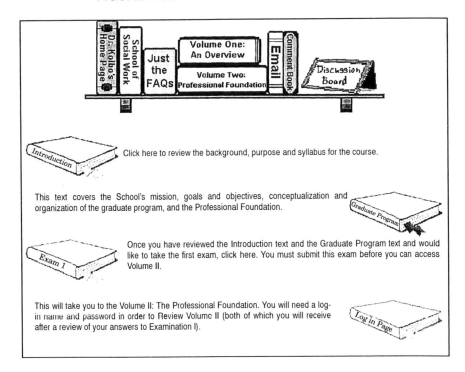

content. Final exam questions are designed to integrate content from the different curriculum areas and courses.

The course is designed to allow both synchronous and synchronous interaction. Students may ask questions or make comments and submit them to an online comment book. These messages are intended for both instructor and other students. Here, neither the student nor the instructor interacts in real time. The messages are public and can be responded to by any of the students or the instructor anytime. Also, the instructor has the means to delete any messages from the comment book anytime. Refer to Figure 4 for examples of comments submitted to the Comment Book.

The course also utilizes a white board designed to allow interaction in real time. Students may interact with each other and the instructor at the same time. The class is set up so that the white board is used at only selected times during each week. This information is also public and the instructor can clear the board anytime. Identification of students is made possible through their

FIGURE 2. Orientation Course Diversity Page

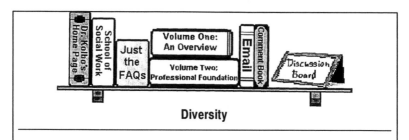

Content on human diversity is infused throughout the curriculum. As indicated in the mission statement, the School of Social Work is committed to preparing students who demonstrate:

- An appreciation for human diversity
- Sensitivity to oppression and discrimination
- Responsiveness to the unserved and under-served
- Concern for social and economic justice and the implications for services
- An ability to provide a wide range of services to vulnerable and at-risk populations

To this end, the faculty regard as a hallmark of competent professional social work practice the ability to bridge differences between people. They are committed to educating students who understand differences related to gender, race, ethnicity, age, language, sexual orientation as well as other personal and cultural characteristics.

Learning purposes, objectives, assignments and readings, theory and skill-building strategies are presented throughout the curriculum emphasizing an appreciation for human diversity. Each course is linked both vertically and horizontally with content on diversity. Click on the icons below to read how diversity is integrated into each course.

HBSE   POLICY   PRACTICE   RESEARCH   FIELD

registered log-on numbers. Private correspondence with other students or the instructor is always available throughout the course via e-mail.

For the purposes of privacy and security, the comment book and white board are available only in the second level. Only students that have received a log-on identification number and password (after completing the first exam) can interact with each other and the instructor. While students may e-mail the instructor for a specific fall course, students are informed that faculty are not expected to be available during the summer.

Implementing the Course

This course is being offered as a complement to the current array of academic support services for incoming graduate students. After the Internet-Based orientation course, students receive, at the beginning of the fall semester, 16 hours of training in preparation for the field practicum. This training includes content on the purpose, goals and objectives of field education and a

FIGURE 3. Orientation Course HBSE Page

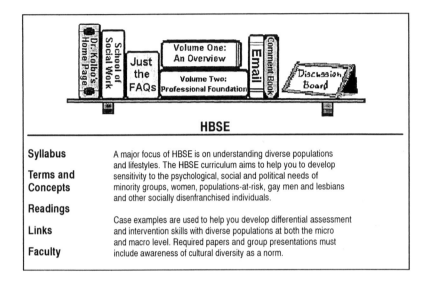

HBSE

Syllabus

Terms and Concepts

Readings

Links

Faculty

A major focus of HBSE is on understanding diverse populations and lifestyles. The HBSE curriculum aims to help you to develop sensitivity to the psychological, social and political needs of minority groups, women, populations-at-risk, gay men and lesbians and other socially disenfranchised individuals.

Case examples are used to help you develop differential assessment and intervention skills with diverse populations at both the micro and macro level. Required papers and group presentations must include awareness of cultural diversity as a norm.

FIGURE 4. Comment Book Entries

Comment Book Submissions
(Last entry appears at the top)

Name: astudent
Email: astudent@usm.edu
Date: Tuesday, July 7, 1998 at 21:31:34
Comments: This is for all my classmates. This web-site really helped me understand some of the terms used in the section on research. (www.ruf.rice.edu/~lane/hyperstat/contents.html)

Name: bstudent
Email: bstudent@usm.edu
Date: Monday, July 6, 1998 at 11:38:35
Comments: Does anyone know where to get the latest information on the status of legislation in the State? Please help!

Click here to return to the Comment Book

practice lab on interviewing and recording and cultural diversity. Students also receive eight hours of training on writing professional papers and another eight hours of training on strengthening library research and study skills.

The Internet-Based course is scheduled for implementation beginning Summer 1999. Once students receive notice of acceptance into the program (May

1999), they will be invited to attend an on-campus orientation to the course (early June 1999). The on-campus component of this course will coincide with the School's general orientation program. During the remaining time in the summer term, students will continue the course online.

Student progress and performance in the Internet-Based course will be determined through their work online. Besides the two exams, the course is designed to assess the number of visits to the Internet site, amount of time each student engaged in course activities online, and the areas and levels of content the student covered. No grade is assigned, because the course is designed as a support service. However, the degree to which the course is completed and the responses given to the exam questions, may be used for diagnostic purposes, identifying students in need of further academic assistance in the fall semester.

Evaluating the Course

To expand knowledge about Internet-Based instruction, process evaluation is occurring in the developmental and implementation phases of this project. Both students and faculty have been and will continue to be given opportunities to review and critique all aspects of the course. Through the interactive nature of the course, students provide feedback during both course levels.

During the first summer (1999) that the course will be offered, not every student will take the course. To assess course effectiveness, two sets of comparisons are scheduled for Fall 1999. Newly admitted students will be randomly assigned to either the traditional or the Internet-Based orientation course. The performance of students taking the Internet-Based course will be compared with their performance in the four fall foundation courses. Since the course is designed to track number of visits, time online and content reviewed, these data will be correlated with student performance in each of the fall foundation courses. In addition, student performance in the fall courses will be compared with those who did not take the course. Despite obvious limitations related to both internal and external validity, this form of evaluation provides valuable data to inform and improve the course and curriculum.

CONCLUSION

Although the development, implementation, and evaluation of this Internet-Based course occurs within a social work education setting, processes and challenges are certainly generalizable to other educational or human service programs. Given limited published descriptions and evaluation studies of Internet-Based courses, educators and human service providers may not consider using Internet-Based technology. This article, however, suggests that the Internet may be effective in preparing students for successful mastery of a graduate social work curriculum and that Internet-Based courses enrich existing academic support services. Those interested in developing similar courses may benefit from a brief discussion of the challenges faced by program developers and the knowledge gained through the program development process.

Financial support was critical to the successful development of this course. Although the final budget for course development was sufficient, overall cost exceeded initial estimates and involved three different funding sources: the School, College and University. Costs for faculty summer salary, a graduate assistant and software were anticipated. Unanticipated costs, however, included faculty development for initial training on Internet-Based technology, new hardware to improve technology capacity and ongoing technical consultation. Given rapid developments in computer technology, faculty training, new hardware and ongoing technical assistance may be recurrent costs.

Program administrators can expect the initial cost of an Internet-Based course to vary depending on hardware and software needs and faculty expertise. Based on the authors' experiences, Internet-Based course development appear to be more costly than courses developed using traditional and interactive video technology (compressed video). Faculty members do not receive course release time or specific training for developing new courses using traditional methods. On the other hand, faculty members developing courses to be taught using interactive video technology (i.e., compressed video) receive one course release time and specific training. Comparatively, faculty members developing an Internet-Based course receive three courses release time (1.0 full-time equivalency) and specific training.

The most time-consuming step in the development of the Internet-Based course was the course design and development phase. Faculty worked closely to reach a consensus about the purpose, nature and content of the course and to develop ownership of the process. Significant coordination, however, was required to identify specific prerequisite content, reading lists and Internet links for courses taught in the foundation curriculum. A concurrent process of preparing self-study documents for program accreditation greatly assisted faculty in this endeavor. Nevertheless, the iterative process of collecting, reviewing and creating content for the course was tedious for most faculty members.

Another challenge related to course design was the lack of appropriate software programs to assist in the development of the courseware. Due to financial and time constraints, course management software programs such as WebCT and Web-in-a-Box were not purchased prior to the development of the course. Thus, course developers had limited software available for the project. The first author and the Graduate Assistant used Netscape Composer, a web-authoring software included within Netscape Communicator for Windows, and Common Gateway Interface programming scripts to design the interactive component of the course (i.e., exams, comment book, discussion board, password). The lack of appropriate software added to the level of difficulty and length of time required for courseware development.

Challenges during the implementation phase can also be expected. Logistical issues related to the admissions and orientation processes may affect program operations. Since the Internet-Based course is completed during the summer, the admission deadline date, review of application materials and notice of acceptance to students must occur early in the spring semester, perhaps requiring changes in the timeline of the admissions process. Further, changes regarding when and how students are oriented to the University and School may also be warranted. While faculty members are not opposed to these changes, potential staffing difficulties may develop, along with increased cost to modify existing admission forms and packets.

Using the Internet to support instruction and prepare students for graduate social work education can present numerous challenges for faculty and program administrators. In spite of these challenges, the Internet can be used as an innovative approach to enhance student readiness for graduate education. This article has described the development of this innovation and discussed challenges that may affect program development in similar or different settings. Future studies will evaluate the effects of the course on student learning and mastery of curriculum content.

REFERENCES

Aubin, A., Galloway, J., Harrington, T., Ickes, E., Jackson, T., Jones, B., & Mesrobian, D. (1998). *SWK 637 research project: Development of an Internet-based orientation course*. Unpublished manuscript, University of Southern Mississippi.

Council on Social Work Education (1992). *The Curriculum Policy Statement for Master Degree Programs in Social Work Education*. Alexandria, VA: Author.

Cyrs, T. (1997). *Teaching at a Distance with the Merging Technologies: An Instructional Systems Approach*. Las Cruces, New Mexico: New Mexico State University, Center for Educational Development.

Freddolino, P. (1996). Maintaining quality in graduate social work program delivered to distant sites using electronic instructional technology. *Tulane Studies in Social Welfare, 20*, 40-52.

Leashore, B., & Wilson, S. (1998, March). *Implication for accreditation: Distance Education*. Faculty Development Institute presented at the 44th Annual Program Meeting of the Council on Social Work Education, Orlando, FL.

Murphy, K., Cifuentes, L., Yakimovicz, A., Segur, R., Mahoney, S., & Kodali, S. (1996). Students assume the mantle of moderating computer conferences: A case study. *The American Journal of Distance Education, 10 (3)*, 20-36.

Raymond, F. (1996). Delivering the MSW curriculum to non-traditional students through interactive television. *Journal of Social Work Education, 34 (2)*, 16-27.

Siegel, E., Jennings, J., Conklin, J., & Flynn, N. (1998). Distance learning in social work education: Results and implications of a national survey. *Journal of Social Work Education, 34 (2)*, 71-80.

Thyer, B., Artelt, T., Markward, M., & Dozier, C. (1998). Evaluating distance learning in social work education: A replication study. *Journal of Social Work Education, 34 (2)*, 291-295.

Thyer, B., Polk, G., & Gaudin, J. (1997). Distance learning in social work education: A preliminary Evaluation. *Journal of Social Work Education, 33 (2)*, 363-367.

The Virtual Community:
Computer Conferencing for Teaching
and Learning Social Work Practice

Diane S. Falk

SUMMARY. This author describes the use of a web-based conferencing program to augment classroom learning in generalist social work practice courses in a BSW program. This "virtual classroom" allows students to have more or less continual access to the instructor and to each other, greatly expanding opportunities for teaching, learning, and communication. *[Article copies available for a fee from The Haworth Document Delivery Service: 1-800-342-9678. E-mail address: getinfo@haworthpressinc. com <Website: http://www.haworthpressinc.com>]*

KEYWORDS. Web-based conferencing, teaching, virtual classroom

Colleges and universities across the nation have been struggling with how best to incorporate a variety of technological advances, including computer technology, into the educational process. The successful integration of computers into teaching and learning has been slow to develop, for a number of reasons. At the university-wide level, these may include: (1) difficulties of finding the financial resources to purchase and continually update equipment,

---

Diane S. Falk is Assistant Professor, Richard Stockton College of New Jersey.

Address correspondence to: Diane S. Falk, Jim Reed Road, Pomana, NJ 08240 (E-mail: dfalk@earthlink.net).

[Haworth co-indexing entry note]: "The Virtual Community: Computer Conferencing for Teaching and Learning Social Work Practice." Falk, Diane S. Co-published simultaneously in *Journal of Technology in Human Services* (The Haworth Press, Inc.) Vol. 16, No. 2/3, 1999, pp. 127-143; and: *Computers and Information Technology in Social Work: Education, Training, and Practice* (ed: Jo Ann R. Coe, and Goutham M. Menon) The Haworth Press, Inc., 1999, pp. 127-143. Single or multiple copies of this article are available for a fee from The Haworth Document Delivery Service [1-800-342-9678, 9:00 a.m. - 5:00 p.m. (EST). E-mail address: getinfo@haworthpressinc.com].

127

(2) possible communication gaps between computing professionals and educators, (3) poor support services, and (4) legal and ethical concerns (Gilbert, 1996). At the program and individual faculty level, there are other obstacles. Many faculty members and students still feel uncomfortable with using computers beyond the word processing level. In addition, not many studies have been done (and published) on incorporating computer technology into teaching and learning. Although the literature in higher education has some reports from individual educators who have developed models that apparently work well for them, studies that demonstrate the effectiveness of any particular model are generally not available (Ehrmann, 1995). This is especially true in social work education, although there are exceptions. Seabury and Maple (1993), for example, reported the successful use of a computer-based interactive video disk program to teach interviewing skills. Patterson and Yaffe (1993) used a hypermedia program to teach DSM-III-R diagnostic skills to graduate social work students and found it to be as effective as using the training manual. An international study, conducted by the International Association of Schools of Social Work, found that the schools of social work that had computers at all did not tend to use them in the core social work courses (Caputo & Cnaan, 1990). Only 23% of schools (mostly those in the USA) used computers in teaching practice (Caputo & Cnaan, 1990). Unfortunately there is no more recent international study available, and the social work literature of the last five years contains very few reports of such use (Patterson, & Yaffe, 1993).

Educators are justifiably not interested in technology for technology's sake; rather they are interested in advances that enhance teaching and learning (Horgan, 1998). This paper describes how one particular teacher used computer technology to supplement "traditional" (i.e., lectures, discussions, exercises, papers, etc.) teaching in social work practice classes. It focuses on the role of technology in *teaching*, rather than on details of the technology itself. First I describe the process of acquiring the skills required in order to use the software, then discuss the pros and cons of using this technology, and finally present some data on how one instructor and her students used it in a social work practice methods course. This is not a controlled study, comparing a group that used technology with one that did not. Rather it is a description of how the technology was integrated into teaching and learning in one of the core BSW-level social work courses, with discussion of how the computer technology added to the educational experience.

OVERVIEW OF WEB CAUCUS

Web Caucus is a web-based synchronous conferencing program that permits a large number of password-protected conferences to be established–and a large number of individual conference members to communicate with the server at once. As such, its communicating capabilities are richer than those of a bulletin board, listserv, or threaded discussion. Unlike in a chat room, users are not generally online simultaneously, although they may be–and may post responses to other users without significant delay. This program allows users to create a variety of topic items and also to respond to each other's posted items and responses. Users can log onto the conference from any computer that has access to the World Wide Web, whether that computer be in the college computer laboratories, in the local public library, or at home. The program also allows users to create hotlinks to WWW sites, post graphics, and upload text files, among other things. In addition, it permits conference organizers to track the number of postings each user has made–and even the number of responses each user has read. This is a valuable feature for course instructors.

Users of Web Caucus do not need to have any computer skills beyond the ability to manipulate a mouse. All of the skills required can be demonstrated within about a half-hour. Students need to have a college computer account number and a password. The course instructor must enter the student account numbers before any students can log on for the first time. Then students need to learn how to:

- Log on
- Join the conference
- Access information

- Post new topic items
- Post responses to existing items
- Log off

Students may encounter some difficulty at first. The log-on process is probably the most difficult task initially. Once students have successfully entered one item into the conference, they usually experience a beginning sense of mastery of the technology. The only real difficulties arise when the college computer network is temporarily "down" or when the program has too many users trying to log on at once. Although the latter problem is frustrating to users, the increased demand for access to Caucus is one measure of its success: every semester more instructors adopt it for use with their classes.

Once students have mastered the basics, some of them may be interested in learning more advanced skills. These include the ability to:

- Cut and paste from other programs
- Post URL's
- Post images

- Upload files
- Download text
- Use HTML (Hypertext Markup Language) to control formatting

The more advanced skills vary in the degree of difficulty involved. Cutting and pasting can easily be mastered by anyone who has learned how to do this in a word processing program. Posting URL's and images is also relatively simple, but usually only students (or instructors) who have considerable experience using the World Wide Web think about adding such creative touches to their entries. Uploading files (e.g., taking a text file from a word processing program and bringing it into a Caucus entry) is also not difficult, but cutting and pasting generally serves the same purpose. Students are very quick to learn how to download text, since this only involves giving the computer a "save" or "print" command. Any of the material from Web Caucus can be printed from any location from which Caucus can be accessed. Students and instructors can learn to use Hypertext Markup Language within a few hours of study, but most students and instructors are not sufficiently motivated to bother learning how to enhance their entries with "frills," such as boldfaced or italicized text.

THE LEARNING PROCESS

I started to use this technology in the second semester of the 1996-97 academic year with my two sections of the junior methods/field seminar course. Although a different non-web-based conferencing program had been used by some of the social work faculty in previous years, this was the first introduction of Web Caucus to students in the Social Work Program. Students in this initial group (there were approximately 45 enrolled in two sections) were quite intimidated. Many of them had never used computers before. Some of the "non-traditional" students had survived 40 or 50 years of life without using computers and could not see why they had to start now. Many of the "traditional" students had chosen social work as their major, partly because they disliked technical subjects, such as mathematics, physical sciences, and computers. They could not understand what computers had to offer to a field of study that focused on humanistic concerns.

To alleviate their anxieties, I scheduled one hour initially in the college computer laboratories to demonstrate the program and enable them to have "hands-on" experience with it. I paired students off to assure that relatively experienced computer users sat next to inexperienced ones. Since the initial session was not enough to alleviate anxieties, I had one hour-long follow-up session for anyone who still felt insecure. Despite their initial reluctance, students realized that this was a course requirement, bowed to the inevitable, and learned enough to get started.

Throughout the semester, some students continued to have problems on occasion. A few students became angry that I would not drop this require-ment: "This is not a *computer* course. It's *social work*." I told the students that I would be irresponsible if I did not prepare them for the job require-ments of the 21st Century. Many of them would be required to maintain records with a computer; some would even be carrying laptops around in the field. This helped them to gain some perspective on the assignment. If they were gaining potential job skills, perhaps it might be worth putting up with some frustration in the present semester. The payoff is that every student (except one) in the two classes learned enough to be able to fulfill course requirements. A few expressed gratitude that I "made them learn this." Many students succeeded in moving beyond the self-consciousness that accompa-nies using a new technology and were able to see the benefits of being able to stay in touch and continue class discussions outside of the class. Since my two sections were linked together in one conference, students also were able to communicate with a broader network of students than the ones they regu-larly saw in class.

During the academic year 1997-98 I again used computer conferencing with my junior practice methods course. Most students in the new junior class had computers at home, whereas only a few the year before did. In addition, several of the students had taken classes where they had been required to use computers. These students were enthusiastic about using computer confer-encing from the beginning. They learned to use the Web Caucus program with less than an hour of demonstration and rapidly began to make entries. Class members demonstrated some creativity as they both fulfilled and moved beyond the assignment I had given them, using the technology for their own purposes. Time will tell whether this group represents a trend among social work students towards more comfort with computers.

BENEFITS OF INCORPORATING COMPUTER CONFERENCING INTO TEACHING AND LEARNING SOCIAL WORK PRACTICE

The main benefits *to students* of using computer conferencing as a supple-ment to face-to-face classes are that it dramatically increases students' access to the instructor outside the classroom setting, and it establishes direct com-munication links among the students. In addition to learning from the instruc-tor, students have more opportunities to learn from each other. The student-to-student exchanges of support, ideas, and experiences that begins in the classroom are continued throughout the week, creating a sense of a "virtual community." Figures 1 and 2 are a pictorial representation of the way in which the use of computer conferencing enhanced communication patterns among students. These drawings are not based on actual data on pre- and post-computer conferencing communication patterns. Rather, they are in-tended to indicate a phenomenon observed and commented upon by students. They reported that by reading each other's online journal entries they got to

FIGURE 1. Communication Patterns Outside the Classroom in a Traditional Class

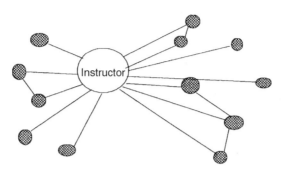

FIGURE 2. Communication Patterns–Classroom Using Computer Conferencing

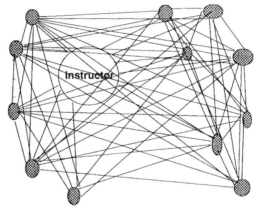

know each other much better than if they had only spent class time together. This enhanced knowledge of–and interest in–each other led them to begin commenting on each other's postings. Students also reported that ordinarily, even if they did talk with each other on the telephone or saw each other in classes, they would not have discussed some of the topics they discussed online (for example, responses to readings or field experiences).

Computer conferencing also increases participation of students who have difficulty engaging in classroom discussions (e.g., shy people). For many such students, this opportunity to be a part of the class discourse increases their motivation and enhances the class learning by including diverse ideas that otherwise might not be shared (Gilbert, 1996; Akers, 1997). Students become very active learners, often creating new ideas about what to include in the conference. They share in the construction of the course by initiating, building upon, and deepening discussions (Akers, 1997). In addition, using computer conferencing helps students to move into other uses of computer technology, such as the World Wide Web, where they become familiar with the rich variety of social work and related web sites.

This technology allows *the instructor* to provide follow-up to class discussions, give assignments and readings, make announcements between classes, and direct students to web sites so that they discover an additional way of learning about resources for themselves and for clients. In addition, the instructor can make comments to one student and know that the message is reaching the entire class. (Communication between student and instructor that needs to be private is conducted by e-mail.) The instructor can be very responsive to individual student needs and learning styles. For example, the conference allows for students to communicate their ideas and questions when they occur, rather than be restricted to the traditional boundaries of access to the instructor and to fellow students. Questions about, or insights into, course material do not occur only during the three to four hours of class time; they can occur at midnight on a weekend. This program allows students to communicate at their convenience, when the question or discovery is fresh in their minds, and it allows the instructor and fellow students to respond well before the next scheduled class meeting (Akers, 1997).

Social work educational philosophy and methodology has been influenced by the principle of andragogy, which posits adult learners as independent persons with a growing fund of experience to draw upon, who are oriented towards fulfilling occupational roles, and who are motivated to apply their newly acquired knowledge immediately (Knowles, 1980). According to this principle, learning is "a cooperative venture in nonauthoritarian, informal learning, the chief purpose of which is to discover the meaning of experience" (Knowles, 1980, p. 55). Computer conferencing fits well with this educational approach.

POSSIBLE DISADVANTAGES
OF INCORPORATING COMPUTER CONFERENCING
INTO TEACHING AND LEARNING SOCIAL WORK PRACTICE

Some of the obstacles to incorporating computer technology into teaching and learning in colleges and universities generally have already been discussed. An additional issue–unequal student access–is a problem for all teachers but perhaps an even more acute problem for teachers of social work. There is no question that some students have serious difficulty getting computer time, even when computers are widely available at their school. Single parents, for example, may not be able to spend time in computer labs. The increased availability of computers with Internet access at local public libraries resolved this problem for a few students. In addition, recent price reductions have made it possible for many students to purchase their own computers.

Another disadvantage of using this technology is that students with less experience with computers may feel extra stress, since they have to master the technology as well as the subject matter of the course. They may need to go to the computer laboratory to practice using the software while other students are moving ahead on other class assignments (Maus, 1996).

A third disadvantage, and a very significant one, is that incorporating a computer conferencing program into teaching may increase the instructor's workload. This is especially true the first semester when the instructor is working through any technical problems that may arise. The benefit (to students) of more or less continual access to the instructor may also prove burdensome; however, the enhanced teaching and learning that results may be worth the extra effort (McKay, 1997).

EXAMPLES OF TEACHING AND LEARNING USING COMPUTER CONFERENCING

Rather than talking *about* how effective computer conferencing can be, I am going to give some concrete examples of how my students and I have used this technology to enhance student learning. My comments will focus on the *additional benefits* that technology adds to teaching. Although at least one study has suggested that virtual teaching in higher education can replace classroom teaching, I am not suggesting that this could be true for teaching social work students practice methods (Schutte, 1996).

The first way in which I used the conference was to post the online journal assignment, as follows:

> [INSTRUCTOR] Social Work Professional Journal: The journal should include your reactions to readings, class discussions, exercises, and field experiences. When you refer to readings, please make specific reference to the author and the concepts that you are discussing. You may also want to bring up other life experiences you have had, especially those that involved receiving or giving help. . . . I encourage you to put your journal entries into the public conference to share with others, because this will enhance the class's learning. If there is something private that you would rather not put in the conference, please send it to me by e-mail. I also strongly encourage you to read each other's entries and respond to each other. You can learn much from your peers. You

should do at least four journal entries over the semester. This 'public' conference can only be accessed by the members of this class and by me. [Student entries are reproduced here with the consent of the class members.]

This got the students started.

Using the data tracking facilities of the Web Caucus program, I was able to extract information on the number of postings per student over the course of the two semesters that students participated in the junior year practice methods course conference. By printing out the entire conference (250 pages of text), I was able to do a content analysis of the ways in which the instructor and the students used the conference for teaching and learning social work practice.

As Table 1 indicates, the two main ways in which *the instructor* used the conference were to provide support and encouragement to the students–and to expand upon the classroom learning. Social work students who are enrolled in practice methodology classes often go through considerable questioning of their ability to use the theory they are learning and actually help

TABLE 1

EXAMPLES OF TEACHING	Instructor Postings	
	Number of Postings	Amount Posted (lines of text)
1. Providing support and encouragement	108	236
2. Expanding class learning	55	427
3. Providing challenges	19	87
4. Providing assistance in use of the technology	9	49
5. Giving assignments	5	147
6. Giving suggestions about field work	4	20
7. Giving information	1	65
8. Responding to student questions	1	3
9. Referring student to WWW sites	1	3
TOTAL INSTRUCTOR POSTINGS	203	1037

people. Important roles of the instructor are to provide reassurance and to encourage students to think more deeply about issues. The provision of support and encouragement–or challenges–to individual students is something that does not so easily occur in a classroom setting, since it is often not possible for the instructor to tune in to the needs of many students at once. The conference presents an opportunity to individualize teaching, within the limits of the instructor's time.

The Table reports both the total number of postings in each category and the total number of lines of text posted. This gives the reader some idea of the quantity of content in each category, as well as the number of postings. Some categories occurred very frequently but were relatively insubstantial in content. A line of text in the conference format contains about 14 words.

I had originally thought that responding to student questions would be a major function of my participation in the conference, but students did not generally use the conference to raise questions. Instead they presented their reflections on class experiences (readings, exercises, field work) and looked for encouragement from the instructor and from each other. At the start of the semester, I responded to nearly every student posting–to encourage the students to deepen their thinking about the course material and to participate actively in the conference. As the semester moved along, there was more and more student-to-student conversation, and I was able to stay in the background much of the time.

A total of 30 students participated in the conference. Seventeen were enrolled the first semester, and 28 the second semester. Sixteen of the original seventeen continued into the second semester, and 12 additional students joined the group during the second semester. Participation in the Web Caucus conference was required of all students each semester. The assignment was to make 4 journal entries during the course of the semester. If each student had done just the minimum required journal entries, there would have been 180 postings in the conference over the course of the year. The actual number of student postings was 560, with a range of between 4 and 56 responses per student and a mean of 18.7. This was approximately three times the required number of postings.

In the next section, *the students* speak for themselves. Table 2 indicates how the students actually used computer conferencing for their own purposes, as well as to meet the class assignment.

Table 2 is divided into two parts: the two columns to the left contain data about postings that students made in order to meet the requirements of the course. The online journal assignment had particularly asked students to share their reactions to readings, assignments, class discussions, and field experiences. Categories 1 and 2 above specifically capture student postings that address this assignment. Categories 3 and 4 capture postings that address

TABLE 2

	Student Postings			
	Postings to Meet Course Requirements		Voluntary Postings	
EXAMPLES OF LEARNING	Number of Postings	Amount Posted (lines of text)	Number of Postings	Amount Posted (lines of text)
1. Sharing reactions to field (and work) experiences	104	1775	14	117
2. Sharing reactions to readings, assignments, class discussions and exercises	95	1583	14	75
3. Contemplating growth of the professional self	9	176	0	0
4. Attempting to integrate theory with practice	6	103	0	0
5. Socializing	0	0	142	268
6. Providing support to each other	3	13	76	315
7. Creating ways to inspire each other	2	46	52	169
8. Commenting on the technology	5	14	18	40
9. Confronting each other	0	0	5	16
10. Giving suggestions to each other	0	0	3	15
11. Sharing information	5	195	2	34
12. Asking for input on field assignment	1	18	2	30
13. Asking questions of the instructor	0	0	1	5
14. Sharing ethical concerns	1	24	0	0
TOTAL STUDENT POSTINGS	231	3947	329	1084

learning at a deeper level–the internal changes that occur when students integrate theory with practice. The other categories in the left-hand column were topics that students addressed within their formal online journal postings.

The two right-hand columns in Table 2 represent additional "voluntary" postings that students made outside of their journals. Here the most frequent posting is for the purposes of socializing. As the numbers indicate, most of these postings were very brief–one or two lines. Students dropped in to say hello. Occurring not quite as frequently, but with more substance, were postings intended to give each other support, encouragement, or inspiration, mostly about field work but also about how to cope with the stress of being a student and carrying multiple roles (worker, parent, friend, and so forth). Students also fairly frequently commented on the use of Web Caucus, either to say how enjoyable it was or to complain about the software occasionally being "down."

The following paragraphs present some excerpts from student postings in the conference that were intended to meet the online journal assignment. Some of the examples contain the instructor's response to the student posting.

Sharing Reactions to Field (and Work) Experiences

Since students are placed in a variety of agencies, and many already have paid employment in the human services field, they need to discuss and get feedback on particular issues. The conference gives them this opportunity. It also gives other students an opportunity to read about issues that arise in the work place, to see how fellow students think about and handle these issues, and to read the instructor's responses. There would not be time for as much of this discussion in the classroom.

> [Student] About a week ago we had a team meeting to review CM's progress. All the team members, agreed he is progressing nicely. The frustrating part came in with DYFS. They seem to be more concerned and unhappy with the activities of the parents. They went as far as to suggest the adolescent should remain in the facility. Correct me if I'm wrong, but why punish the child for his parent's shortcomings. I did vocalize my thoughts. . . . We shall see how it went over.
>
> [Instructor response to above] One thing you might consider with the CM case is whether being in a residential facility is really a punishment for this child. If he is doing very well now, is there a possibility that he would regress significantly if he were to be returned home to a situation that is not as stable as the residential facility?
>
> [Student response to instructor response above] Thanks! I really didn't look at the positive effects this facility had on this child. The

structure and therapeutic components are probably why CM is doing so well . . .

Sharing Reactions to Readings, Assignments, Class Discussions and Exercises

The professional journal assignment asks students to integrate readings, class discussions and exercises, and personal experiences–and articulate the growing sense of becoming a "professional self." As students write about their struggles with this assignment, the instructor has the opportunity to provide direction and clarification, give support, and ask challenging questions. This student fulfilled the professional journal requirement quite effectively.

> [Student] When I read about the roles that weren't so obvious, I realized that there is more to social work than I thought. Social work, to me was about helping people. So the roles of an advocate, a counselor, a teacher and even a workload manager did not come surprising to me. However, an administrator and a staff-developer are not about dealing with clients, those roles deal with a social worker's co-workers. A social worker has a very difficult job, and honestly when I completed this chapter I wondered if I would ever be able to see how these all came together. That is why I am so glad that we role played in class. J's situation, for the most part, seemed realistic to me. As the counselor I found myself trying to help her and find out what I could do for her. Although I was supposed to be thinking and acting like strictly a clinician, I found myself wanting to advocate for her and teach her new skills so that she could get a job. To my surprise, I also thought about trying to delegate responsibility to people, like telling the broker to find out about how we could find J's husband. As I was thinking all of these thoughts I realized that I was all of the different roles at once. I couldn't believe that I even thought like an administrator. This chapter and exercise in class really helped me to see that I am capable of being a social worker.
>
> [Instructor response to above] C, you did a very nice job in your first journal entry. I like the way you tied together your initial feelings, as you contemplated the readings, with your experience in the class role play, then gave us a clear sense of the learning process you experienced.

Contemplating Growth of the Professional Self

Students are continually encouraged to examine themselves and to grow personally and professionally. This student used the conference to summarize his growth over the course of his junior year.

[Student] I think that if I were to sum up the two most important lessons that I learned this semester, the first would be "Condemn the sin and not the sinner." . . . The second would be not to get too full of myself and my abilities. This class made me painfully aware of my limitations at this point in time, as well as some weaknesses that I have chosen to learn from and turn into strengths. One weakness is that I constantly find the need to solve the problem. I guess that I always knew that I shouldn't do that, but I couldn't figure out an alternative approach, so I tried to solve it any way. . . . I'd like to thank everyone for sharing and listening.

[Instructor response] Thank you for . . . having the humility (and confidence) to examine yourself and consider making some changes. Empowering clients to make changes in their lives requires some self-containment on the part of the social worker. Rather than rush to the rescue, we learn to hold back a little and find ways to encourage clients to learn how to help themselves.

Attempting to Integrate Theory with Practice

Integrating theory with practice is one of the most essential, and also one of the most difficult, tasks for a social work student. The conference enables students to articulate their insights and share the effect of interventions with other students.

[Student] Recently a young girl who has been having a hard time with several issues was having a difficult day. I asked her if she wanted to talk. . . . As we were talking she was saying she wanted to go home and she didn't want to be here anymore. When she said, "I wish I could just wake up tomorrow in my own house and my own bed." In the handout, How to Interview for Client Strengths, by Peter De Jong and Scott D. Miller, there was a part about the "miracle" question. Even though I didn't propose the question I thought this would be an opportunity to use the solution-focused approach. After she had finished venting I asked her what she would have to do to make her wish come true. She thought for a second or two and told me that her behavior would have to improve, and that had to compete the program. . . . This conversation took place over three weeks ago and her attitude has changed. . . .

Providing Support to Each Other

Often students are very supportive of each other. The conference provides them with an opportunity to reach out to a much wider group of their fellow students than would be possible in a traditional classroom.

[Student] I missed you at our final group this week. I gave much thought to the things you shared with us about not rushing through life. . . . Thank you so much, what might have seemed to you like a little contribution, has left a lasting/life changing impression on me.

Creating Ways to Inspire Each Other

This year students went beyond the instructor's assignment and created an item designed to bring inspiration to each other. One student posted an inspiring saying each day, and another added a lighter touch by posting a joke of the day. The "virtual community" encourages students to be creative and make the course more meaningful to them. Here is another example of a student trying to inspire other students:

[Student] I was very glad that J brought up the topic of domestic violence. . . . I also read the post that J left on caucus about domestic violence and I found it very interesting. I would like to close with a poem that I read about domestic violence that reflects how society turns their backs on battered women. [reproduces long inspirational poem]

Commenting on the Technology

Students often comment on how much they enjoy reading about the thoughts and experiences of other students. For example:

[Student] I love the idea of a class conference room on Web Caucus. There will be a particular question running through my mind, and just when I know that I've exhausted every possible approach to solve it, I'll read someone's journal entry, smack myself in the head and say, 'Hey! I didn't think of that.'

Confronting Each Other

In addition to support, students occasionally benefit from confrontation. They are often much more open to listening to fellow students than to the instructor. Although this also can occur in the classroom, some students find it easier to address what other students write, rather than face-to-face.

[Student] D., you were not kidding when you said you went off in your journal. Our group is supposed to be focusing on the group process. What you expressed in your journal would have made a great topic for discussion in the group on Thursday. We are not there to work on personal problems. We are there to help everyone get an experience within a group. Just a suggestion, but you should have a more positive attitude.

CONCLUSION

The above excerpts give the reader some idea of the range and type of communication that occurs among students enrolled in a social work practice methods course who use computer conferencing as a supplement to traditional classroom learning. In social work classes, especially practice classes, responses to readings and class discussions do not always happen in class. Students need time to process what they are learning, some more than others. Computer conferencing allows each student to reflect on learning at his or her own pace—and then to articulate and share insights with the instructor and other students in written form. The use of computer conferencing greatly expands the amount of interaction between students and instructor—and among students. This is the real power of this technology. Students benefit from their own ideas and experiences but also get to read about a wide range of ideas and experiences that their fellow students are having—and the instructor's comments to other students as well as to them. This would not happen in a class where students did the same type of writing but turned their journals in to the instructor. With computer conferencing, students and instructor join together to construct a virtual community where learning can take place in a flexible fashion that is very responsive to student need. Although there are shortcomings to using this method, such as unequal access to computers, students with previous computer experience having an advantage, and the requirement of a greater investment of time from the instructor, the advantages appear to outweigh the disadvantages. Further evaluation of the effectiveness of computer conferencing in teaching social work practice is recommended.

REFERENCES

Akers, R. (1997). Web discussion forums in teaching and learning. *Case Studies (August). http://horizon.unc.edu/ts/cases/1997-08a.asp.*

Caputo, R.K. & Cnaan, R.A. (1990). Information technology availability in schools of social work. *Journal of Social Work Education, 26 (2),* 187-98.

Ehrmann, S.C. (1995). Asking the right questions: What does research tell us about technology and higher learning? In American Association for Higher Education. *Teaching, learning, and technology roundtable program, regional TLTR workshop workbook, version 1.51,* 213-20.

Gilbert, S.W. (1996). Making the most of a slow revolution. *Teaching, learning, and technology roundtable program, regional TLTR workshop workbook, version 1.51,* 187-200.

Horgan, B. (1998). Transforming higher education using information technology: First steps. *Vision* (January). *http://horizon.unc.edu/ts/vision/1998-01.asp.*

Knowles, M.S. (1980). *The modern practice of adult education,* (rev. ed.). Chicago: Associated Press.

Maus, D. (1998). Walking the line: Rectifying institutional goals with student realities. *Vision* (February). *http://horizon.unc.edu/ts/vision/1998-02.asp.*

McKay, J. (1997). Paradigms and practices: Creating different strategies for learning. *Case Studies* (November). *http://horizon.unc.edu/ts/cases/1997-11.asp.*

Patterson, D.A., & Yaffe, J. (1993). An evaluation of computer-assisted instruction in teaching axis II of DSM-III-R to social work students. *Research on Social Work Practice, 3 (3),* 343-57.

Patterson, D. & Yaffe, J. (1994). Hypermedia computer-based education in social work education. *Journal of Social Work Education, 30 (2),* 267-77.

Schutte, J.G. (1996). Virtual teaching in higher education: The new intellectual superhighway or just another traffic jam? *http://www.csun.edu/sociology/virexp.htm.*

Seabury, B.A., Maple, Jr., F.F. (1993). Using computers to teach practice skills. *Social Work, 38 (4),* 430-39.

Computer-Facilitated Instructional Strategies for Education: Designing WebQuests

Debra Gohagan

SUMMARY. This article describes the use of WebQuests, a computer-facilitated instructional strategy for social work education. Pedagogical constructs relevant to the use of WebQuests as a computer-facilitated instructional strategy are identified and discussed. Examples of the application and integration of WebQuest activities in an undergraduate social work curriculum are presented. *[Article copies available for a fee from The Haworth Document Delivery Service: 1-800-342-9678. E-mail address: getinfo@haworthpressinc.com <Website: http://www.haworthpressinc.com>]*

KEYWORDS. Computers, instructional strategies, World Wide Web

Educators are fascinated with the Internet and are finding a variety of ways to incorporate Internet-based resources in their professional and teaching activities (Finn, 1995; Crook & Brady, 1998; Galambos & Neal, in press; Holden, Rosenberg, & Weissman, 1995, 1996; Karger & Stoez, 1998; Marson, 1997; Stocks & Freddolino, in press; Yaffe, 1998). However, Internet-based information is so rich, so varied, and changing so rapidly that educators are often unsure how to harness the power of this technology for classroom use. The lack of a framework by which to develop and integrate Internet-based

Debra Gohagan, MSW, is Assistant Professor, Department of Social Work, Minnesota State University, Mankato, Mankato, MN 56001.

[Haworth co-indexing entry note]: "Computer-Facilitated Instructional Strategies for Education: Designing WebQuests." Gohagan, Debra. Co-published simultaneously in *Journal of Technology in Human Services* (The Haworth Press, Inc.) Vol. 16, No. 2/3, 1999, pp. 145-159; and: *Computers and Information Technology in Social Work: Education, Training, and Practice* (ed: Jo Ann R. Coe, and Goutham M. Menon) The Haworth Press, Inc., 1999, pp. 145-159. Single or multiple copies of this article are available for a fee from The Haworth Document Delivery Service [1-800-342-9678, 9:00 a.m. - 5:00 p.m. (EST). E-mail address: getinfo@haworthpressinc.com].

resources as teaching tools can lead to a pragmatic or 'add and stir' approach. This, in turn, leads to chaos, frustration, and failure to effectively use technology as teaching tools. These uncertainties, subsequent frustrations, and occasional failures fuel the debate about the effectiveness of using Internet-based information to teach the knowledge, values, and skills of the social work profession.

This article provides a brief overview of the core pedagogical constructs that are relevant to understanding and designing instructional approaches for use in all teaching activities. These constructs are then applied to the development of pedagogically-sound web-based instructional approaches. The first construct defines two types of teaching styles most frequently used by educators. A second pedagogical construct, the development of teaching goals based upon the teaching of thinking skills (lower-order and higher-order) across the cognitive, affective and psychomotor teaching domains is also briefly reviewed. These constructs are then specifically applied to the development of computer-facilitated instructional strategies (CFIS) using an instructional design approach called WebQuests. Finally, general CFIS applications for social work education using a WebQuest framework are discussed. Specific examples of the integration of WebQuests in two courses are also presented.

TEACHING PEDAGOGY

Educators in their eagerness to integrate technology into their teaching activities tend to add technology without explicitly considering the pedagogical requirements for successful and effective integration of this technology. Pedagogical requirements for designing effective technology-based instructional activities include (a) knowledge about and an awareness of educators' teaching philosophies, (b) identification of teaching goals appropriate for the specific course objectives, and (c) choosing the appropriate computer-facilitated instructional strategy (CFIS).

The primary emphasis when integrating CFIS into any teaching activity should first be on the instructor's teaching pedagogy, not the technology (Florini, 1989). Traditional and constructivist teaching approaches are two of the most widely recognized teaching pedagogues and are closely associated with the use of CFIS in education (Ehrmann, 1998; Facciola, 1997; Jonassen, 1988; Jonassen, Wilson, Wang, & Grabinger., 1993; Weston & Cranton, 1986). The often quoted phrase "sage on stage to guide on the side" is an apt description of the philosophical differences in teaching principles and behaviors represented by these two theoretical approaches (King, 1993).

Teacher-centered is an accepted term for 'traditional teaching pedagogy' and is the most widely practiced teaching style in higher education settings

(Bell-Gredler, 1986; Magner, September 13, 1996; Roblyer, Edwards, & Havriluk, 1997; Grasha, 1996). Many of today's educators are products of or are trained in this teaching philosophy. The philosophical base of this theory is that knowledge exists outside the student, that reality, which this knowledge represents, is fixed and that through instruction this knowledge and reality is made known to the student. In teacher-centered teaching, educators are the experts and their role is to transmit this ordered, rational approach of understanding knowledge and reality to students. This has been described as the 'empty vessel' technique (Walz & Uematsu, 1997) or the 'banking' approach (Freire, 1993). Freire's 'banking' metaphor describes the teacher-centered process in which the educator deposits knowledge into the student's head. As the recipients of this knowledge, students develop skills in receiving, filing, and storing (collecting and cataloging) these knowledge 'deposits.' The sharing of information is usually one-way—from teacher to student—with the student acting as the recipient of information. Teacher-centered pedagogy is used frequently when the course content is prescribed and when established segments of knowledge, considered standard in the field, are to be transmitted. For example, this teaching style would most likely be used in teaching classes, such as introduction or foundation courses or research courses, in which a specific and concrete knowledge base must be transferred to the student. Traditional approaches for transmitting the educator's information are through lectures, textbooks, and assigned readings.

Student-centered teaching is the generally accepted term for describing 'constructivist teaching pedagogy.' In this approach, the teacher places the student at the center of her or his teaching activities. Teaching is anchored in multiple aspects of the teaching environment. The student's knowledge and prior 'lived' experiences (i.e., the student's social, historical, personal, and community context) are an important part of the student-centered classroom. Student-centered pedagogy is an appropriate teaching model when teaching goals are to develop or to expand student thinking skills. Instructors guide students in their efforts to understand the causes or effects of their ideas or actions. This teaching style supports the student's capabilities for critical, reflective, and creative thinking, for solving problems, and for making decisions. It is particularly effective when teaching students to become self-directing and self-initiating learners (Grasha, 1996; Weston & Cranton, 1986). Student-centered teaching activities integrate collaboration and communication. It is likely that constructivist teaching approaches are used in courses in which knowledge development and the ability to apply values and skills must be addressed, such as direct practice, policy analysis or other advanced skill development courses. Instructional methods include, but are not limited to, the use of dialogue, problem-solving activities, case studies, group work, and experiential exercises.

TEACHING GOALS

Instruction is a set of events external to the learner that are designed to support the internal process of learning (Montezumi & Wang, 1995). The goal of all instruction is to develop and strengthen thinking skills in the cognitive, affective, and psychomotor domains (Angelo & Cross, 1993; Bell-Gredler, 1986; Frayer, 1997; Grasha, 1996; Knowles, 1975; Laurillard, 1993; Merriam & Brockett, 1997; Roblyer et al., 1997; Weston & Cranton, 1986). The term 'teaching goals' describes the directing of instructional activity to the development of thinking skills and teaching domains (affective, cognitive, and psychomotor). Many educational theorists have since incorporated these domains into their teaching pedagogues and instructional design models. In addition to teaching domains, the teaching of thinking skills is a necessary component of teaching goals.

Teaching Domains

Cognitive domain. The development of cognitive or intellectual skills is the primary focus of all teaching activity. It is usually the first skill addressed by any instructional strategy. These skills are retention, recall, and transfer of facts and data. These facts are the building blocks of the body of knowledge required for professional certification or competency. As with most disciplines, much of the instructional activity for teaching the social work profession's body of knowledge is directed to this domain. Traditionally, many of the cognitive teaching goals are accomplished with lecture, assigned readings, and the expectation that the student learn the facts and details being transmitted.

Affective domain. Affective domain refers to attitudes. An attitude is an acquired internal (motivational) state that influences students' choice of personal action and is a predisposition to choose one alternative course of action over another (Wager & Gagne 1988; Weston & Cranton, 1986). Teaching goals in the affective domain are geared toward changing attitudes of awareness, interest, attention, concern, responsibility, and the ability to listen and respond in interaction with others (Barron, May 21, 1997). These values should be an integral part of the student's socialization and preparation for entry into the profession. Generally, instructional strategies related to social work values are directed to the affective teaching domain.

Psychomotor or behavior domain. This domain refers to the development of actual physical skills or activities required by individuals to complete the tasks of their profession (Barron, May 21, 1997). Psychomotor skill development for helping fields such as social work is more than kinesthetic or physiology-based skills. Skills for social work are similar to those suggested by Schon (1987) in his 'knowledge in action' and 'reflection in action' concepts (Weston & Cranton, 1986). Examples of social work specific skills include interviewing, counseling, assessment, and evaluation.

Levels of Thinking Skills

Another construct related to the development of teaching goals and that is required to develop instructional strategies is the concept of *lower-order thinking skills* and *higher-order thinking skills*. Lower-order thinking skill describes the concrete learning activities related to the acquisition, analysis, and integration of knowledge. Lower-order thinking skills include the intellectual or cognitive skills of retention, recall, and transfer. These skills are usually the first addressed by a particular instructional strategy whether teaching to the cognitive, affective or skill domains. The teaching of lower-order thinking skills is also consistent with teacher-centered instructional theory.

Higher-order thinking skills are at the other end of the thinking skill continuum. The teaching activities that involve higher-order thinking skill development moves students beyond the acquisition of knowledge (information) towards the development of critical thinking and problem-solving skills. These higher order thinking capacities involve the ability to think critically and creatively. It also includes the ability to construct knowledge from facts and data gathered through the use of lower order thinking activities (Bell-Gredler, 1986; Grasha, 1996; Roblyer et al., 1997; Merriam & Brockett, 1997; Weston & Cranton, 1986). The primary skills in which all social work students should develop expertise include critical thinking and problem solving. Students who are actively engaged in acquiring, assessing and evaluating social work's knowledge, values, and skills will use higher order thinking or critical thinking.

These domains and levels of thinking skills are consistent with the social work curriculum content goals for knowledge, values, and skills established by Council on Social Work Education (1994). These guidelines stated that baccalaureate programs "must provide a professional foundation curriculum that contains a common body of the profession's knowledge, values, and skills" (p. 98) and that masters' programs "concentration content includes knowledge, values, and skills for advanced practice . . ." (pp. 138-9). In addition, social work students must graduate with not only improved cognitive, affective and psychomotor skills, but also with critical thinking skills, problem-solving, and decision-making skills.

INSTRUCTIONAL STRATEGIES

Instruction is an essential part of all pedagogical activities and instructional strategies are designed to meet the cognitive, attitudinal or behavioral objectives of the curriculum content. Instructional strategies or methods are goal-directed activities used to deliver this instruction (Romiszowski, 1988; Weston & Cranton, 1986). Educators use numerous instructional strategies. These include but are not limited to strategies such as lecture, audio and video media, and experiential activities (group discussions, role-plays, and debates). Computer-facilitated instructional strategies (CFIS) merge traditional instructional processes and procedures with computer-based technologies and support systems. Teaching with computers assumes that the computer-based application is an instructional method or resource that is used to deliver or manage some aspect of instruction (Jonassen, 1988). CFIS describes the act of teaching using computer-based technology as a medium for delivering or participating in instruction. Computer-facilitated strategies range from CFIS use as a tool for collecting, presenting, storing, and disseminating information to teaching students to solve problems and to think critically about the information that is being presented (Heerman, 1986; Jonassen, 1988; Roblyer et al., 1997).

DESIGNING INTERNET-BASED INSTRUCTIONAL STRATEGIES

There are several challenges to designing effective CFIS using internet-based activities. The first challenge is to design activities consistent with teaching philosophy of the instructor as reflected by his or her teaching style. An educator's teaching style is his or her pattern of beliefs, knowledge, and performance or behaviors in the classroom that reflects his or her teaching pedagogy, such as teacher-centered or student-centered (Airasian, Gullick-son, Hahn, & Farland, 1995; Grasha, 1996). A teacher-centered educator will likely select different approaches for technology use in their teaching activities than their student-centered counterparts. Having a framework in which to select and design CFIS allows the educator to select teaching activities that best suit his or her teaching style while allowing the educator to compensate for teaching areas that are not addressed by personal teaching styles.

A second challenge is to structure assignments so that teaching goals specific to lower-order and higher-order thinking skills are addressed as needed. It is important that educators ensure that teaching goals reflect the knowledge, values, and skills required by the course. Educators should also structure their teaching activities to help students develop their critical thinking skills while building their knowledge acquisition efforts to move from lower-order thinking skills to higher-order thinking skills.

A final challenge, and usually one of the easiest, is to structure assignments so students develop or strengthen their technology skills in using the Internet (computer literacy and competency). This includes adding the relevant knowledge/value/skills components to course content to assist students in becoming competent technology users. In spite of the assumption that today's students are computer literate, it is quite common to find that many social work students are inexperienced or uncomfortable in using technology, in particular, using Internet-based activities.

WEBQUESTS

WebQuests is one example of an instructional design model or framework for designing effective web-based instructional activities (Dodge, 1997). WebQuests are an inquiry-oriented activity in which some or all of the information that learners interact with is Internet-based. This instructional strategy or framework allows the educator to integrate teaching style, teaching goals, and computer-based technology as medium for delivering instruction. To achieve efficiency and clarity, WebQuests should contain the following parts: (1) an introduction which sets the stage and provides background information; (2) tasks that are possible and interesting; (3) a list of information resources needed to complete the tasks; (4) a description of the process that learners should go through in accomplishing the tasks–this process should be clearly defined; (5) instructions or suggestions related organizing the information as it is acquired; (this can take the form of guiding questions or specific instructions for organizing and presenting the information) and (6) a conclusion that brings closure to the quest, reminds students of what they learned, and offers opportunities to extend or disseminate the experience (Dodge, 1997).

WebQuests should include information about resources that point to specific information and addresses on the World Wide Web. Examples of these information resources are web documents, experts available through electronic mail or videoconferencing, searchable databases on the Internet, and books or other documents available in the learner's academic setting. Providing these resources keeps the student from drifting aimlessly through cyberspace looking for relevant resources.

Dodge (1997) describes two types of WebQuests: short-term and long-term. Short-term projects are best suited for individual activity, can be completed in one or two classes, and can be integrated as part of longer term projects. Teaching goals for short-term WebQuests primarily involve the development or use of lower-order thinking skills in the cognitive and skill teaching domains. Short-term WebQuests give students the opportunity to develop skills in accessing and integrating information. Another teaching goal for the use of short term WebQuests is that learners will have grappled with a significant amount of new information and made sense of it.

Long-term projects can last several weeks to several months, and are best suited for group projects where, for example, students are assigned case studies and asked to develop projects that integrate course content and their learning activities. Teaching goals for long-term WebQuests involve the development and use of higher-order thinking skills for cognitive, affective and skill domain teaching. Problem-solving and critical thinking skills are also addressed, as long-term WebQuests allow students to expand and refine their knowledge base and strengthen their skills for finding and integrating new knowledge. At the end of these long-term activities, students should have analyzed a body of knowledge deeply, transformed it in some way, and demonstrated an understanding of the material by creating something that others can respond to, on-line or off line. Frequently, in long-term WebQuests, students are assigned roles and instructed to search for information on pre-selected topics. Final products or assignments are usually the completion of a special project that can take the form or class presentation or paper. The content of these presentations or papers can also be published on-line for dissemination to a larger audience.

For example, a group of social work students in a policy analysis class, using computer-based resources such as the Internet and computer-mediated communications applications, can function as 'legislative assistants' or as a 'special-interest committee' to search for information about social welfare services, laws and policies, or case-examples related to a specified policy. These students, using this WebQuest approach, can present this information in the form of a policy statement or a debate that is presented in class, turned in as a written product or even published on-line.

APPLICATION TO SOCIAL WORK EDUCATION

WebQuests, when designed using pedagogically sound principles, can be useful approaches to teaching the knowledge, values, and skills of the social work profession. The flexible structure of WebQuests allows educators to adapt many activities to meet the learning needs of students. First, short-term WebQuests can be designed to provide students with the opportunity to expand their knowledge base while teaching students skills in finding information on the Internet. For example, short-term WebQuest assignments can be related to gathering information and facts such as building a time-line for a specific aspect of social welfare history or participating in an on-line scavenger hunt for information about curriculum content areas. As an exercise for finding information, lower-order thinking skills are addressed. Another example of the use of short-term WebQuests to teach basic skill development is to give students' assignments to find and evaluate the content of web pages. Requiring the student to report orally or in written format further strengthens their presentation and/or writing skills. However, if the educator structures these WebQuests assignment to teach students how to ask questions, find more than one answer, compare and contrast the answers, and ask more questions, then a student's higher-order thinking skills can be strengthened.

Short-term and long-term WebQuests can be used across the curriculum in the constructivist classroom. In one example of a short-term WebQuest, students can be assigned to work groups in a direct practice course with instructions to find information about populations-at-risk or ethnic groups and to report on this information in either written or oral form. A long-term Webquest would add other steps to the assignment by having students communicate with persons or organizations that provide services or support web-based activities for these groups and to evaluate the quality and content of these Internet-based resources. If web-based research and reports are part of a larger group process, students learn teamwork and group work, both of which are valuable social work skills. The addition of a requirement for a group product such as a paper, presentation, web page, or poster session provides students with the opportunity to practice team work and group work related skills and to develop advanced thinking skills in the content area.

In addition to the benefits that pedagogically designed WebQuests have for student learning, WebQuests are particularly useful strategies for teaching students technology literacy and competency skills. They provide a consistent structure or framework by which to integrate purposefully technology as a teaching tool for social work education. In addition, well-designed WebQuests help students to use their time more efficiently on the Internet and teaches skills that will be invaluable for their future as practitioners.

WebQuests can be applied as instructional strategies across the social work curriculum. WebQuests in human behavior and social environment courses can address searching the Internet for information related to issues of diversity, stages of human development, and to individual, family or group systems. Practice classes can use WebQuests to teach students to identify resources on the web and evaluate their usefulness for providing services to clients. In addition, WebQuests that structure student' experiences with list-serves can introduce them to the skill of evaluating communications applications while increasing their skills in communicating with professionals, peers, and consumers. Policy classes will find an unlimited supply of information about legal and social problem issues for use in class assignments related to policy analysis. In research courses, students can search for information while learning evaluation skills, to find specific sites to access data for analysis, or to support the learning of statistics. In fact, many of today's educators who use computer-facilitated instructional strategies for more than presenting, storing, or accessing information actually are applying one or more parts of the WebQuest framework.

CASE EXAMPLES

Long- and short-term WebQuests were integrated as instructional strategies in two undergraduate social work courses at a large southern university. In one class, child welfare, several of the course assignments were designed as short-term WebQuests. In the second class, school violence, all course assignments were designed as components of an ongoing long-term WebQuest.

Example 1: In the first class, one of the first WebQuest activities was designed as a scavenger hunt for topics related to child welfare history. Each student was given a date, event, name, organization, and/or place and instructed to find information to report to class. Students reported in chronological order, thus building an oral time-line for child welfare history in the classroom. This assignment can be translated easily to a written or on-line product. Lower-order thinking skills and teaching goals to access knowledge and develop reporting skills were addressed by this initial assignment. Asking students to search specific web sites for information related to social work history assisted in their cognitive and skills domain development. Adding specific Internet addresses to guide the students in their initial forays as a cyberspace detective is useful. For example, the first short-term WebQuest activity is to read the NASW code of ethics (http://www.naswdc.org/toc.html).

A second short-term WebQuest assignment for the child welfare course was to complete an on-line search for organizations that provide services to professionals and/or to consumers. Student work groups were organized by fields of specialization or system levels within child welfare, such as international children's' rights organizations, adoption, welfare, or juvenile justice. Students completed individual searches and summarized this information using an outline provided by the instructor.

Example 2: Using a team approach is an integral part of most long-term WebQuests and one that this instructor employs regularly in her classes. Students in the child welfare course were assigned to work groups and each student was asked to assume the role of a child welfare team composed of educators, parents, judicial, and legal representatives. Students in the child welfare class were instructed to conduct their WebQuests activities from the perspective of their assumed role. In the school violence course, all students were 'informed' that they had been selected to take part in a special commission formed by the President of United States. The goal of this commission was to study, evaluate, and report on the problem of violence in the nation's public schools. Students were assigned to small work groups (i.e., subcommittees) during the class, which were supported by this 'Commission on School Violence.' Each of these sub-committees in the school violence course identified a school violence case to study throughout the course. The instructor functioned as the facilitator for the commission and provided research and reporting support for each subcommittee.

For each of these group-based activities, students in both courses were given a set of Internet-based resources with related instructions to explore weekly or bi-weekly as their starting point. These resources were supplemented with a series of questions to guide their explorations. These questions ranged from fact finding (lower-order thinking) to critical thinking (higher-order). Topics for each weekly or bi-weekly group activities were specific to the topics being covered in each unit, such as diversity, legal issues, child abuse and neglect, or community and educational systems. For these courses, follow-up WebQuests activities included providing the addresses for (1) an on-line newspaper (http://www.pathfinder.com) with directions for using search techniques to find case study information about violence in schools and (2) large web cites <http://www.census.gov/>Census; <http://www.abacom.com/sociologylinks.html> Allyn & Bacon; < http://www.mincava.org/> MINCAVA. Specific instructions were to look for demographic information about the cities in which the assigned school violence case was located (Census web page), to find information about individuals, families, and diversity issues that affect children and communities (Allyn and Bacon web page), and to find information about potential solutions for violence (MINCAVA web page). The final product for both courses was a group presentation or paper using information gathered throughout the course from all the assignments. The instructor was careful when designing the teaching strategy to assure that the content and results would be useful for integrating into student presentations.

A very important teaching goal in these courses was to develop students' research and thinking skills by learning to ask questions, to think critically about the information, and to evaluate the usefulness of the available information. Each WebQuest activity included a series of questions related to the development of these skills. For example, questions were asked for each WebQuest activity: (1) What questions did you have about this subject/topic before you started this assignment? (2) What new questions did you have when you finished this assignment? (3) What biases, if any, did you find in these web pages content?

A final teaching goal for these WebQuests was to increase students' technology use skills. This was addressed through a range of activities that included providing information about specific web pages, giving detailed instructions to access specific web pages as well as providing general instructions to find other resources within large web sites.

DISCUSSION

There are several limitations to be considered when developing Web-Quests. The first is that of student access to technology. Many students do not have easy access to technology to complete the assignments. One way to compensate for this limitation is to structure the WebQuests as an Information quest. Students are instructed to use other legitimate and more traditional resources to complete the required activities. It is often helpful to have at least one student who uses the more traditional resources. This provides a rich opportunity to discuss the differences in quality, teach skills in comparison, and expand everyone's awareness of the variety of information resources available to students.

The final step, a conclusion, does not address adequately the need to have students evaluate their own experiences in using this approach to learning. It is important to add an evaluative component that encourages student to assess their own learning responses as well as give the instructor comments about what was most useful and what was least useful about the WebQuests assignments. This instructor supplements her WebQuests and other teaching activities with critical thinking inventories or classroom environment scales to assess student change in these areas.

The description provided for WebQuests do not clearly describe the use of multiple WebQuests over the course of the semester. Yet, the addition of several WebQuests, each of which are not related, can add to students' confusion, anxiety and frustration as they attempt to shift their attention from one WebQuest activity to another. It is possible to develop a series of WebQuests in which the information gathered from each is useful in completing the final assignments. It is also beneficial to develop WebQuests that teach skills in a sequential and logical manner such as when research and technology skills are addressed. Information gathered while completing these activities should be relevant to course outcomes and should be useful in completing the class final product. This will significantly increase student satisfaction with their learning experiences in using WebQuests.

CONCLUSION

The importance of computer-based technology in the curriculum has been discussed in the social work technology-based literature for more than 20 years. Educators, many of whom are considered technology leaders in social work education, have written numerous articles and books to inform and convince other educators to use computer-facilitated instruction in social work education. Historically, these authors recommended the integration of computer-facilitated instruction in the curriculum as either a separate course on technology use and, more recently, as an integrated component across multiple curriculum areas (Caputo & Cnaan, 1990; Ezell, Nurius, & Balassone, 1991; LaMendola, 1987; Nurius & Nicoll, 1989; Reck, 1996; Smith, 1984). However, the use of a model for designing social work technology-based instructional strategies can assist educators with the infusion of technology across the curriculum. Purposeful integration of technology across the curriculum better prepares students to work in a technology-enhanced work environment. Using a pedagogically sound instructional strategy model increases the profession's capacity to evaluate the effectiveness of technology use as a teaching tool. WebQuests can provide a clear and pedagogically-sound framework for developing computer-facilitated instructional strategies across the curriculum.

REFERENCES

Angelo, T.A., & Cross, K.P. (1993). *Classroom assessment techniques: A handbook for college teachers*. San Francisco: Jossey-Bass.

Airasian, P., Gullickson, A., Hahn, L., & Farland, D. (1995). *Teacher self-evaluation: The literature in perspective*. Kalamazoo, MI: Center for Research on Educational Accountability and Teacher Evaluation: The Evaluation Center.

Barron, D. (May 27, 1997). *School library media activities monthly: Keeping current*. <http://www.LibSci.sc.edu/dan/classes/jungle/psychart.htm>

Bell-Gredler, M.E. (1986). *Learning and instruction: Theory into practice*. New York: Macmillan.

BlueWeb'n (1998) online at <http://www.kn.pacbell.com/wired/bluewebn>

Caputo, R.K., & Cnaan, R.A. (1990). Information technology availability in schools of social work. *Journal of Social Work Education, 26 (2)*, 187-198.

Council of Social Work Education. (1994). *Handbook of accreditation standards and procedures* (4th Edition). Alexandria, Virginia: Commission on Social Work Accreditation.

Dodge, B. (1997) San Diego State University. <http://edweb.sdsu.edu/courses/edtec596/about_webquests.html>

Ehrmann, S.C. (February 13, 1998). The flashlight project: Spotting an elephant in the dark. <http://www.aahe.org/etchnology/elephant.htm>

Ezell, M., Nurius, P.S., & Balassone, M.L. (1991). Preparing computer literate social workers: An integrative approach. *Journal of Teaching in Social Work, 5(1)*, 81-99.

Facciola, P.C. (1997, September). Building an effective computer learning environment in the dynamic learning classroom. *Syllabus, 11(5)*, 12-14.

Finn, J. (1995). Use of electronic mail to promote computer literacy in social work undergraduates. *Journal of Teaching in Social Work, 12(1/2)*, 73-83.

Florini, B.M. (Ed.). (1989). *Teaching styles and technology*. (Vol. 43). San Francisco: Jossey-Bass.

Frayer, D. (1997, April). *Creating a new world of learning possibilities through instructional technology: Part one*. Paper presented at the American Association of Higher Education Teaching Learning Technology Roundtable Information Technology Conference, Fitchburg, MA.

Freire, P. (1993). *Pedagogy of the oppressed* (Myra Bergman Ramos, Trans.). (20th Anniversary Edition, Revised). New York: Continuum.

Galambos, C., & Neal, C.E. (in press). Macro practice and policy in cyberspace: Teaching with computer simulation and the internet at the baccalaureate level.

Grasha, A.F. (1996). *Teaching with style: A practical guide to enhancing learning by understanding teaching and learning styles.* Pittsburgh, PA: Alliance.

Heerman, B. (1986). Strategies for adult computer learning. In B. Heermann (Ed.), *Personal computers and the adult learner* (Vol. 29). San Francisco: Jossey-Bass. 5-15.

Holden, G., Rosenberg, G., & Weissman, A. (1995). Gopher accessible resources related to research on social work practice. *Research on Social Work Practice, 5 (2)*, 235-245.

Holden, G., Rosenberg, G., & Weissman, A. (1996). World wide web accessible resources related to research on social work practice. *Research in Social Work Practice, 6(2)*, 236-262.

Jonassen, D.H. (Ed.). (1988). *Instructional designs for microcomputer courseware.* Hillsdale, New Jersey: Lawrence Erlbaum Associates.

Jonassen, D.H., Wilson, B.G., Wang, S., & Grabinger, R.S. (1993). Constructivist uses of expert systems to support learning. *Journal of Computer-Based Instruction 20(3)*, 86-94.

Karger, H.J., & Stoez, D. (1998). *The Internet and social welfare policy. A supplement to American social welfare policy, a pluralist approach.* New York: Longman.

King, A. (1993). From stage on stage to guide on side. *College Teaching, 41(1)*, 30-35.

Knowles, M.S. (1975). *Self-directed learning: A guide for learners and teachers.* Chicago: Association Press, Follett.

LaMendola, W. (1987). Teaching information technology to social workers. *Journal of Teaching in Social Work, 1(1)*, 53-69.

Laurillard, D. (1993). *Rethinking university teaching: A framework for the effective use of educational technology.* London: Routledge.

Magner, D.K. (September 13, 1996,). Faculty survey highlights: Drift from western canon. *The Chronicle of Higher Education*, p. A12.

Marson, S.M. (1997). A selective history of Internet technology and social work. *Computers in Human Services, 14(2)*, 35-49.

Merriam, S.B., & Brockett, R.G. (1997). *The profession and practice of adult education.* San Francisco: Jossey-Bass

Miller-Cribbs, J.E., & Chadiha, L.A. (1998). Integrating the Internet in a human diversity course.

Montazemi, A.R., & Wang, F. (1995). An empirical investigation of CBI in support of mastery learning. *Journal of Educational Computing Research, 13 (2)*, 185-205.

Nurius, P.S., & Nicoll, A.E. (1989). Computer literacy preparation: Conundrums and opportunities for the social work educator. *Journal of Teaching in Social Work, 3(2)*, 65-81.

Reck, E.T. (1996). *Modes of professional education II: The electronic social work curriculum in the twenty-first century.* In E.T. Reck (Ed.) (Vol. XX). New Orleans: Tulane University School of Social Work. 1-6; 157-162.

Roblyer, M.D., Edwards, J., & Havriluk, M.A. (1997). *Integrating educational technology into teaching*. Upper Saddle River, New Jersey: Merrill.

Romiszowski, A.J. (1988). *The selection and use of instructional media*. (Second ed.). Kogan Page, London: Nichols Publishing (New York).

Schon, D. (1987). *Educating the reflective practitioner*. San Francisco:Jossey-Bass.

Smith, N.J. (1984). Teaching social work student about computers: Outline of a course. *Journal of Social Work Education, 20 (2)*, 65-70.

Stocks, J.T., & Freddolino, P. (in press). Evaluation of a world wide web-based graduate school of social work research methods course. *Computers in Human Services, 15(2/3)*, 51-69.

Taylor, R. (Ed.) (1980). *The Computer in the school: Tutor, tool, tutee*. New York: Teachers College Press, Teachers College, Columbia University.

Wager, W., & Gagne, R.M. (Eds.) (1988). *Designing computer-aided instruction*. Hillsdale, New Jersey: Lawrence Erlbaum Associates.

Walz, T., & Uematsu, M. (1997). Creativity in social work practice: A pedagogy. *Journal of Teaching in Social Work, 15(1/2)*, 17-31.

Weston, C., & Cranton, P.A. (1986). Selecting instructional strategies. *Journal of Higher Education, 57(3)*, 259-288.

Yaffe, J. (1998). *Quick guide to the Internet for social work*. Boston: Allyn & Bacon.

Perspectives from Consumers (Students) in a Distance Education Program

Jo Ann R. Coe
John Gandy

SUMMARY. This paper presents a literature review of social work programs' distance education evaluation studies with an emphasis on the strengths distance education programs offer to students relative to standard programs. The authors discuss quality issues in relation to teaching and learning in distance education programs with a panel of distance learners who will discuss their experiences. *[Article copies available for a fee from The Haworth Document Delivery Service: 1-800-342-9678. E-mail address: getinfo@haworthpressinc.com <Website: http://www.haworthpressinc.com>]*

KEYWORDS. Distance education, student's perceptions of distance teaching

Recent technological advances have had a significant impact on social work education. These developments have enhanced the potential for social work educators to provide what is know as "distance education" (Raymond

Jo Ann R. Coe, PhD, is Assistant Professor and Technology Coordinator, University of South Carolina, College of Social Work.

John Gandy, PhD, is Associate Dean, and Director of the Distance Learning Program, University of South Carolina, College of Social Work.

Address correspondence to either author at: USC College of Social Work, Columbia, SC 29208 (E-mail: jocoe@sc.edu, or johng@cosw.cosw.sc.edu).

[Haworth co-indexing entry note]: "Perspectives from Consumer (Students) in a Distance Education Program." Coe, Jo Ann R., and John Gandy. Co-published simultaneously in *Journal of Technology in Human Services* (The Haworth Press, Inc.) Vol. 16, No. 2/3, 1999, pp. 161-174; and: *Computers and Information Technology in Social Work: Education, Training, and Practice* (ed: Jo Ann R. Coe, and Goutham M. Menon) The Haworth Press, Inc., 1999, pp. 161-174. Single or multiple copies of this article are available for a fee from The Haworth Document Delivery Service [1-800-342-9678, 9:00 a.m. - 5:00 p.m. (EST). E-mail address: getinfo@haworthpressinc.com].

and Pike, 1997). "Distance education" is used to describe those formal teacher-learner arrangements in which the teacher and learner are geographically separated most or all of the time, and the communication between them is through a technology medium such as audiocassette, telephone, radio, television, computers, interactive videodisc and print. Schools of social work have increasingly used distance learning to deliver undergraduate, graduate and continuing education credit. In October 1995, the Council on Social Work Education (CSWE) conducted a survey to determine the usage of distance education technology among social work programs. Of a total of 126 programs responding, 22 (17%) indicated that they offer distance education courses and 43% indicated a moderate to high probability of offering distance education courses (Lockhart and Wilson, 1997).

As distance education programs have continued to grow, the Council on Social Work Education (CSWE) has been faced with accreditation and evaluation issues regarding these programs. Historically, social work education has utilized a deficit model in which all new innovative and experimental programs were compared to traditional full-time course of study. In addition to distance education programs, part-time and international efforts were evaluated from the perspective that the full-time course of study is the ideal and most effective way of delivering social work education. Yet no conclusive evidence exists that the full-time model is the most effective. While this seems a logical place to start for evaluating new social work programs, there is also logic to indicate that these new programs may offer something that the full-time model does not and may be the reason for their development in the first place. By utilizing a deficit approach that focuses on comparability and effectiveness to a traditional full-time model, there is less emphasis on the particular strengths that these programs may offer to consumers (students) who benefit from the development of these programs.

Despite this dilemma, CSWE has developed criteria for approving distance education programs as experimental and/or alternative programs. A key factor in obtaining approval from CSWE has been social work programs designing evaluation components that address the comparability and effectiveness of the program relative to the standard program. As a result, a number of evaluative studies have been completed by social work programs that compare distance learners with traditional on-campus learners (Coe & Elliott, 1997; Forster & Rehner, 1998; Freddolino, 1996, 1997a, 1997b; Haga & Heitkamp, 1995; Kalke, Rooney & Macy, 1998; Patchner, Wise & Petracchi, 1998; Petracchi & Morgenbesser, 1995; Raymond, 1996; Thyer, Artelt, Markward & Dozier, 1998; Thyer, Polk & Gaudin, 1997; Weinbach, 1985; Weinbach, Gandy & Tartaglia, 1984). While these studies are important to the development and advancement of distance education programs in social work education, the authors suggest that studies are also needed that address the strengths these distance education programs offer that may not be relative to the standard program. It is clear that other types of alternative and experimental programs such as part-time and international programs have been demonstrated as comparable and as acceptable to the standard program. However, there are some particular strengths that these programs offer that are not comparable to the criteria set up for traditional programs. Kalke, Macy, and Rooney (1998) raise the issue that the evaluative standard of alternative programs being comparable has led them from seeing some of the particular strengths of distance education.

Thus, the authors suggest that a new model is needed for approving experimental and/or alternative programs. In viewing these programs from a strengths perspective (Gutierrez, Parsons & Cox, 1998; Saleeby, 1992) that includes consumers (students) highlights areas traditionally ignored by a deficit approach. This model would continue to focus on the comparability and effectiveness of programs relative to the standard program but also include the particular strengths that experimental and/or alternative programs offer that are not relative to the standard program. Also, important to this model are the perspectives of those that participate and receive the programs such as students. Focusing on distance education program evaluations, the authors decided to conduct a literature review of all the social work distance education evaluation studies to date and determine if there are particular strengths that these programs offer to students that are not relative to the standard program. All of the studies to date have utilized the deficit model as mandated by the Council on Social Work Education, through its Curriculum Evaluation Standards 6 and 7. This requires that alternative programs "document the equal quality of its alternative programs relative to its standard program" (Commission on Accreditation, 1994). The purpose of this study was threefold: (1) to conduct a literature review of distance education evaluation studies to date and identify those areas that may be considered strengths of distance education programs that are not relative to standard programs, (2) interview a panel of consumers (students) on the areas identified as strengths in the literature review and compare their feedback with the evaluation studies' findings, and (3) discuss a model for future distance education evaluation studies.

LITERATURE REVIEW

An exhaustive systematic review of the distance learning research and evaluation studies in social work education was completed to identify peer-reviewed studies. Since distance learning is an exploratory area of research and just beginning to emerge in the social work literature, conference papers and internal evaluations of distance education programs that the authors had copies of were also reviewed. The authors did note other conference presentations in the Council on Social Work Education Annual Program Meeting Distance Education Symposium that were program evaluations but were not able to obtain copies of the papers presented and thus could not be reviewed for this study. The search identified a pool of 13 relevant articles and reports (see Table 1). Articles and reports were selected if they: (1) were empirical studies rather than conceptual, theoretical or programmatic reports, (2) discussed student and/or faculty perceptions, (3) instruction occurred when the student and teacher were at a distance at least fifty percent of the time, and (4) utilized television as the primary learning media. The authors identified a number of studies utilizing the computer and the Internet as the learning media and recognize the impact this medium will have on distance education programs in the future. However, since this area is just beginning to emerge and most distance education programs being approved by CSWE utilized television, these studies were omitted. Table 1 categorizes the studies selected by author and year, type program, distance learning format, sample size and focus of evaluation.

LITERATURE REVIEW FINDINGS

The literature review identified three main areas that were considered strengths of distance education programs not highlighted utilizing a deficit model. These included: (1) access to education, (2) socialization and acculturation of students, and (3) acquisition of technology skills. These three areas are discussed in terms of the studies reviewed.

ACCESS TO EDUCATION

Demographics of Students

Nine of the studies reviewed discussed student demographics. However, it should be noted that many of the studies focus on the same social work program but at different times. Generally, the studies indicate similar demographic characteristics of students participating in distance learning programs despite different types of programs. Also, most of the studies indicated that the distance learners were a distinctly different population when compared with the on-campus learners. Most of the studies indicated that the distance learners were older and had more social work experience than on-campus learners. They also tended to work full-time in social service agencies while they took courses in distance education programs and had longer travel times

TABLE 1. Studies Selected for Literature Review

AUTHOR(S) YEAR	TYPE PROGRAM	DISTANCE LEARNING FORMAT	SAMPLE SIZE	FOCUS
Referred Journal Articles				
Forster & Rehner (1998)	University of Southern Mississippi MSW Program	Two-Way Interactive Television	18 MSW Students	Student and Faculty Perceptions
Thyer, Artelt, Markward & Dozier (1998)	University of Georgia 2 Practice Courses	Two-Way Interactive Television	57 MSW Students	Student Perceptions
Thyer, Polk & Gaudin (1997)	University of Georgia MSW Practice Course	Two-Way Interactive Television	17 MSW Students	Student Demographics and Attitudes
Freddolino (1997a, 1996)	Michigan State University MSW Program	Two-Way Interactive Television	122 MSW Students	Student and Faculty Perceptions
Raymond (1996)	University of South Carolina MSW Foundation Courses	One-Way Closed-Circuit Interactive Television	Not Stated	Student and Faculty Perceptions
Rooney & Bibus (1995)	University of Minnesota School of Social Work Continuing Education Course	Two-Way Interactive Television	129 Participants 113 Distance Learners 16 In-Person Learners 361 In-Person Previous Learners	Student Perceptions
Weinbach, Gandy & Tartaglia (1984)	University of South Carolina MSW Foundation Courses	One-Way Closed Circuit Interactive Television	140 MSW Students 7 Faculty	Student and Faculty Perceptions

to classes than on-campus students (Coe & Elliott, 1997; Haga & Heitkamp, 1995; Forster & Rehner, 1998; Freddolino, 1996, 1997b; Raymond, 1996; Weinbach, 1985; Weinbach, Gandy & Tartaglia, 1984). The only exception to these findings are Thyer et al. (1997), Thyer et al. (1998) and Patchner, Wise and Petracchi (1998) who found no significant differences in the mean ages of students in both groups and social work or volunteer experience. However, this study only focuses on courses and not an entire program that may indicate differences when distance education is set up as a program or just for course delivery.

These findings indicate that distance education programs meet the needs of a different type of student than those enrolled in a traditional full-time program. This would be expected, as many of these students cannot attend a regular on-campus program due to their work and family responsibilities as well as their community ties. The findings also indicate that distance is a critical factor and that many distance learners must travel from rural areas to enroll in classes and/or continuing education. Rooney and Bibus (1995) found in their study which used distance learning for continuing education that comments from participants indicated appreciation for the convenience of less expense and travel. Many of the studies reviewed indicated student's tremendous appreciation for the distance education social work program and statements indicating that students would not have been able to pursue their degree otherwise. Weinbach (1985) in an evaluation of their distance education program from 1983-85 indicates in his evaluation report: "It (the distance education program) is clearly serving a group of potential social work students who might otherwise be unable to avail themselves of graduate education. It also provides an opportunity for some persons to acquire the MSW degree who would not be able to do so if all courses were required to be taken in the traditional classroom setting" (p. 8). From student comments in their program, they found that at least 90% of the distance learning students would not enroll in a graduate level social work course if the distance learning program were discontinued.

Rationale for Developing Distance Education Programs

Most of the studies reviewed also discussed the rationale for setting up a distance education program. Some of the studies reviewed indicated reasons such as requests from prospective students and social service agencies in rural areas that were underserved and fulfilling the school's land grant mission to provide education to all areas of the state (Forster & Rehner, 1998; Freddolino, 1997b, 1996; Kalke, Rooney, & Macy, 1998). Geographical factors such as size of state (i.e., Texas) and cold weather (i.e., North Dakota) that make commuting impossible for students are also reasons cited for developing distance education programs (Coe & Elliott, 1997; Haga & Heitkamp, 1995).

Discussion of Literature Review Findings

These findings indicate that distance education is a means to provide social work education and training to individuals in remote areas so that they do not have to relocate in order to participate. Distance education programs also address the needs of adult learners who are already employed and have family responsibilities. One of the strengths of distance education programs is that it allows Schools of Social Work to accomplish their mission of increasing access to education as a means of promoting social change and justice for all people in all areas. Kalke, Rooney, and Macy (1998) indicate in their evaluation findings that their distance learning graduates are serving underserved populations around the state by remaining in their distance locations to work and serve those communities

SOCIALIZATION AND ACCULTURATION OF STUDENTS

Seven of the studies reviewed discussed socialization of students (Coe & Elliott, 1997; Freddolino, 1996, 1997a, 1997b; Kalke, Rooney & Macy, 1998; Weinbach, 1985; Weinbach, Gandy & Tartaglia, 1985). Again, many of the studies focus on the same social work programs and on the socialization experiences of distance learners compared with on-campus learners. An important factor in the evaluation studies reviewed is whether the distance learning program met the Council on Social Work Education (CSWE) standards in providing students with professional knowledge as well as offering students an opportunity to acculturate into the profession. Generally, the studies indicated that distance learners reported as much socialization and acculturation with the instructor and classmates as on-campus learners. In some evaluation studies reviewed, distance learners reported more interaction and socialization than on-campus learners did. Coe and Elliott (1997) found that the distance learners tended to interact more with other classmates than on-campus learners do. Many of the distance learners worked together and were able to complete assignments together. Also, the distance learning program was a joint cooperation with the child welfare agency that encouraged interaction and socialization while attending school and working full-time. Freddolino (1996, 1997a, 1997b) has done the most work in this area. Utilizing the ACES (Adult Classroom Environment Scale), he found that distance learners rated one dimension, affiliation, higher than on-campus learners did. However, most of the distance learners in this study also worked together.

Although there is some criticism about the fact that many distance learning programs allow students to move through the program as a group, there have been some strengths identified with this format. Kalke, Rooney, and Macy (1998) found that students in their distance learning program would form a cohort and would interact with one another around themes and information presented in their courses as well as in their professional roles in work settings. Many of the students in field seminars would interact with other students from other agencies that helped to enhance their professional inter-action and socialization. Their findings also indicate that distance learners develop special rapport and cohesiveness not often found in the on-campus groups. Weinbach (1985) concluded that the research on their program sug-gests that distance learners were not deficient in professional socialization. He found that because the distance learners tended to be older and have considerably more practice experience than on-campus learners do, these factors contributed to their high levels of socialization. Weinbach, Gandy, and Tartaglia (1985) also found that the distance learning program was hav-ing a positive effect on professionalization of existing social work manpower within the state. Freddolino (1997b) indicated other findings in his evaluation studies. Distance learners, who had higher levels of practice experience, reported that the largest benefit they received from the distance learning program was the increased knowledge from field instruction and the applica-tion of theory. Distance learners also reported increased knowledge of social work ethics, roles and theory as well as professional growth and develop-ment. Distance learners in many of the studies also cited how they enjoyed the opportunity to interact with other social workers throughout the state through their television courses. Many students cited networking as one of the most important benefits they received from participating in a distance education program. These studies also indicated that on-campus students liked being exposed to the perspectives of older and more experienced stu-dents which is an added benefit to those programs who combine on campus learners with distance learners (Coe & Elliott, 1997; Freddolino, 1997b).

Discussion of Literature Review Findings

The studies reviewed indicates that distance education is a means to pro-vide unique opportunities for networking and interaction that students may have not gotten otherwise. One of the strengths of distance education pro-grams is that it allows Schools of Social Work to accomplish their mission of promoting professionalization amongst those already employed in social ser-vice agencies which in turn impacts the delivery of services to promote social change and justice in all communities.

ACQUISITION OF TECHNOLOGY SKILLS

Most of the studies discussed the issue that distance teaching requires additional technology skills than those required in traditional face-to-face classroom instruction for both faculty and students. Raymond (1996) re-ported that most faculty teaching in distance education had to make greater use of audio-visual materials. For example, the use of graphics, promoting interaction, managing the equipment, the use of questioning techniques and learning assessment as well as on-camera presentation are skills faculty must utilize in teaching a distance learning course. In order to promote more interaction and organization to distance education courses, some studies reported the use of presentation packages such as *PowerPoint* to prepare computer-generated graphics and outlines and/or overhead and ELMO projectors to convey the lecture material more succinctly (Freddolino, 1997b; Kalke, Rooney & Macy, 1998). Other studies discussed how faculty and students enjoyed the opportunity to experience an electronic classroom or technology environment that are usually equipped with projectors, computers, Internet access, telephones, televisions and VCR. In one study, instructors commented on how they wished all classrooms were equipped in this way (Forster & Rehner, 1998; Freddolino, 1997b).

This increased use of technology by faculty impacts students in the classroom as they become exposed to technology skills they may not receive in a traditional classroom where they are not needed as much to enhance teaching. Most program evaluations reviewed discussed the use of e-mail accounts for all students, toll-free telephone numbers and the use of listservs and bulletin boards to enhance communication between faculty and students. Studies indicate that as faculty increase their involvement with distance education technology, attitudes about the experience become more positive which affects their comfort level in teaching students to use the technology (Dillon, 1989; Mani, 1988). Thus, students become more exposed to using these skills in the classroom and practice. Kalke, Rooney and Macy (1998) have noted that their distance education students are more comfortable with technology and use it more after graduation than students receiving in-person instruction. As distance education programs expand to include the use of the computer and Internet, these skills should only continue to be enhanced by both faculty and students participating in these type of programs.

Socialization

The studies reviewed indicates that distance education is a means to provide unique opportunities for networking and interaction that students may have not gotten otherwise. One of the strengths of distance education programs is that it allows Schools of Social Work to accomplish their mission of promoting professionalization amongst those already employed in social service agencies which in turn impacts the delivery of services to promote social change and justice in all communities.

Discussion of Literature Review Findings

The studies reviewed indicate that students and faculty participating in distance education programs are being exposed to technology skills that are not always available in the traditional classroom. The use of electronic classrooms lend themselves to faculty and students being able to use a wide array of technology to help promote interaction and organization to distance learning courses. It seems that the unique challenges of not being face-to-face force students and faculty to rely on electronic medium which in turn enhances their skills and development for education as well as practice in the field. This will only continue to expand as technology rapidly increases to include the delivery of education via the computer and Internet and represents a unique strength of distance education programs.

It is clear from a review of distance education evaluation studies that there are several strengths noted that these programs offer in terms of areas discussed above. These are important factors to consider in evaluating a distance education program and are often ignored when utilizing a model that only looks at comparability to a standard program.

FINDINGS FROM A PANEL OF STUDENTS

The literature review was conducted in order to identify strengths of social work distance education programs. As part of the presentation, a panel of three students who have participated in distance education courses were interviewed to obtain qualitative data regarding their perspectives. The purpose of the panel was to add their comments and remarks under each of the three areas identified to compare findings with the studies reviewed. The perspectives of students was obtained as part of this study to further the model suggested by the authors for evaluating distance education programs.

Demographics of Panel and Access to Education

The three students included on the panel fit the typical characteristics of distance education students discussed in the literature. All of them were older and already employed in social work agencies. Two of the panel members stated that they would not be able to obtain their MSW without the distance education program as it was impossible for them to move their family to where the university was located. Another student who attended the on-site distance education sessions in the evening stated that her work schedule made it impossible to attend traditional classes offered during the daytime.

Socialization and Acculturation of Students

None of the students on the panel indicated that they had met prior to taking a distance education course. Although all of them were located in different sites, they indicated that they felt they knew each other through the course. One of the panel members indicated that they had interacted with others in the class through professional meetings and groups offered state-wide. Another panel member indicated that they developed a contact in the same agency he was employed in a different part of the state. The three students stated that they gained different ideas about practice in other geographical areas of the state from the perspectives of others in their distance education courses. All of the panel members indicated that they developed more professionally through the distance education courses by being exposed to other perspectives from students in all of the sites.

Acquisition of Technology Skills

All of the panel members indicated that they felt they gained skills in the use of technology skills such as e-mail, research on the Internet and the use of presentation software. One of the panel members discussed using *Power-Point* for a presentation in the class and now uses it regularly in his work. All of the panel members agreed that they were "forced" to rely on technology such as e-mail and the Internet in order to communicate with the instructors and others in the class. The panel members stated that the level of use depended on how much the faculty utilized it in course assignments and in communicating with students. The panel members indicated that they felt they were more exposed to technology in their distance education course than when they took a traditional face-to-face course.

Overall, the three panel members supported the information found in the literature review findings. Although this was only three student's perspectives, it was helpful to get the student feedback on their experiences regarding these three areas.

FUTURE DISTANCE EDUCATION EVALUATION RESEARCH

It is clear from the literature review findings that distance learning in social work education is growing. The findings also indicate that these distance learning programs are comparable and as effective as traditional on-campus programs. With this effectiveness demonstrated, distance education evaluation research needs to begin to focus on the experiences of students, faculty and administrators. Utilizing the strengths perspective, researchers need to focus their research on such questions as:

• What types of experiences do distance education students and faculty have that are different from traditional on-campus students?

- How can these positive and negative experiences be considered utilizing a strengths perspective?
- How should administrators view distance education programs within the context of their traditional on-campus program?

An emphasis on these type of questions for distance education research will further the adoption and development of these programs in education. It will help strengthen and enhance the quality of these programs by focusing on ways to improve distance education programs rather than just comparing them to a traditional model. This in turn may help to strengthen traditional programs by combining the strengths of both models.

CONCLUSION

It is clear from this literature review of that there are three strength areas that can be identified that are unique to distance education programs. Although this is a beginning attempt to identify those areas, the findings do indicate a need to reevaluate how experimental and alternative programs are evaluated. The findings suggest that the deficit model that is currently in use does not highlight the particular strengths that a program may offer when just compared to a standard program. This literature review highlighted only three areas in the area of distance education programs. One of the limitations of this study is that all studies of distance education programs were not available for review. Another limitation is that the review only focused on perceptions of students. Further study would probably identify strengths for faculty, administrators and institutions that also need to be highlighted. The authors hope that this initial review of the literature highlights the need for a strengths perspective to be included when evaluating new and experimental programs. It is clear that distance education programs are meeting a need that is different from a traditional, standard program and their unique strengths need to be emphasized.

REFERENCES

Coe, J. & Elliott, D. (1997). *An evaluation of teaching direct practice in distance education programs for rural settings.* Paper presented at the Annual Program Meeting of the Council on Social Work Education, Chicago, IL. Commission on Accreditation (1994). *Handbook of Accreditation Standards and Procedures* (4th ed.), Alexandria, VA: Council on Social Work Education.

Dillon, C. (1989). Faculty rewards and instructional telecommunications: A view from the telecourse facility. *American Journal of Distance Education,* 3 (2): 35-43.

Forster, M. & Rehner, T. (1998). Part-time MSW distance education: A program evaluation. *Computers in Human Services*, 15(2/3): 9.

Freddolino, P.P. (1996). Maintaining quality in graduate social work programs delivered to distant sites using electronic instruction technology. In E.T. Reck (Ed.). *Modes of Professional Education II: The Electronic Social Work Curriculum in the Twenty-First Century. Tulane Studies in Social Welfare*, 20. New Orleans, LA: Tulane University.

Freddolino, P.P. (1997a). The importance of relationships for a quality learning environment in interactive TV classrooms. *Journal for Education for Business*, 71 (4): 205-208.

Freddolino, P.P. (1997b). *Building on experience: Lessons from a distance education MSW program.* Paper presented at the Information Technologies for Social Work Education: Using to Teach-Teaching to Use, Charleston, SC.

Gutierrez, L.M., Parsons, R.J. & Cox, E.O. (1998). *Empowerment in Social Work Practice: A Sourcebook.* Pacific Grove, CA: Brooks-Cole.

Haga, M. & Heitkamp, T.L. (1995). *Evaluation results of an innovative social work distance education program.* Paper presented at the Annual program Meeting of the Council on Social Work Education, San Diego, CA.

Kalke, N.L., Rooney, R. & Macy, J. (1998). *Providing effective education in distance education.* Paper presented at the Annual Program Meeting of the Council on Social Work Education, Orlando, FL.

Lockhart, L. & Wilson, S. (1997). Distance education: a summary of survey results. *Social Work Education Reporter*, 45 (2): 5.

Mani, G. (1988). Attitudes of external faculty towards distance education. In D. Stewart and Daniel, J. (Editors), *Developing Distance Education* (pp. 197-300), Oslo: International Council for Distance Education.

Patchner, M.A., Wise, S. & Petracchi, H. (1998). *Teaching research: an evaluation of ITV and face-to-face instruction.* Paper presented at the Annual Program Meeting of the Council on Social Work Education, Orlando, FL.

Petracchi, H.E. & Morgenbesser, M. (1995). The use of video and one-way broadcast technology to deliver continuing social work education: A comparative assessment of student learning. *Journal of Continuing Social Work Education*, 6 (3): 18-22.

Raymond, F.B. (1996). Delivering the MSW curriculum to non-traditional students through interactive television. In E.T. Reck (Ed). *Modes of Professional Education II: The Electronic Social Work Curriculum in the Twenty-First Century. Tulane Studies in Social Welfare*, 20. New Orleans, LA: Tulane University.

Raymond, F.B. & Pike, C.K. (1997). Electronic technologies for social work education. Copy of paper submitted for inclusion in the *Supplement to the Encyclopedia of Social Work*, 19th ed.

Saleeby, D. (1992). *The Strengths Perspective in Social Work Practice.* New York: Longman.

Thyer, B.A., Artelt, T., Markward, M.K. & Dozier, C.D. (1998). Evaluating distance learning in social work education: A replication study. *Journal of Social Work Education*, 34 (2): 291-295.

Thyer, B.A., Polk, G. & Gaudin, J.G. (1997). Distance learning in social work education: a preliminary evaluation. *Journal of Social Work Education*, 33 (2): 363-367.

Weinbach, R.W. (1985). *Evaluation of the Interactive Closed Circuit Television (ICCT) Method.* Columbia, SC: University of South Carolina, College of Social Work.

Weinbach, R.W., Gandy, J. & Tartaglia, L. (1984). Addressing the needs of the part-time student through interactive television: An evaluation. *Arete*, 9: 12-29.

Reframing from Site Bias to Site Identity: Pedagogic Issues in Delivering Social Work Courses via Interactive Television

Ronald H. Rooney
Elena Izaksonas
Jane A. Macy

SUMMARY. Tension between instructors and students at distance sites has been called site bias. Additional sources of site tension sometimes occurs between cohorts at different sites and within the originating site cohort. This paper describes how site tension can be reframed as site identity and utilized to promote goals of teaching about social justice and diversity. *[Article copies available for a fee from The Haworth Document Delivery Service: 1-800-342-9678. E-mail address: getinfo@haworthpressinc.com <Website: http://www.haworthpressinc.com>]*

KEYWORDS. Distance education, site identity, student's perceptions

Ronald H. Rooney, PhD, is Professor, School of Social Work, University of Minnesota.

Elena Izaksonas, MSW, LICSW, is a Doctoral Student, School of Social Work, Univeristy of Minnesota, and Adjunct Faculty, Augsburg College.

Jane A. Macy, PhD, is Educational Specialist, School of Social Work, University of Minnesota.

Address correspondence to either author at: School of Social Work, 105 Peters Hall, 1401 Gortner Avenue, St. Paul, MN 55108.

[Haworth co-indexing entry note]: "Reframing from Site Bias to Site Identity: Pedagogic Issues in Delivering Social Work Courses via Interactive Television." Rooney, Ronald H., Elena Izaksonas, and Jane A. Macy. Co-published simultaneously in *Journal of Technology in Human Services* (The Haworth Press, Inc.) Vol. 16, No. 2/3, 1999, pp. 175-192; and: *Computers and Information Technology in Social Work: Education, Training, and Practice* (ed: Jo Ann R. Coe, and Goutham M. Menon) The Haworth Press, Inc., 1999, pp. 175-192. Single or multiple copies of this article are available for a fee from The Haworth Document Delivery Service [1-800-342-9678, 9:00 a.m. - 5:00 p.m. (EST). E-mail address: getinfo@ haworthpressinc.com].

175

Distance education refers to formal teacher-learner arrangements in which the teacher and learner are geographically separated most or all of the time and the communication between them is through a technology medium such as satellite, computer, compressed video or fiber optics (Kahl and Cropley, 1986; Verduin and Clark, 1991). Social work's response to distance education has included "fascination, reservation and caution" (Siegel, Jennings, Conklin and Napoletano Flynn, 1998, p.71). Social workers have been fascinated by the potential to reach underserved populations and to increase access for students (Raymond, 1996; Coe and Elliott, 1997). Indeed, distance education has been described as an ideal way to deliver education to non-traditional students who live at locations distant from the social work school. Such students are frequently older than traditional students, work full-time and hence often must complete degrees on a part-time basis. In addition, the population includes single parents and members of disadvantaged groups who cannot afford to attend full-time (Raymond, 1997). Reservations and caution are urged by some who suggest that social work is moving too quickly to adopt this new form of technology without adequate evaluation (Krueger and Stretch, 1997; Thyer, Polk and Gaudin, 1997). As Thyer, Artelt, Markward and Dozier (1998) express it: "It would indeed be tragic if social work faculty enthusiastically embraced selected distance learning technologies and applied them to thousands of graduate students, only to find out that instructional quality suffered as a result" (p. 294).

Such caution has led social work educators to focus on demonstrating that educational results achieved through distance learning are "as good as" or "not worse than" traditional programs. Based on the criteria applied by CSWE to assess the adequacy of alternative programs, evaluation has focused upon demonstrating that the students receiving their education through distance formats receive grades, skills and other outcomes that are comparable to students receiving their education through in-person formats. Emphasis on comparability is understandable but may distract us from recognizing the special characteristics, qualities or strengths inherent in distance education (Gutierrez, Parsons and Cox, 1998; Saleeby, 1997). This paper will introduce the concepts of originating site dissatisfaction, distant site cohesion, site tension, and site identity. The paper will then describe how purposeful use of these concepts can utilize the strengths of distance education for teaching social work students content related to social justice and diversity.

PEDAGOGY IN DISTANCE EDUCATION

Higher education faculty across fields join social work educators in their combination of fascination and reservation about the potential of technology to enhance education. They express a sense of potential and the opportunity to be creative and also apprehension about change. Hezel describes these concerns by noting that "The drive to use technology has initially complicated the process of educational delivery. The focus on education and, according to many observers, the emphasis on program delivery has been displaced by a disproportionate concern with the implementation of technology" (Hezel, 1990, p. 59).

The current technological experimentation follows a decade or more of research about how adults learn and the development of increasingly sophisticated theories of adult learning. Widely used and recognized theories of adult learning, including those of Knowles, Knox, and Cross, highlight common characteristics of adult learners. For example, adult learners bring a rich experience repertoire with them. The adult motivation for learning comes from the developmental tasks associated with their social roles as workers, parents and supervisors. Adult learners want to immediately use their learning and are present-focused. And finally, adult learners are independent and self-sufficient and have less use for traditional kinds of college activities or services (Merriam, 1987).

Social work distance education students tend to fit the profile of adult learners as they are often older, more likely to be married, have more job experience and/or are working more currently than traditional students (Freddolino, 1997; Haga and Heitkamp, 1995; Lessons Learned: California State University at Long Beach, 1997). Many studies of distance education student/learner success find that interactivity is a common element to student achievement. Zirkin and Sumler suggest that: "The weight of the evidence from the research reviewed was that increasing student involvement by immediate interaction resulted in increased learning as reflected by test performance, grades, and student satisfaction. The critical factor seemed to be the degree of intellectual and emotional involvement of the student in the learning process. Therefore, interactivity could perhaps best be defined as 'involvement'" (Zirkin and Sumler, 1995, p. 101). In another four year study investigating pedagogical styles and interaction patterns possible utilizing ITV in educational settings, the researchers concluded "Although lecturing can be as engaging as any other method of teaching in a conventional classroom, we have found the most effective uses of interactive television to be those designed to sustain the interaction of participants in dialogue. We believe that interactive television supports learning in a number of social contexts and types of interaction" (MacKinnon, Walshe, Cummings, and Velonis, 1995, p. 191). The researchers found that the moderator/facilitator role was critical in structuring various kinds of interaction such as deciding when to "spontaneously move in and out of the dialogue" (p. 92). They noted that moderators could at some times capitalize on regional differences to encourage disparate points of view among the participants. At other times, moderators could encourage tolerance and cooperation among participants with differing opinions and needs in order that they work collaboratively in negotiating solutions to a problem.

Hence, the above research suggests that social work educators should be concerned with utilizing active learning and knowledge about adult learners in distance education endeavors. Bringing together groups of students separated by space allows social work educators the opportunity to develop new learning activities which can support the educational objectives of the social work curriculum. This paper will describe how interactive television offers us an opportunity to teach students to appreciate diversity and to strive for social justice.

SITE BIAS, ORIGINATING SITE DISSATISFACTION, SITE TENSION AND DISTANT SITE COHESION

Distance education researchers MacKinnon et al. (1995) have used the term site bias to describe difficulties arising from the location of the instructor/moderator of an interactive television course. Specifically, when the instructor paid more attention to one site than others, participants in those other sites felt frustrated and neglected.

The site bias phenomenon in social work appears to be experienced similarly in some respects and differently in others by students in the originating site and the distant sites. An emerging finding in social work is the circumstance that students, if they have a choice of live or distant ITV instruction, often prefer the "live" instructor. In the first study by Thyer et al., when live instruction rotated from a central to a distant site, students in the course significantly preferred live instruction to interactive television (Thyer et al., 1997). In a replication study, while students in one course did not differ significantly in their appraisals of the quality of live and interactive television, students in a second course significantly favored live instruction (Thyer et al., 1998).

Preference for live instruction is described elsewhere in the social work literature. The Southern Mississippi program reported that: ". . . it is clear that given a choice both faculty and students prefer on-site instruction . . . students want regular on-site contact with instructors and seem to experience a sense of 'second class status' when the instructor appears in the flesh at the other site" (Forster, 1997, p. 14). Similarly, Freddolino, in describing the response of Michigan State students in the site from which most instruction originated, reports that they ". . . felt that the group of students where the instructor was located always routinely received more attention. Consequently, when the instructors visited different sites and originated the class at a site other than on the main campus–a move taken to permit closer contact with the distant site students–the students in the on-campus section felt slighted. All participants craved additional contact time" (Freddolino, 1996a, p. 49).

Freddolino notes that once technical problems in delivery and reception were alleviated, students in the distant sites appeared willing to accept some costs. For example, loss of time to technology was a price they were willing to pay for the advantage of attending a program relatively close to home without the need for an even greater commute. Hence, a critical issue in student response to distance education in social work appears to be whether in-person instruction is a ready alternative. For example, Coe and Elliott report in their study of University of Texas distance students that while 75% would prefer on-site instruction near home, two thirds of the distance learners said that their second and third choices were a combination of satellite and in-person instruction or all near home via satellite (Coe and Elliott, 1997, p. 2). Distance education has greatest attraction in areas in which access to education is only made possible by such means. In those circumstances, students appear to find that interactive television, delivered with adequate technological sophistication, is an invaluable way to complete their education without having to relocate to a distant site (Rooney et al., 1998).

Freddolino describes a version of site bias in which the students in the originating site from which the instructor teaches most sessions feel particularly disadvantaged by distance education: "The students on the main campus could not perceive any such benefit accruing for their sacrificed instructional time. They were already here and thus saw no benefit from the broadcast of the signal to other students in other places. In some semesters, there were no unlinked sections of these required courses for students on the main campus to choose, so they were truly *involuntary participants* [italics added]. From their vantagepoint it was simply a waste of time" (Freddolino, 1996a, p. 47). Another example can be found in reports from North Dakota "on-campus students were upset that the class was being taught through IVN and resented distant learning students being in 'their' classroom" (Haga and Heitkamp, 1995, p. 20). We will describe this version of site bias as *originating site dissatisfaction*.

Such originating site dissatisfaction is not restricted to the experience of students. Faculty reports as part of the program evaluation of the distance program at California State-Long Beach include the comment: ". . . I do not believe that the 'live' audience of Long Beach students added anything to my teaching ability, comfort level or classroom dynamics. In fact, I often felt that I was expending so much energy reaching out over the airwaves that I tended to ignore the live audience. . . . [we should] drop live audience: they were basically a distraction in light of energy needed to deal with technology and I don't think their experience was as positive for that reason" (Lessons Learned, pp. 14-15, 1997). Indeed, the solution of transmitting from a site with no live participants was suggested in the original report of site bias (MacKinnon et al., 1995).

There are also reports of strained relations between site which we will refer to as site tension. Forster describes relations between the originating site and the remote site in the Southern Mississippi program as polarized and strained: "Instructors found that students interacted well–about the same as they experience in on-site classes–at each site, but that interaction between the Hattiesburg and Gulf Park sites was minimal and frequently 'strained'; the classroom facilitator in particular was aware of a polarization of the two classes that began in the first semester, abated somewhat over time, but continues to a significant degree still" (Forster, 1997, p. 11). Comments from students in that program included the following "I felt a good deal of antagonism from the other site. . . . It was almost as if we were in competition with one another. . . . I don't know where it came from, but I picked up a lot of 'attitude' from the other students. . . . There was tension in the classes. . . . Those guys couldn't take a joke, it got to where you didn't want to say anything to them. . . . I heard through the grapevine that Gulf Park students would criticize us when the mikes were off" (p. 11).

In addition to tension between sites, some reports describe special rapport and cohesiveness developing among students at the same distant site. We call this *distant site cohesion*. For example, Freddolino and Sutherland report that students in distant sites had higher levels of affiliation on the Adult Classroom Environment Scale than originating site students (Freddolino and Sutherland, 1994, 1995). Freddolino hypothesized that these higher ratings were explained by the fact that distant students often had work-related connections outside the classroom and would complete classes together in a group while students in the originating site were reconfigured for each class (Freddolino, 1996b). In our own program at the University of Minnesota, we have reports of distant site cohorts who continue to meet, to communicate via email and telephone years after graduation. The California State-Long Beach program reported phenomena which appear to fit both the site tension and distant site cohesion concepts: ". . . in the first year report, there was discussion about students appearing to bond well with their same site classmates, but not relating as well to the other sites (Lessons Learned, 1997, p. 5). Instructors in the CSU-LB program reflected on "the inability to build a cohesive 'class' between the sites. I think this is mainly due to the newness of distance education and problem solving could address this issue for future classes" (p. 5). This bonding between students at the same site was described as having both positive and negative elements: "some of the class 'stays together' for all classes and a bond is formed between the students. I believe that results in an increase in complaints and bonding through negatives. . . . ; for many of them, their workloads are too intense outside of class, so they get overwhelmed by school easily . . ." (p. 9).

One of the strengths of distance education in social work so far has been the openness in sharing both the potentials and advantages of the medium and also frank discussion of unresolved difficulties. We hope that expanding our conceptual vocabulary from site bias to include site tension, originating site dissatisfaction and distant site cohesion can assist us in being able to more precisely describe phenomena which both present challenges for distance education and also opportunities to reach instructional goals of the social work curriculum. Day and Blue (1997) acknowledged the frequent occurrence of "differences between sites" in distance education and suggest that these differences can be used to assist students in learning about and understanding the concept of privilege. Following their lead, we believe that the distance education format presents opportunities for teaching social work content on social justice and diversity.

SOCIAL WORK COMMITMENT TO SOCIAL JUSTICE AND DIVERSITY

Social work education has an expressed commitment to prepare students to effectively work in an increasingly multicultural society, to address issues of marginalization and oppression and to work for social justice (CSWE, 1982). However, there seems to be little consensus regarding the best way to achieve these goals and there appear to be inconsistencies between policy development and implementation. According to Van Soest (1995), the problem is not that there are different perspectives about multiculturalism operating in social work, but rather that the role of social work in the multiculturalism debate is passive, indirect, and submerged.

The use of a strengths perspective for reframing site tension to site identity can be an effective tool to bring to the surface issues relating to culturally relevant practice. The strengths perspective guides us to assess situations in a holistic fashion which encompasses deficits, obstacles and challenges augmented by current or potential strengths or resources (Saleeby, 1997). Hence when a classroom obstacle or challenge occurs, we also think about the potentials for reaching our educational goals through our handling of the situation. The distance education classroom environment is well situated to mirror the circumstances and conditions found in marginalized and oppressed groups. Day and Blue (1997) found that the ITV classroom setting provided unique opportunities for developing cross cultural skills. Day and Blue developed a specific strategy which employed the metaphor of "on site privilege" and suggested that ITV strategies seem to provide a powerful potential for cross-cultural learning situations.

In describing a framework for practice that is pertinent to oppressed groups, Van Voorhis (1998) advocates a pedagogy that prepares social work students to understand "the experience of oppression for those at the margin and privilege for those in the center" (p. 122). The variety of geographic settings in distance education provides a rich 'in situ' laboratory where students can begin to be directly exposed to issues of marginalization. The variety of geography brings students to each site who share certain unique, bounded, demographic characteristics common to urban, rural, or small city locales. They come together via interactive television to encounter their own differences and similarities in ways that would be less likely to occur through traditional classroom instruction in any one site. Such an encounter can echo, through the parallel process, the dynamics of marginalization that help students increase their skill development in diversity issues since at any given point one site (usually the main campus as originating site) will be at the center while the others will be located at the margin. This structure provides a powerful metaphor to which the instructor can continually refer to illustrate the psychosocial dynamics of power. Such an understanding posits that people in positions of privilege are associated with power and resources while those at the margins are identified as having less power and resources with which to make viable choices. The different geographic locations provide for students the direct experience of understanding the "difference that difference makes" (Van Voorhis, 1998, p. 122). Although geographic differences constitute the primary structural basis embedded in distance education which makes it unique for the enhancement of culturally relevant practice skills, sometimes classroom composition can become 'value added' when students in one setting are culturally different (in sufficient numbers) from students in another site. Van Voorhis suggests a strategy of assessment of clients identity formation as members of marginalized population groups in order to encourage the development of identity pride and to build on their strengths and positive coping responses.

FROM SITE TENSION TO SITE IDENTITY

The University of Minnesota School of Social Work has offered an advanced standing MSW distance education program via ITV since 1994 to students who attend sites in Moorhead and Rochester. Instructors teach from each distant site at least once per quarter. The system uses two-way compressed video. While the microphones in the Twin Cities are always open, students in the Moorhead site must push a button to activate their microphone. While most instruction occurs from the Twin Cities, Moorhead and Rochester each have site coordinators who manage the site, assist students in coordination of local resources and provide liaison with the School of Social

Work and instructors (Kalke, Rooney and Macy, 1998). About half of the students in the Moorhead site, located on the North Dakota border, come from the Fargo-Moorhead metropolitan area with a population of over 150,000. The other half of the students come from small towns in Minnesota and North Dakota such that some students commute from as far as 200 miles. Rochester, meanwhile, has a population of 80,000 and students come from both small towns and cities in Southern Minnesota and Iowa generally within a one hour driving distance. A majority of students at the Twin Cities site come from the metropolitan area but also include weekend students who drive from surrounding rural areas and small cities in Minnesota, Iowa and Wisconsin. Twin Cities students are enrolled in the weekend program including both distance classes and traditional, in-person instruction in other classes. Hence, our Twin Cities students are reconstituted for each class while students from Rochester and Moorhead are part of cohorts who attend most classes together and each have a site coordinator. Students in both the Moorhead and Rochester sites are primarily of European American descent. Composition of the Twin Cities site varies with the course, but in the example to be described below, 7 of the 14 students were African American or Southeast Asian.

An advanced practice course in Social Work with Involuntary Clients was taught via distance education by the senior author at the University of Minnesota School of Social Work in the winter of 1997. The course instructor and his teaching assistant (the second author) traveled to each distance site twice during the quarter. While we had observed instances that in hindsight we would describe as site tension, a particular series of incidents in this course crystallized the concept for us. We will also describe our efforts to use an exercise designed to help us refocus our attention from the deficits of site tension to the potential strengths of site identity and its utility for teaching content related to social justice and diversity.

Event 1. The third session of the quarter was taught by the senior author from the Rochester site, and focused on ways to increase client choice when circumstances are constrained. A South East Asian American student from the Twin Cities site asked what a social worker is to do when his or her client's circumstances are so constrained as to constitute no real choice. He described a situation in which a South East Asian immigrant with limited English language skills had previously been able to select education options prior to registering for immediate job training and work. The immigrant client's welfare benefits were about to run out and he would no longer be able to attend classes as an alternative to job training and job search. The instructor then initiated a brainstorming exercise in which students from all three sites could suggest ways in which the student social worker might increase choices for his client. Students from Moorhead had briefly lost audio contact during the explanation of the exercise and asked that the instructions be repeated.

A student group at Moorhead was asked to report on the options they considered. They suggested that the client be encouraged to seek employment as an interpreter and that he attempt to find work that might permit him to continue his language courses in the evening. At this point, two hundred miles away in the Twin Cities (thanks to an open microphone), students responded to these suggestions with the comments "get real" and "read the class material." These comments, perhaps shared in a private aside, were heard clearly by distant students, though perhaps not by all Twin Cities students. Later content in the session included a discussion about the use of punishment and reward with involuntary clients. The instructor solicited anonymous feedback at the end of the class, as he did in all sessions, by posing questions which students in all sites were asked to answer on a 3 × 5 card. On this occasion, students were asked to describe whether they had felt rewarded, threatened or punished in this class session and, if so, to describe the instance and their response to it.

When the instructor and teaching assistant reviewed the cards during the next week, they found that several Moorhead students felt punished by the 'get real' remark and further elaborated that they often felt discounted or disrespected by the Twin Cities students: ". . . Comment 'get real' was offensive–[it] would not support continued comments/opinions from students if these comments continue; it would not lend to me feeling comfortable to comment . . . I found it very offending that Twin Cities made rude comments such as 'get real,' 'read the material' when prior to going into the activity we tried to explain that the ITV went down and we didn't know what was expected of us. The whole situation was confusing and afterwards no one wanted to say anything. I would like to say that most of us had read the material . . . I am offended by the Twin Cities lack of vision and acceptance when brainstorming for options with clients. We all need to be more open minded here . . . I feel that the learning climate was not primarily respectful in this session . . . I thought our goal was to look at 'possible' alternatives that may be the basis for client negotiation. I would hope we can be respectful of each others contribution. . . . The reinforced behavior was that I should keep quiet because it was assumed I did not read my lesson when in actuality ITV had a blackout."

In addition, one Twin Cities student responded as follows: ". . . My thoughts have been taken up by the underlying, unsaid or not directly said class and race issues which taint many of our works with involuntary clients. Who are we talking about when we say "involuntary clients"? What are the unsaid implications of their color and economic status being different from that of the practitioner? Honestly, coming from a welfare background, I am offended by the attitudes and underlying class bias that comes from some classmates. If these future practitioners offend me in subtle ways to the point where I feel like being non-participatory in class, how will they deal with clients?" None of the other Twin Cities students commented about this issue and, as it happened, comments from Rochester students were not received prior to the following class session.

Event 2. The next session of the class was taught by the second author when the lead instructor was away from campus for a planned commitment. They consulted together, however, about the feedback received and decided to share what was written and give students an opportunity to clarify their viewpoints. It was hoped that this airing of the issues would provide useful material for planned course content for this session. Instead of leading to de-escalation, further elaboration seemed to solidify students in both the Moorhead and Twin Cities site in their feelings that they were being labeled by students in the other site. Specifically, a student from the Moorhead site commented: ". . . We feel like the ugly sister; we try to intermingle with you guys when we come down there, but nothing happens. Why is it that we have to travel down to the Cities every year and teachers have to come out here, but you students from the Cities, you never come out here?" While none of the Twin Cities students offered to travel to Moorhead, one Twin Cities student, who presumably made one of the offensive remarks, commented: "I own what I say; I want to learn, you can enhance my learning by letting me know how I come across." Her comment was supported by another Twin Cities student who noted "We are all here to learn; don't take it so personal, we are here to help each other." Efforts to broaden the scope of the discussion to a consideration of regional differences and to bring Rochester students into the discussion fell flat despite diligent efforts by the teaching assistant. The South East Asian student who had suggested the example which led to the controversy apologized for causing disharmony by saying "I feel bad; I provided a bad example."

So, instead of reducing tension and being able to link it with planned content on persuasion, tensions had further expanded as reflected in the post-session feedback cards. From the Twin Cities students, comments included: "Taking this ITV class is the most frustrating experience of my graduate career! . . . The discussion of offendedness by other sites had/will have an effect on my sharing comments from now on . . . I appreciate your reading the comments of the last class but it might have been better if you didn't; it was hard for me to understand why one made a big deal of 'big deal.' . . . Regarding parallel process and comments last week of 'get real,' I wonder if we could revisit the conversation next week to see if there are additional comments. I understand that we had to stop for the sake of time but I didn't feel that the conversation came to a natural pause. . . . I however feel that we should be allowed to discuss about the difference among us of the various sites. We started it, we should end it, just a thought. . . . This wouldn't happen if we were all one big class."

Event 3. The senior author had the benefit of reviewing videotapes from the previous sessions as well as the written feedback and the teaching assistant's impressions. The instructor and teaching assistant were convinced that tension between the Moorhead and Twin Cities site was clearly inhibiting communication on both sides. The senior author taught the next session from the Twin Cities site while the teaching assistant make a previously planned trip to the Rochester site. The senior author concluded that an instructional exercise was needed to both alleviate site tension and also hopefully link their experiences with course content. By focusing on possibilities in addition to obstacles, the exercise could become a model application of the strengths perspective. The instructor first noted to the student who had suggested the case that his example was not a bad one at all, but a rich one which was providing the mechanism for conveying much course content. The in-class discussions of the last two weeks were described as a "marvelous laboratory" for exploring planned course content related to communication barriers and opportunities and about the experiences of oppressed groups. Next, a systems communication diagram was shared in which the key events of the last few weeks were depicted including the increasingly strained communication. That is, the student's example was followed with a request for brainstorming. When the Moorhead students suggestion was followed by the "get real" comment, Moorhead students reported on feedback cards that they felt punished and disrespected by the Twin Cities students. Similarly, Twin Cities students had reported what they experienced to be racist and classist overtones in the Moorhead suggestions. The following efforts to clear the air had resulted in further charges and negative reactions. After this summary, the instructor attempted to link the experience with course content by asking whether students from Moorhead and the Twin Cities were experiencing themselves as members of an oppressed group, in this case oppressed ITV students? The question lightened the mood briefly as students noted that they did feel unhappy about some issues in their interaction, but not at the level of the kinds of oppression studied in the course whereby groups such as persons of color, single parents, and children often experience a kind of impersonal oppression as involuntary clients. Part of the tension appeared to come from feeling inappropriately labeled by students from other sites. Rather than continue to react to inappropriate labels, students in each site were next asked to help clarify their own *site identities* by describing characteristics they shared and did not share with other students from their own site. They were further asked to describe ways they were similar and different from students in other sites and, finally, ways in which they were similar and different as a whole class.

Moorhead students described themselves as very diverse geographically, coming from large cities and small communities; they described as a strength of their site the support received from their site coordinator. Rochester students described themselves as a tightly knit, cohesive group composed completely of women, who were more reserved than students in either of the other sites. Students in the Twin Cities site identified their site as having a "home field advantage" which became an appropriate metaphor for privilege (Day and Blue, 1997). They noted that they had greatest access to the instructor, were less bothered by technological difficulties and had easier access to school facilities and the teaching assistant. They acknowledged the privilege of other sites being dependent in some ways on transmission from the originating site. As a class across sites, students agreed that they were MSW degree-seeking students in a weekend program, often working, with complex family obligations, at times suffering from technological difficulties, and reflecting great ethnic and geographic diversity.

Tension between students and sites appeared substantially reduced, perhaps influenced by the acknowledgement of privilege, according to feedback received after the session and spontaneously reported by site coordinators. The incident led to discussions of technological differences between sites. Twin Cities students were asked to remember that their mikes were open and avoid rustling papers and making unguarded comments lest they be heard hundreds of miles away. Distant students in the "margin" also recognized that one advantage of their lack of open mikes was that they had control over what comments they would share with others across the state.

INTERGROUP TENSIONS IN SOCIAL WORK EDUCATION

Similar tensions between students may occur in traditional classrooms in which older students fear younger students and see them as better adapted to college life, paper writing, test taking, and other academic tasks. Meanwhile, younger students fear older students because they are seen as having much more experience and depth of understanding. However, there are additional challenges that need to be recognized in using an ITV system to teach. Distinct groups of students are usually separated by space, unlike a traditional classroom. In our experience, in an ITV teaching situation there are all the same tensions that a group of traditional classroom students may experience with each other (differences due to ethnicity, gender, age, social class, sexual orientation, etc.) and there are additional tensions when distinct sub-groups have limited physical contact with each other. They have limited opportunities for informal interaction with one another during breaks and in either nonclassroom settings. Among the interventions we are now also using to broaden their contact with one another is to plan for informal contact possibilities in their in-person contact opportunities, and exploring the development of email connections between students in different sites (Huff and Johnson, 1998). In addition, students can be asked to consult with one another about classroom projects across sites.

Social work's growing exploration of internet and web-based learning raises additional obstacles and opportunities for reaching educational goals. Use of e-mail, web and chat groups increase access to the instructor outside the classroom setting, establish direct communication links among students which permit them to learn from one another and elaborate exchanges carried on that begin in the classroom, creating a virtual community. In addition, use of such formats can increase participation of students who have difficulty engaging in classroom discussions including diverse ideas which might not otherwise be shared (Falk, 1998). However, some report that non-traditional students with limited computer experience can be intimidated by the opportunity (Falk, 1998). Similarly, students who have limited time or access to computers can find the experience frustrating (Faux and Black-Hughes, 1998). Such experiences both raise challenges and create opportunities for connecting such experiences to social justice themes and for creative problem solving. That is, the realities of differential access and experience can be addressed and the implications for obstacles to equal access to learning. Those challenges can be explored through pairing up students of different experience levels and exploring opportunities for easier access.

Consistent with our strengths perspective, we conclude that each educational format (including the traditional in-person class) includes realities of student similarities, differences, strengths, resources and obstacles which enhance or detract from learning. By including all, opportunities are created with each format for learning and problem solving.

CONCLUSIONS

Social work distance education is very new and, to date, most reports understandably focus on the comparability of the outcomes of distance students when compared to traditional in-person students. In this paper, we have examined phenomena described in the literature as site bias and suggested additional descriptive terms for the varied circumstances revealed. We have suggested the concepts of originating site dissatisfaction, distant site cohesion, site tension and, finally, site identity as having potential utility for both describing recurring phenomena and also forming the basis for proactive instruction. While the ITV medium contributes to the potential for greater diversity of experience across sites, it also appears to be susceptible to stereotyping. That is, students who do not have contact with one another outside of the televised interaction may respond to each other in more limited roles than occurs when they experience one another in more spontaneous contact over breaks, and through other classes. Stereotyping is not a problem unique to distance education and the class experience can hence be used to clarify the phenomena. Understanding such dynamics can help us in harnessing them in productive ways to further social work education roles and to recognize strengths. Site identity identification offers a learning opportunity for students regarding diversity. That is, the very differences embedded in the sites are ideally suited as didactic metaphors for students to experience as they engage in their learning process. For example, dynamics pertinent to marginalization, privilege, and insider-outsider status can be utilized and illustrated through the parallel process. Instructors can both anticipate site tension and proactively deal with it through exercises such as exploration of site identity to contribute to course goals.

Thyer et al. (1998) have suggested that ". . . caution is warranted before adopting distance learning technology on a wide scale. Analogous studies examining student learning, not simply attitudes toward instruction, are urgently needed in social work education. On the other hand, if novel teaching tools are superior or equivalent to conventional pedagogical methods, their adoption will be legitimately promoted by well-crafted research studies empirically demonstrating such favorable outcomes" (Thyer et al., 1998, p. 294). We don't think that distance education needs to demonstrate that it is superior to traditional in-person education. Distance education and in-person education are not in competition. When students can gain access to quality in-person education, many prefer it. When their choices are quality interactive television or no education, they prefer the quality ITV. The challenge to students and faculty in distance programs is to go beyond good second choices to recognize and build on strengths available in the medium to teach content important to the social work curriculum in ways not as easily accessibly through in-person instruction at any one site. That challenge includes implicit requirements to provide education in a fashion which is active, recognizes and builds upon the strengths of adult learners across a wealth of geographic and cultural differences.

We must also work to diminish originating site dissatisfaction. As noted by Freddolino (1996a), the experience of students in the originating site is such that "We must do a far better job identifying and then making real the potential benefits to the students on campus who may be participating in the [distance education] courses. Having multiple perspectives in the classroom, exposure to rural social work practice, and opportunities to learn about new technologies are all possible benefits that have to be communicated to the students" (p. 47). Similarly, we must recognize the potentials of strength arising from distant site cohesion that could be emulated by our in-person sites.

Freddolino further suggests that "Electronically mediated distance education is here to stay; for fiscal, administrative and even pedagogical reasons, will only increase; new types of students; geographic monopolies will be diminished" (Freddolino, (1996b, p. 207). The issue, again as noted by Freddolino, is to focus on the expansion of quality distance education. In that regard, we are suggesting that social work not only carefully evaluate distance education but creatively explore pedagogical potentials for reaching the instructional goals of our curriculum. We need to broaden our scope of inquiry in distance education and in-person formats to include: What kind of pedagogy produces what kind of results? What content or curriculum areas lend themselves best to different media? What is the influence of learner traits and learning styles and their interaction with pedagogical methods? (Rooney et al., 1998). We now add to this list: how can we recognize and utilize the various relationships and strengths students and sites develop with one another to better reach our educational goals?

REFERENCES

Coe, JoAnn and Elliott, Doreen. (1997, March). *An evaluation of teaching direct practice in distance education programs for rural settings.* Paper presented at Council on Social Work Education Annual Program Meeting, Chicago, IL.

Council on Social Work Education (1982). *Curriculum Policy Statement for Master's Degree and Baccalaureate Degree Programs in Social Work Education.* New York: Author.

Day, Priscilla A. and Blue, Elizabeth T. (1997, March). *Teaching cross-cultural skills: a metaphor for integration using interactive television.* Paper presented at the Council on Social Work Education Annual Program Meeting, Chicago, IL.

Falk, Diane S. (1998). The virtual community: Computer conferencing for teaching and learning social work practice. 114-123 in *Proceedings of Information Technologies for Social Work Education and Practice Conference.* Charleston, SC

Faux, Tamara and Black-Hughes, Christine (1998). Results of pretest and posttest data to analyze the effectiveness of using computer technology (internet) to teach social work history. Pages 124-132 in *Proceedings of Information Technologies for Social Work Education and Practice Conference.* Charleston, SC, August.

Forster, Michael (1997, September). *Evaluating a part-time graduate social work distance education program at the University of Southern Mississippi.* Paper presented at the Information Technologies for Social Work Education Conference, Charleston, SC.

Freddolino, Paul P. (1996a). Maintaining quality in graduate social work programs delivered to distant sites using electronic instruction technology. In Modes of Professional Education II: The Electronic Social Work Curriculum in the Twenty-first Century. *Tulane Studies in Social Welfare, 20* (May), 40-52.

Freddolino, Paul P. (1996b). The importance of relationships for a quality learning environments in interactive TV classrooms. *Journal of Education for Business, 71 (4)*, 205-208.

Freddolino, Paul. (1997, September*). Building on experience: Lessons from a distance education MSW program.* Paper presented at Information Technologies for Social Work Education, Charleston, SC.

Freddolino, Paul P. and Sutherland, C.A. (1994, November). *Assessing the effectiveness of graduate social work education delivered via interactive instructional television (ITV).* Paper presented at the Annual Meeting of the American Evaluation Association, Boston, MA.

Freddolino, Paul P. and Sutherland, C.A. (1995). *Factors affecting student perceptions of quality in courses delivered via interactive instructional television (ITV).* East Lansing, MI: Michigan State University School of Social Work.

Gutierrez, Lorraine, Parsons, Ruth J., and Cox, Enid O. (1998). *Empowerment in Social Work Practice.* Pacific Grove, CA: Brooks/Cole.

Haga, Myrna, and Heitkamp, Thomasine L. (1995, March). *Evaluation results of an innovative social work distance education program.* Paper presented at the Council on Social Work Education Annual Program meeting, San Diego, CA.

Hezel, Richard T. (1991). *National policy in distance education: The issues and research.* (Research Monograph No. 8). University Park, PA: The Penn State University, American Center for the Study of Distance Education.

Huff, Marie T. and Johnson, Miriam M. (1998). Students' use of email and a listserv in distance education courses. Pp 203-211 in *Proceedings of Information Technologies for Social Work Education and Practice Conference.* Charleston, SC, August.

Kahl, T.N. and Cropley, A.J. (1986). Face to face versus distance learning: Psychological consequences and practical implications. *Distance Education, 7,* 38-48.

Kalke, Nan L., Rooney, Ronald H., and Macy, Jane A. (1998, March). *Providing effective education in distance education.* Paper presented at the Council on Social Work Education Annual Program Meeting, Orlando, FL.

Krueger, Larry W. and Stretch, John J. (1997, September). *Hyper-technology is destroying social work.* Paper presented at Information Technologies for Social Work Education Conference, Charleston, SC.

Lessons learned: Second year report (1997, August). Long Beach, CA: California State University, Master of Social Work Distance Education Program.

MacKinnon, Allan, Walshe, Bridget, Cummings, Michael, and Velonis, Ursala (1995). An inventory of pedagogical considerations for interactive television. *Journal of Distance Education, 10 (1),* 75-94.

Merriam, Sharon (1987). Adult learning and theory building: A review. *Adult Education Quarterly, 37 (4),* 187-198.

Raymond, Frank B. III. (1996). Delivering the MSW curriculum to non-traditional students through interactive television. In Modes of Professional Education II: The Electronic Social Work Curriculum in the Twenty-first Century. *Tulane Studies in Social Welfare, 20* (May), 16-27.

Rooney, R.H., Kalke, N., Macy, J., Freddolino, P., Raymond, F., Jacobsen, M.,

Siegel, E., Black, J., Hagen, C., Potts, M., and Wilson, G. (1998). Letter to editor. *Journal of Social Work Education, 34 (2)*, 317-318.

Saleeby, Dennis (1997). *The Strengths Perspective in Social Work Practice.* Second edition. New York: Longman.

Siegel, Elbert, Jennings, Joanne G., Conklin, Jack, and Napoletano Flynn, Shelly A. (1998). Distance learning in social work education: Results and implications of a national survey. *Journal of Social Work Education, 34 (1)*, 71-80.

Thyer, Bruce A., Polk, Gerald and Gaudin, James G. (1997). Distance learning in social work education: A preliminary evaluation. *Journal of Social Work Education, 33 (2)*, 363-367.

Thyer, Bruce A., Artelt, Thomas, Markward, Martha K., and Dozier, Cheryl D. (1998). Evaluating distance learning in social work education: A replication study. *Journal of Social Work Education, 34 (2)*, 291-295.

Van Soest, Dorothy (1995). Multiculturalism and social work education: The non-debate about competing perspectives. *Journal of Social Work Education, 31 (1)*, 55-66.

Van Voorhis, Rebecca, M. (1998). Culturally relevant practice: A framework for teaching the psychosocial dynamics of oppression. *Journal of Social Work Education, 34 (1)*, 121-133.

Verduin, J.R. and Clark, T.A. (1991). *Distance Education: The Foundations of Effective Practice.* San Francisco: Jossey-Bass.

Zirkin, Barbara G., and Sumler, David E. (1995). Interactive or non-interactive? That is the question!!! An annotated bibliography. *Journal of Distance Education, 10 (1)*, 95-112.

Index

Abramowitz, S., 48
ACCENT system (Tennessee), 89
ACES
    Adult Classroom Environment
        Scale (ACES). *See* Adult
        Classroom Environment
        Scale (ACES)
    Automated Client Eligibility
        System (ACES) (Washington
        State). *See* Automated Client
        Eligibility System (ACES)
        (Washington State)
Adult Classroom Environment Scale
    (ACES), 167
Afifi, M.A., 53
Airasian, P., 150
Akers, R., 132-133
Allen, A., 32
Allyn and Bacon (Web site), 154
ALMIS. *See* America's Labor
    Management Information
    System (ALMIS)
America's Labor Management
    Information System
    (ALMIS), 88
Andrews, J., 64
Angelo, T.A., 106,148
ANNs. *See* Artificial neural networks
    (ANNs)
Artelt, T., 162,165f,176
Artificial neural networks (ANNs)
    as clinical decision support tools,
        2,47-49
    benefits of, 58-59
    historical perspectives, 49-54
    introduction to, 2,47
    models, Bayesian, 47,52-54,58-59
    models, graphic, 50f
    research studies using, 54-59

statistical software, use with, 50-61
Ask 2000 initiative (Hawaii), 83-84
Aubin, A., 117
Automated Client Eligibility System
    (ACES) (Washington State),
    86
Azab, M.E., 53

Bacsich, P., 25
Baker, W., 98,100
Balassone, M.L., 156
Barone, N.M., 37
Barr, R., 99
Barron, D., 148
Bart, W.G., 52
Bayesian artificial neural networks
    (ANNs), models,
    47,52-54,58-59
BCLP. *See* Blandin Foundation
    Community Leadership
    Program (BCLP)
BCSG. *See* Breast Cancer Support
    Group (BCSG), Marquette
    General Hospital (MGH)
Bell-Gredler, M.E., 147-149
Berger, A., 48
Bias, site, in distance learning,
    175-192
Biner, P.M., 37
Black-Hughes, C., 188
Blakley, T.J., 37
Blandin Foundation Community
    Leadership Program (BCLP),
    36-44
Blue, E.T., 180
Boshuizen, H.P.A., 7
Brawley, E.A., 64